THE LAZY ENVIRONMENTALIST

The Lazy
Environment-alist

Your Guide to Easy, Stylish, Green Living

Josh Dorfman

Stewart, Tabori & Chang
NEW YORK

Published in 2007 by Stewart, Tabori & Chang
An imprint of Harry N. Abrams, Inc.

Text copyright © 2007 by Josh Dorfman

All rights reserved. No portion of this book may be reproduced, stored in a retrieval system, or transmitted in any form or by any means, mechanical, electronic, photocopying, recording, or otherwise, without written permission from the publisher.

Library of Congress Cataloging-in-Publication Data
Dorfman, Josh.
  The lazy environmentalist : your guide to easy, stylish, green living / by Josh Dorfman.
     p. cm.
  Includes index.
  ISBN-13: 978-1-58479-602-2
  ISBN-10: 1-58479-602-2
  1. Environmental protection—Citizen participation. 2. Environmentalism. 3. Organic living. I. Title.

TD171.7.D67 2007
640—dc22   2006100976

Editor: Dervla Kelly
Designer: Pamela Geismar
Production Manager: Jacquie Poirier

The text of this book was composed in Perpetua and Rotis Sans.

The Lazy Environmentalist was printed on Rolland Enviro 100 made with 100% post-consumer waste and processed chlorine free. Rolland Enviro 100 is certified Ecologo and FSC Recycled, and manufactured using BioGas energy.

Printed and bound in the United States of America
10 9 8 7 6 5 4 3

HNA

harry n. abrams, inc.

a subsidiary of La Martinière Groupe

115 West 18th Street
New York, NY 10011
www.hnabooks.com

CONTENTS

Designers are saving rain forests. Fashionistas are clearing toxins from the soil. Architects are rolling back global warming. A new wave of eco-conscious activists is stimulating fresh approaches to environmental challenges. The market is their arena. Organic cotton, bamboo, and certified sustainable woods are their materials. Hybrid engines and solar power are their technologies. Stylish, high-performing products and services are their tools of change.

These innovators make it easy for us to integrate environmental awareness into our lives. They understand that while so many of us are concerned about the environment, we don't always have the time, energy, or inclination to do something about it.

We are lazy environmentalists. This is our moment.

Environmentally savvy products are now in kitchens, bathrooms, bedrooms, and living rooms. They're the new paint on your walls and the contemporary rugs on your floors. They're everything from your toothbrush to your laundry detergent to your flat-screen TV. They inform your life easily without compromise.

The Lazy Environmentalist is your hands-on guide to the best of easy, stylish green living. You can start today.

1

FASHION
FIRST
Clothing
and Accessories

Forward-thinking designers

around the globe are merging fashion with eco-awareness, creating sexy, chic apparel that supports a cleaner planet. Global brands like Levi's are creating eco-conscious apparel alongside visionary eco-fashion designers like Linda Loudermilk and Deborah Lindquist. Wal-Mart, the world's largest retailer, is touting organic clothing alongside eco-design boutiques like The Green Loop near Portland, Oregon, and Gomi NYC on the Lower East Side of Manhattan. Bono, U2's indefatigable front man, is a leading voice for the eco-fashion crusade through his Edun line, and the movement is creating its own rising stars like eco-fashion model, spokesperson, and industry expert Summer Rayne Oakes. Eco-fashion may not change the planet, but it will certainly change your look. Indeed, doing good never looked as good as it does today.

The shift toward eco-conscious apparel mirrors the rising popularity of organic foods. Just as we choose to put healthier foods inside our bodies, today we can also choose to put healthier clothing on our bodies. Conventionally grown cotton, for example, is one of the most heavily sprayed crops in the world, accounting for nearly 25 percent of all insecticides and 10 percent of all pesticides used worldwide—which rely on hazardous chemicals that are suspected or known to be carcinogenic by the Environmental Protection Agency (EPA). The chemicals remain in the fiber of the clothing, which leaves the wearer susceptible to toxicity. Opting for nontoxic, organically grown apparel is the healthiest choice, for both you and the planet. Chemicals from clothing can not only seep into the human body, but also contaminate groundwater, soil, air, and food supplies.

Organic cotton is at its finest when under the skillful hands of designers Karen Stewart and Howard Brown. The couple was inspired to develop their Stewart+Brown label after the birth of their daughter, and their designs succeed in mixing style and eco-consciousness with serious comfort. Rich, subtle details can be seen in camis and long-sleeve shirts, plunging V-neck and scoop-neck sweaters, and hoodies and jackets. Every Stewart+Brown design uses organic cotton, factory surplus materials, or Mongolian cashmere—straight from a co-op in northwestern Mongolia that helps to ensure the nomadic herders' survival and maintain their traditional way of life.

Jeans are also receiving an eco-makeover. Organic cotton denim collections by eco-fashion newcomer Del Forte, longtime eco-label Of The Earth, and original denim pioneer Levi Strauss are creating attractive options for greening your wardrobe staples. But it's Loomstate that has elevated denim to new heights with the launch of its eco-intelligent label in 2004. Under the talented hands of designer Rogan Gregory—also widely renowned for Rogan, his namesake fashion label—Loomstate provides a wide collection of low-slung distressed jeans for men and women, weaving each item with raw organic cotton yarn in homage to nineteenth-century manufacturing methods. The rapidly expanding collection also features organic cotton chinos and corduroys along with designer T-shirts and hoodies. The New York City–based clothing label is sharply focused on ecological principles, yet knows first-hand what it takes to create a successful fashion label. According to co-founder Scott Hahn, "It [Loomstate] ultimately has to be cool. It's got to have sex appeal. It's got to be street credible. We're really going after people who are pretty discerning about what they're wearing." Pushing the eco-envelope still further, Gregory and Hahn have teamed up with Ali Hewson and husband Bono to introduce the Edun fashion label, which emphasizes fair-trade wages with an emphasis on manufacturing in Africa and strives to integrate Earth-friendly materials.

Sustainable style encompasses far more than organic cotton. Fashion innovators are developing new fabrics from unexpected sources. Bamboo is at the top of the list. The versatile, rapidly growing grass can be transformed into furniture, flooring, home goods, paper, and now more than ever, fabric. A special manufacturing process turns bamboo pulp into fiber, which can then be woven into luxuriously soft fabric that's comparable to silk or cashmere. Bamboo fabric is also antibacterial, breathable, and biodegradable. Linda Loudermilk, the mind behind "Luxury Eco," is garnering well-deserved attention for chic, elegant designs made of bamboo and other eco-exotic materials like sasawashi, a blend of Japanese paper, herbs, vitamins, and amino acids. Forward-thinking designers like Loudermilk are shaping an entirely new fashion ethic using materials made out of soy, corn, and even the cellulose found in wood pulp (it's called Tencel and it has an excellent drape). Many of these materials feature prominently in Loudermilk's new twenty-six-piece denim line, one of the most ambitious eco-fashion endeavors yet, and are also present in her tops, jackets, coats, pants, and dresses.

Eco-fashion designer to the stars Deborah Lindquist also works with a wide palette of materials. Lindquist has dressed celebrities such as Sharon Stone, Gwen Stefani, Demi Moore, Hilary Duff, Jessica Simpson, and Charlize Theron in her edgy eco-glam garments made of hemp, organic cotton, organic wool, and an array of repurposed vintage materials like silk scarves and recycled materials like cashmere. Lindquist's synthesis of materials continues to evolve as quality eco-aware materials become increasingly available.

One designer who is taking it upon herself to create her own eco-aware materials is Annie Langlois of On and On écolo chic. Langlois, a former model and designer for Dior and Guess, creates her collection of one-of-a-kind design-forward styles from fabrics that have been recovered and recycled from used garments such as sweaters, tweed jackets, men's suits, silk scarves, and dresses. On and On deconstructs the garments and refashions them into cutting-edge styles. Langlois also provides a unique one-on-one service to create fully customized fashions. Bring her your own used clothing, and together with you in consultation, she'll refashion your tired outfits into a fresh, new look.

Accessories designers are also turning used materials into fun, stylish products. Bazura Bags uses discarded juice containers and recycled aluminum soda and beer cans to make funky purses, handbags, and messenger bags. The bags are designed by a women's cooperative in the Philippines where workers receive fair wages for their labor. Escama makes eye-catching handbags out of recycled aluminum soda tabs. The bags are made by two women's cooperatives on the outskirts of Brasília, Brazil, and each Escama bag contains a card with the name of the artisan. Salvation Sacks turns recycled leather miniskirts into stylish, durable over-the-shoulder bags. Again NYC transforms an eclectic mix of used fabrics into stunning, one-of-a-kind accessories such as handbags, clutches, yoga bags, and laptop bags. Again NYC designer Allison Teich is intent upon creating beautiful, useful products by reusing available materials that have already been created.

Shopping for the latest eco-fashion trends is easy too. Greenloop represents about fifty of today's most exciting eco-fashion clothing, accessories, and beauty product collections. Purchase products at the company's online store and Greenloop will offset the greenhouse gas emissions generated through shipping by purchasing renewable energy credits. Founder Aysia Wright is an extraordinary visionary who continues to raise the profile of the entire sustainable style industry. If you're in Portland, Oregon, visit the company's retail location in nearby West Linn. Elsewhere on the web quality eco-finds can be had at Pangaya.com, Btcelements.com, Beklina.com, Cocosshoppe.com, Hipandzen.com, and Adili.com.

New York City has always been the ultimate destination for fashion purposes, and eco-design is no exception. The Lower East Side is the place to start. It's there that you'll find Gomi NYC, which has been open since 2004. Founder Anne Hettinger has a sharp eye for design and is always on the lookout for eco-fashion labels like Loomstate, Del Forte, Majestic, Delano Collection, and coming soon from Europe, Kuyichi. Nearby is Kaight, a boutique that features eco-fashion labels like Linda Loudermilk, Undesigned by Carol Young, Amira and Ciel. Also be sure to stop into Ekovaruhuset—"house of organics" in Swedish—where European eco-labels share shelf space with local eco-fashion talent. Across the bridge in the über-hip Williamsburg neighborhood of Brooklyn you'll find Sodafine, which showcases the work of emerging Brooklyn designers and artists and also offers quality eco-fashion clothing from designers like Loyale Clothing.

Big-name companies are thinking about the planet too. Until very recently, Nike had been the world's largest purchaser of organic cotton, and the company aims to incorporate at least 5 percent of the material into every one of its cotton products by 2010. Patagonia is also making giant strides and uses 100 percent organic cotton for its clothing line. But it's now Wal-Mart that garners top honors as the world's largest purchaser of organic cotton—10 million pounds' worth in 2006. Today Wal-Mart and its subsidiary, Sam's Club, feature organic cotton baby clothing and teenage fashion. This is just the beginning. Look for new organic fashion on Wal-Mart's shelves by 2008. The endeavor is part of Wal-Mart's comprehensive environmental action plan that calls for massive reductions in greenhouse gas emissions by switching to renewable energy sources and producing gains in energy efficiency inside stores through a host of initiatives. The global retailing giant has awakened to the realities of pressing eco-challenges, and both consumers and the planet will benefit as a result.

Clothing Labels

AMERICAN APPAREL

Americanapparel.net

American Apparel's flamboyant CEO, Dov Charney, shows signs of shifting the company beyond its admirable "made in the USA" fair wage mission to incorporate environmentally conscious fabrics. The "organic" collection features T-shirts for babies, kids, men, and women.

ANNA COHEN

Annacohen.com

Anna Cohen makes efforts to create cutting-edge fashion along the lines of "Italian Street Couture," using sustainable materials joined with globally responsible business practices. This ultra chic line of women's fashion apparel succeeds in its mission by using a combination of recycled, organic, and local materials, while being mindful of the planet.

BAMBOO CLOTHES

Bambooclothes.com

Collection includes activewear, intimates, and casual wear for both men and women designed by EcoDesignz using sustainable bamboo. Bamboo yarn is also available in various colors for do-it-yourselfers.

BAMBOOSA

Bamboosa.com

Bamboosa supplies clothing and accessories for men, women, and children made from bamboo fiber, which is softer than cotton, naturally antimicrobial, and one of nature's most sustainable resources. Bamboo apparel is also comfortable and thermal regulating, keeping you cooler, drier, and warmer.

COVET

Covetthis.com

Covet's men's and women's clothing collections are inspired by Japanese culture, designed for contemporary customers who are looking for something fashionable yet socially aware. All items offered include prevalent use of sustainable materials, including organic cotton, bamboo, and soy fabrics.

DEBORAH LINDQUIST

Deborahlindquist.com

Deborah Lindquist creates environmentally friendly women's apparel using recycled materials and vintage fabrics, resulting in standout designs. Many

A-list celebrities have been styled by Deborah, bringing awareness to her ecologically sensitive collections.

DEITY ATON

Deityaton.com

All of Deity Aton's clothing contains at least 98 percent organic cotton, from T-shirts to hoodies, and is unique and fashionable. Also offered on the site are handmade jewelry pieces as well as organic oil soaps and lip balm.

DEL FORTE

Delforte.com

Started by designer Tierra Del Forte, the company offers premium denim apparel for women, made in the USA with 100 percent organic cotton. These stylish items are Earth-friendly, and a portion of Del Forte's proceeds go to support the Sustainable Cotton Project.

DELANO COLLECTION

Delanocollection.com

Delano Collection features a range of luxury brands for sustainable and sophisticated apparel, furniture, and home ware. All items are designed and made in the U.S., using only high-quality, sustainable, and organic materials like bamboo, soy, organic cotton, and organic wool.

ECOGANIK

Ecoganik.com

Ecoganik offers contemporary designs for women using only certified organic or eco-friendly fabrics, which are pesticide free and use only low-impact-dye fiber. These vibrantly colored items are meant for the social and eco-conscious woman who still wants to look hip and young.

EDUN

Edun.ie

This powerhouse collaboration between Bono, his wife Ali Hewson, and Rogan Gregory has created a fashion line that emphasizes fair-trade wages, with an emphasis on manufacturing in Africa, and strives to integrate Earth-friendly materials.

ENAMORE

Enamore.co.uk

Enamore is a U.K.-based design house that creates beautiful women's wear made from natural organic textiles and recycled fabrics, including hemp, cotton, silk, and bamboo. Line includes clothing, lingerie, and accessories, including a one-of-a-kind shoulder bag made from vintage print fabric and black hemp/Tencel.

HORNY TOAD

Hornytoad.com

This playful company offers eco-friendly apparel for men and women using working organic cotton and Mambo, a cellulose-based fiber, derived from things like wood chips, that breathes, wicks, and dries quickly. Horny Toad offers a lifetime guarantee on their products.

JONANO

Jonano.com

Jonano's mission is to provide exceptional apparel that both promotes healthy living and environmental preservation, deriving its materials from certified organic and eco-friendly fabrics, like organic cotton, bamboo, hemp, and recycled polyester. The company has a variety of clothing items, including yoga outfits and scrubs for medical personnel.

LOYALE CLOTHING

Loyaleclothing.com

This eco-fashion company uses bamboo fabrics, organic cotton, and surplus fabrics to make sophisticated apparel for women including workout clothing and casual wear. All products are made domestically in the United States and 3 percent of Loyale's annual products are donated to the Green Corps, an environmental leadership training program for students.

LEVI'S

Levis.com

The pioneer of denim is going organic. Levi's now offers organic cotton denim jeans for men and women.

LINDA LOUDERMILK

www.lindaloudermilk.com

Through Luxury Eco, Linda Loudermilk is helping to shape a new fashion ethic using materials like organic cotton, sasawashi, Tencel, and others made from bamboo, soy, and corn, many of which feature prominently in Loudermilk's new twenty-six-piece denim line and are also present in her tops, jackets, coats, pants, and dresses.

LOOMSTATE

Loomstate.org

Rogan Gregory revolutionized jeans with his eponymous label, and he's taken it a step further with Loomstate, an organic denim collection that does not skimp on style.

MARGARET O'LEARY

Margaretoleary.com

This upscale line of apparel and accessories uses sustainable materials like bamboo, silk, and hemp to promote Earth awareness, while maintaining a city chic feel meant for the stylish yet socially conscious female.

NATURAL HIGH LIFESTYLE

Naturalhighlifestyle.com

California-based Natural High Lifestyle celebrates the local yoga, surfing, and environmentally aware culture with fashion-forward activewear using materials like hemp and bamboo. The clothing line is well-suited for relaxing at the beach, the boardwalk, or the local café. Visit the company's flagship store on Main Street in Santa Monica.

NAU

Nau.com

Blending performance, beauty and sustainability, Nau offers a line of outdoor performance and lifestyle clothing that is equally suitable for scaling remote mountain peaks or lounging with a cappuccino at the corner café. Sustainbility is considered at every turn and is reflected in high-tech, high-performance materials that are healthier for humans and the planet.

NIKE

Nike.com

The sneaker giant is about more than jump shots. Nike is one of the world's biggest purchasers of organic cotton and aims to incorporate at least 5 percent of the material into every one of its cotton products by 2010. Nike's Considered footwear line pushes eco-awareness into new shoe styles too.

OF THE EARTH

Oftheearth.com

A company committed to eco-conscious performance wear, Of The Earth utilizes eco-aware fabrics like organic cotton, merino wool, cashmere, silk, linen, ramie, hemp, Tencel, soy, and bamboo in its apparel. The Of The Earth line is one of the most extensive eco-collections available for men and women.

ON AND ON ÉCOLO CHIC

Onandon.ca

Designer Annie Langlois creates her collection of one-of-a-kind design-forward styles from fabrics that have been recovered and recycled from used garments such as sweaters, tweed jackets, men's suits, silk scarves, and dresses. On and On deconstructs the garments and refashions them into cutting-edge styles.

PATAGONIA

Patagonia.com

Patagonia provides high-performance outdoor clothing for men, women, and children and has implemented some of the most forward-thinking eco-initiatives in the industry. Patagonia uses organic cotton and recycled PET, a fleece-like fabric derived from recycled plastic soda bottles, in its clothing lines and has begun one of the industry's first garment recycling programs to transform used, worn-out clothing into spun materials for new garments. Patagonia is also now branching into eco-aware footwear.

PEOPLE TREE

Peopletree.co.uk

People Tree is all about the environment and the community, with its eco-friendly, fair-trade clothing and home products. People Tree also creates jobs within communities, promotes sustainability, and pays special attention to their products to ensure they adhere to their Earth-conscious mantra.

SAMEUNDERNEATH

Sameunderneath.com

A collection of hip and edgy apparel for both men and women, with an emphasis on environmental and social awareness, Sameunderneath brings a "street" feel to organic living. Clothing is derived from a blend of bamboo and cotton, with style written all over it.

SANS

S-a-n-s.com

This Brooklyn-based eco-fashion label started turning heads in the fashion world with the introduction of its fall line at New York Fashion week in February, 2007. Deconstructed shapes made of materials like bamboo, organic cotton, and wool inform the latest collection ranging from T-shirts to dresses to overcoats.

STEWART+BROWN

Stewartbrown.com

Designers Karen Stewart and Howard Brown were inspired to start an all-natural clothing company when their daughter was born. Every Stewart+Brown design uses organic cotton, factory surplus materials, or Mongolian cashmere—straight from a co-op in northwestern Mongolia that helps to ensure the nomadic herders' survival and maintain their traditional way of life.

TIMBERLAND

Timberlandserve.com

Timberland's company-wide environmental commitment starts with performance footwear that eliminates toxins and utilizes recycled and eco-aware materials. Timberland is also one of the world's largest purchasers of organic cotton. Many of its operational facilities are powered by renewable energy like solar energy.

TURK AND TAYLOR

Turkandtaylor.com

Based in San Franciso, Turk and Taylor's limited-edition T-shirts are made of organic cotton and hand dyed with their unique designs. These fun, casual, and eco-friendly creations are available in long-sleeve T-shirts, hoodies, and shorts as well.

TWICE SHY

Twice-shy.com

With a newly launched line of organic children's clothing named "Fig," Twice Shy adds to its already hip and trendy men's and women's fashion wear. Items are fashionable and distinctive, with peasant- and tunic-style tops for women and an aviator jacket and chinos for men, all made with organic materials, among their offerings.

UNDER THE CANOPY

Underthecanopy.com

One of the early eco-fashion pioneers, Under The Canopy continually reinvents itself and now offers a broad collection of stylish, eco-aware clothing for women using materials like organic cotton and soy. Men's and baby clothing collections are in the works.

UNDESIGNED

Undesigned.com

Undesigned contains Carol Young's line of eco-conscious clothing, constructed with recycled fabrics, including fleece made from recycled soda bottles. In addition to its green practices, Undesigned also raises money for various nonprofits and is a proud member of One Percent for the Planet, an alliance of socially and environmentally responsible businesses that donate one percent of all sales to environmental organizations.

Accessory Labels

AGAIN NYC
Againnyc.com
These distinctive bags are made in the U.S. using rescued and repurposed materials to create accessories that will blend in with your style while maintaining environmental awareness. Portions of the profits are donated to environmental charities.

ALCHEMY GOODS
Alchemygoods.com
Alchemy Goods, whose motto reads "Turning useless into useful," certainly does just that, with their chic bags constructed with eco-friendly materials, including recycled seat-belt straps for handles. They also offer a clever line of "accessories" consisting of seat-belt buckles sold as bottle openers.

BAZURA BAGS
Bazurabags.com
Bazura Bags uses discarded juice containers and recycled aluminum soda and beer cans to make funky purses, handbags, and messenger bags. The bags are designed by a women's cooperative in the Philippines where workers receive fair wages for their labor.

ECOIST
Ecoist.com
Even though they're made from recycled trash (candy wrappers, soft drink labels, and food packages), these hip, flashy bags have been seen on the arms of A-list celebrities including Paris Hilton and Lindsay Lohan. But the overall goal for Ecoist is not fame, but to inform consumers and inspire positive changes for our planet.

ESCAMA
Escama.com
Made by two women's cooperatives on the outskirts of Brasília, Brazil, these bags are constructed with recycled aluminum can tabs, giving the appearance of fish scales, hence the name Escama, which means "fish

scales" in Portuguese. Enclosed in every bag is a card with the name of the artisan.

HER DESIGN
Her-design.com
This is the site for designer Helen E. Riegle's trendy, contemporary handbags and accessories made with various eco-friendly materials, including organic cotton, hemp canvas, silk, microsuede, vegan leather, eco wool, and silk. Her Design also donates 2 percent of gross sales to environmental and youth-oriented causes.

MOONRISE JEWELRY
Moonrisejewelry.com
A collection of high-quality, handcrafted jewelry made locally in Virginia to promote women's economic empowerment, while also being Earth-friendly, using natural, recycled, and renewable materials in their crafts. Items are unique and colorful, with influences in cultural traditions worldwide, including Hawaiian-, Asian-, and South American–styled jewelry.

PRO'TECH'D
Protechd.com
Organic can mesh with high-tech. Ruben-Salama's organic cotton iPod cozies cover your music player in eco-goodness.

RED FLAG DESIGN
Redflagdesign.ca
Red Flag Design creates stylish bags from materials that are as historically valuable as they are sustainable. Bags are comprised of recycled boat sails washed in cold water and bio-friendly detergents, and no two bags are the same.

SALVATION SACKS
Salvationsacks.com
It doesn't get much more unique or eco-friendly than these original bags by Salvation Sacks, constructed with vintage, salvaged, and recycled clothing, linens, accessories, jewelry, and other objects. To make ownership special no two bags are exactly the same.

TERRA PLANA
Terraplana.com
Striving to become the most sustainable shoe brand on the planet, Terra Plana creates shoes for men and women, which are based on stitched

artisan constructions with water-based adhesives. Shoes are hip and stylish, made with recycled materials like coffee bags, clothing scraps, 100-percent-recycled foam footbeds for interior comfort, and, of course, recycled card for shoe boxes.

Retailers

ADILI

Adili.com

Named for the Swahili word meaning "ethical and just," Adili strives to showcase items made ethically, using fair-trade standards, including no child exploitation or sweatshops, and environmental consciousness. The company mainly features women's wear, but it has a limited selection of items for men and children, and beauty products.

BEKLINA

Beklina.com

Beklina is an organic boutique run by a three-woman family operation based in Northern California offering clothing, accessories, and stationery. All items are organic, sustainable, and/or fair trade, from a variety of eco-conscious designers.

BTC

Btcelements.com

BTC (Be The Change) Elements is an eco-style boutique founded by Summer Bowen to present organic garments for men, women, and children, as well as home accessories and beauty products made from sustainable and natural materials. The site also offers a wedding registry, items on sale, and gifts.

COCO'S SHOPPE

Cocosshoppe.com

Coco's Shoppe is a boutique carrying fashion, accessories, and beauty products that are sustainable and eco-conscious. Some of the unique items that can be bought here include Ananas handbags made from banana plants, Brickhouse organic body care products, and Jezebelle handmade jewelry.

EKOVARUHUSET

Ekovaruhuset.se

Ekovaruhuset—meaning "house of organics" in Swedish—is a New York City boutique where European eco-labels share shelf space with local eco-fashion talent.

GOMI

www.gominyc.com

Tucked on a side street in NYC's East Village, Gomi sells cutting-edge, eco-aware clothing and accessories. Founder Anne Hettinger is always on the lookout for eco-fashion labels like Loomstate, Del Forte, Majestic, Delano Collection, and coming soon from Europe, Kuyichi.

GREENLOOP

Thegreenloop.com

Greenloop carries a wide array of sustainable items from a number of responsible brands, including clothing by Loomstate, Stewart+Brown, and Edun. Among the collection are modern, stylish bags, belts, footwear, and jewelry, not to mention premier organic and natural body care products.

THE HEMPEST

Hempest.com

Founded in 1995 to bring quality, eco-aware hemp clothing and accessories to a broad audience, The Hempest is fulfilling its mission. A quality online store is complemented by retail store locations in Burlington, Vermont; Boston, Cambridge, and Northampton, Massachusetts; and Santa Barbara, California.

HIP & ZEN

Hipandzen.com

Hip & Zen's easily navigated website includes a handy product key labeling which products are organic, recycled, handmade, natural, and/or fair trade. Products range from apparel to home products, all of which were chosen carefully to reflect sophistication, style, and eco-awareness.

KAIGHT

Kaightnyc.com

This newcomer to the Lower East Side of New York City offers quality eco-fashion labels that continually push aesthetics in new and exciting directions. You'll find many cutting-edge designers represented under one roof.

NOT JUST PRETTY

Notjustpretty.com

Not Just Pretty is an eco-boutique offering a broad selection of hip, stylish clothing from forward-thinking international designers, hair and beauty products, and accessories. Everything sold is sustainable, made from organic fibers or recycled materials.

ORGANIC AVENUE

Organicavenue.com

Get your raw food and your organic denim jeans all at once by visiting this Lower East Side store in Manhattan. Del Forte and Natural High Lifestyle are just two of the featured labels in this eco-lifestyle store, where you'll also find stylish collections of tabletop and bath and bedding products.

SATYA

Satyaboutique.com

The City of Brotherly Love gets its sustainable style groove on thanks to Philadelphia-based Satya. This eco-fashion boutique offers many top labels, including Loomstate, Of The Earth, and Delano Collection.

SODAFINE

Sodafine.com

Based in Brooklyn, New York, Sodafine specializes in unique handmade clothing, accessories, and gifts, with an emphasis on eco-friendly collections. Aside from being Earth-friendly, Sodafine also assists young artists and individuals to market their wares.

WAL-MART

Walmart.com

Wal-Mart garners top honors as the world's largest purchaser of organic cotton—10 million pounds' worth in 2006. Today Wal-Mart and its subsidiary, Sam's Club, feature organic cotton baby clothing and teenage fashion. This is just the beginning. Look for new organic fashion on Wal-Mart's shelves by 2008.

ZANISA

Zanisa.com

This online boutique offers stylish, eco-aware accessories like bags, belts, and jewelry. The full collection includes spa products, stationery, and a nice selection of tabletop furnishings.

Information/Education

FABULOUSLY GREEN

fabulouslygreen.blogspot.com

Fabulously Green tracks the latest trends, styles, and products in eco-fashion and accessories and green interior design. Find products ranging from the newest clothing fashions to hip handbags to plant-able greeting cards that will sprout organic herbs like basil or chives—it's the gift that keeps on giving.

FIFTYRX3.COM

Jill Danyelle's eco-fashion blog is an essential destination for tracking the fast-moving product introductions and trends at the crossroads of fashion and the environment.

GREAT GREEN GOODS

greatgreengoods.com

A dedicated green shopping blog, Great Green Goods scours the Internet for stylish and funky green finds. Products highlighted are typically made from recycled or sustainable materials.

ORGANIC EXCHANGE

Organicexchange.org

A nonprofit organization committed to expanding the use of organic cotton by retailers and manufacturers, Organic Exchange is working with retail giant Wal-Mart to encourage its continued adoption of organic cotton products. The website's database lets you easily find organic cotton products available from the brands of its member companies.

SUMMER RAYNE OAKES

www.summerrayne.net

The model with a mission is not new, but Oakes takes it to another level as the face of the eco-fashion movement and founder of SRO, a think tank and consultation and project-development firm that aims to connect fashion, media, education, and sustainability. SRO's newsletter, *S4*, is a must-read for industry insiders and fashionistas seeking insight into sustainable trends in fashion.

SUSTAINABLE STYLE FOUNDATION

Sustainablestyle.org

If it's stylish and green, you'll probably find it here. The daily showcase features green products. The daily spotlight covers sustainable style information and resources. The online sourcebook provides yet another resource for great products and services to plug into your eco-lifestyle. SSF also publishes a quarterly online magazine called *SASS* and hosts the annual Outstanding Style Achievement Awards.

TREEHUGGER.COM

The top green destination on the web, this fast-paced blog is dedicated to everything that's green with a modern aesthetic. Get the latest updates on green trends and search more than ten thousand categorized posts. Contributing writer Kyeann Sayer provides insights into the latest product introductions, fashion shows, and trends shaping the eco-fashion industry.

2

Outdoor Gear

Ahh, the great outdoors. That bastion of bugs, bites, and restless nights in cramped tents. Hardly my favorite activity, but still, I like to think of myself as an intrepid adventurer who's always prepared to spend months in the wilderness equipped with the ultimate in high-performance gear. Luckily, the outdoor industry has made supreme eco-advances. Many manufacturers of recreational products are ahead of the curve when it comes to creating goods that respect nature and running businesses that leave a minimal environmental footprint. It makes sense: the majority of people drawn to work at outdoor companies are nature enthusiasts themselves, and many of the CEOs and founders are outdoor legends and preservation pioneers.

There is perhaps no greater eco rock star than Yvon Chouinard, founder of Patagonia. Not only has he single-handedly (actually he used both hands) scaled the imposing rock faces of Yosemite National Park, Chouinard has also succeeded in creating outdoor eco-performance gear that lives up to its promise to keep you warmer, cooler, and drier. And it all starts with plastic soda bottles. Since 1993, the company has been making top-quality fleece garments out of recycled soda bottles through a process that melts the plastic down into pellets, transforms them into yarn, and spins the yarn into a polyester fabric. It's not just a few bottles here and there, but 86 million that have successfully been kept out of the trash heap. Through continuous innovation, Patagonia now combines recycled soda bottles with unusable fabrics and worn-out garments to create polyester fibers that are used for fleece clothing, Capilene—Patagonia's signature moisture-wicking polyester fabric—base layers, shell jackets, and board shorts.

Upping the eco-ante further, when cotton is called for, Patagonia relies exclusively upon certified organic cotton for its men's, women's, and kids' clothing, so no toxic pesticides or insecticides need to touch your skin. The company has also created the world's first customer-garment recycling program. Drop off your used Patagonia Capilene base layers at any Patagonia store or mail them into the company's service center, and Patagonia will break down the fabric, give it a good scrubbing, and integrate the material into new garments. Sure, the program would be more appealing if customers received store credit for the materials they gave back to Patagonia, but it's a good start and an exciting example of how companies can create continuous product life cycles that limit the need for more raw materials.

For outdoor adventurers who depend upon rugged high-performance footwear to ascend tall peaks, and for those adventurers who depend on stylish oxfords to climb corporate ladders, Timberland offers quality eco-aware options. To advance its company-wide commitment to a cleaner planet, Timberland has gone after the most noxious ingredients found in conventional footwear: the toxic solvents used to bind components together. Timberland has sought alternatives and hit upon high-performance, nontoxic, water-based adhesives. Timberland has found that shoes with healthier ingredients outperform their conventional counterparts. Additional eco-footwear innovations include the introduction of recycled rubber for rugged outer soles and eco-friendly SmartWool for thermal-regulating interior comfort.

Yet, where the environment is concerned, a shoe is not just a shoe. It's also a box. Every pair of shoes comes packaged in its own box. So making that shoe box out of eco-friendly materials is an important challenge, one that Timberland meets head-on. In 2006, the company began packaging all footwear in boxes made from 100 percent recycled cardboard accompanied by a "nutritional" label printed with soy-based inks that describes the company's environmental and community footprint.

Timberland's commitment to a cleaner planet also extends deep into its own operations. Timberland's European distribution center in the Netherlands is powered entirely by wind energy, waste steam, and small-scale hydro power. The company's manufacturing facility in the Dominican Republic draws power from wind and solar energy. And Timberland's product distribution center in California is powered by one of the fifty largest solar panel systems in the world, providing over 60 percent of the distribution center's energy needs and eliminating 480,000 pounds of annual carbon emissions.

Timberland is now rolling out the industry's first eco-labeling program to help consumers quickly understand and verify the eco-impact of its products. Green Index tags found on select Timberland items rate a product's eco-performance from zero to ten across three key categories: greenhouse gas emissions specific to the production of the product, chemicals and solvents used in the production of the product, and organic, renewable, and recycled materials used in the product itself. Green Index tags help consumers easily choose the most eco-aware products. Stay tuned as the rest of the industry follows Timberland's lead.

Okay, you've got your Timberlands for mountain climbing and your Patagonia clothing to keep you acclimated to the weather. Now you're ready to do whatever it is that people who enjoy camping do. For me, it's enough just to know that Mother Nature is out there, but for others who need the real thing, I suggest packing along an array of Freeplay Energy products for your campsite. Freeplay is a U.K.-based provider of radios, lanterns, and flashlights that have regenerative energy sources built right into them. With integrated solar panels and hand cranks, you never have to worry about dead batteries when trekking in the wilderness (though if you happen upon an electric outlet you can always recharge the internal batteries and run your Freeplay products using the AC adapter). The Freeplay Eyemax radio offers impressive sound quality in a sleek compact design that doubles as an LED flashlight. Leave it in the sun to charge up or turn the hand crank for thirty seconds to get thirty minutes of light and radio pleasure. The Freeplay Summit is a multiband global radio and alarm clock that offers the same self-sufficient energy technology as the Eyemax and when fully charged can play continuously for twenty hours. Other products like the Weather Band radio enable you to tune into AM/FM stations as well as seven NOAA (National Oceanic & Atmospheric Administration) emergency weather broadcast channels. Factor in the integrated LED flashlight, and the Weatherband radio becomes a super-reliable product for both everyday and emergency use.

Let's say you're already an eco-enlightened adherent of Digital Convergence—the rapidly advancing technological trend enabling single electronic devices to perform multiple functions that formerly required multiple products. You depend upon an all-in-one gadget like the Palm Smartphone for GPS navigation, phone calls, emails, surfing the web, listening to MP3s, taking photos, and shooting videos. To keep your all-purpose gadget consistently charged and at the ready, turn to a Voltaic Systems backpack or attachable daypack. Voltaic Systems offers a line of bags that are embedded with solar panels and which feature a battery that stores the sun's energy. Each pack also comes with a wide assortment of plug tips that can be fitted to power virtually any handheld device. Sleekly designed and built to withstand harsh outdoor conditions, Voltaic Systems bags provide an elegant solution for powering up with nothing more than a bit of daylight. Convenient plug-charge-and-play capability is enabled with cords that are woven through the pack's shell, which makes charging up as easy as placing your cell phone or iPod inside the shoulder strap pouch. "This is wearable electronics—where the electronics are fully integrated in a seamless way," explains company founder Shayne McQuade. "You will see things like an LED charge indicator light integrated into the logo that it actually lights up when the panels are collecting the sun's energy. We're aiming for a full integration of textile and electronics." The Voltaic Systems line of backpacks, daypacks, and messenger bags are built with padding to protect laptops and other valuables, as well as plentiful pockets and storage compartments. A pack capable of powering a laptop is in the works.

Other portable solar power options include the line of Reware Juice backpacks, which are equipped with solar panels, and Reware Power Pockets—travel-size solar panels that are capable of delivering up to twelve watts of power—enough to power some small laptops—and can be easily folded and stowed away. When folded, Power Pockets measure only five inches wide by nine inches long and three-quarters of an inch thick, and weigh less than a pound, making them your convenient energy accessory. Or opt for a tent with solar panels like the Solar Intent, which is roomy enough to sleep up to six people. The Eclipse Intent comes with an LED light source and rechargeable batteries that can illuminate the tent's interior for up to eight hours when fully charged. It might not deliver enough light to comfortably read, but it will prevent you from stomping on your brother's head when heading out to relieve yourself in the middle of the night.

Should your outdoor adventure lead you to pristine mountain peaks where the air is crisp, the snow is deep, and the snowboarding is calling your name, then you will probably want to have an Arbor snowboard strapped to your boots. Makers of top-quality snowboards and skateboards, Arbor relies upon responsibly harvested wood and fast-growing bamboo to enhance the style and performance of its boards. The Arbor Mystic, for example, has been called the Mercedes-Benz of snowboards. This board is a radical performer thanks in large part to a bamboo-reinforced core that is both lightweight and durable. You can go for big air, and if you don't land it, your board will still be intact—even if your pride isn't.

Performance Wear

OF THE EARTH

Oftheearth.com

A company committed to eco-conscious performance wear, Of The Earth utilizes eco-aware fabrics like organic cotton, merino wool, cashmere, silk, linen, ramie, hemp, Tencel, soy, and bamboo in its apparel. The Of The Earth line is one of the most extensive eco-collections available for men and women.

PATAGONIA

Patagonia.com

Patagonia provides high-performance outdoor clothing for men, women, and children and has implemented some of the most forward-thinking eco-initiatives in the industry. Patagonia uses organic cotton and recycled PET in its clothing lines and has begun one of the industry's first garment recycling programs to transform used, worn-out clothing into spun materials for new garments. Patagonia is also now branching into eco-aware footwear.

PRANA

Prana.com

Prana believes that performance and design integrity should be mirrored by eco-integrity. The company integrates materials like organic cotton into its line and also offsets the carbon emissions of 250 of its national retailers through the purchase of renewable wind energy credits.

SAHALIE

Sahalie.com

Sahalie has been making outdoor performance wear for more than thirty years. The company integrates eco-innovative materials like bamboo and soy into clothing. Organic cotton is also prominently featured in many items.

SMARTWOOL

Smartwool.com

SmartWool is revolutionizing performance wear through its natural wool garments that are not only thermal regulating but also extremely comfortable. Founded by two ski instructors in New England, SmartWool makes base layers and mid-weight layers that will have you on the go in comfort and style.

TEKO SOCKS

Tekosocks.com

Teko's high-performance socks are made from a variety of eco-advanced materials like merino wool, organic cotton, recycled polyester, and ingeo—a material derived from corn. The warm, soft, non-slip socks are made in a North Carolina facility that offsets 100 percent of its energy use through the purchase of wind energy credits.

TIMBERLAND

Timberland.com

Timberland's company-wide environmental commitment starts with performance footwear that eliminates toxins and utilizes recycled and eco-aware materials. Timberland is also one of the world's largest purchasers of organic cotton. Many of its operational facilities are powered by renewable energy like solar energy.

Outdoor Gear

CLEAR BLUE HAWAII

Clearbluehawaii.com

When a waterproof pack is called for, check out Clear Blue Hawaii's stylish solar-paneled pack that will keep your gear dry and gadgets charged. Integrated solar panels enable you to charge your devices even while surrounded by water.

EUREKA SOLAR INTENT

Eurekatent.com

Roomy enough to sleep six people, the Solar Intent is equipped with flexible solar panels that power an LED light to illuminate the tent's interior and deliver up to eight hours of light when fully charged.

FREEPLAY ENERGY

Freeplayenergy.co.uk

Freeplay is a U.K.-based provider of radios, lanterns, and flashlights that are equipped with integrated, regenerative energy sources such as solar panels and hand cranks. With Freeplay products you never have to worry about dead batteries, which makes them great for the campsite and emergency situations.

REWARE

Rewarestore.com

Reware Juice bags integrate solar panels directly into backpacks and messenger bags. Some bags are made from recycled materials, creating quite possibly the most eco-friendly product in the world. Reware also offers Power Pockets—foldable, stowable solar panel kits that you can take along wherever your travels lead.

SIERRA STOVE

Zzstove.com

The tiny yet powerful Sierra Stove relies upon a small fan powered by a single AA battery to create a forced ventilation system that generates intense heat for cooking. Fuel the fire with twigs, bark, pinecones, and other small kindling and your meal will be prepared in short order. When collapsed, the Sierra Stove measures 5.5 inches by 3.5 inches and weighs just 2 pounds. Use rechargeable batteries for a fully eco-enlightened alfresco dining experience.

SOLIO
Solio.com
A sleek, ultra-portable solar power solution, the Solio fits in your pocket and fans out to reveal three solar panels that can charge your mobile gadgets when on the go.

VOLTAIC SYSTEMS
Voltaicsystems.com
Voltaic Systems offers quality-constructed backpacks and messenger bags that have solar panels and battery storage integrated directly into them. With your Voltaic pack you'll always have a power source with you.

Sporting Gear

ARBOR
Arborsports.com
Arbor designs and manufactures snowboards and skateboards for high performance thanks to innovative eco-aware materials like lightweight yet extremely sturdy bamboo. Arbor also makes clothing base layers using bamboo fabric, which naturally wicks moisture to keep body temperatures regulated while you're active.

BODY GLOVE
bodyglove.com
Body Glove, a leader in action sports wear, offers its ECO wetsuit, the first of its kind in the industry. The high-performance wetsuit is made of Body Glove's BIO-stretch rubber and ECO-flex materials that are stretchy yet non-petroleum based. Using healthier materials enables Body Glove to create a wetsuit that is nontoxic and requires only one-tenth the amount of energy to produce as standard petroleum-based wetsuits.

COMET SKATEBOARDS
Cometskateboards.com
Comet Skateboards produces high-quality skateboards using bamboo and FSC (Forest Stewardship Council) certified woods—attesting that the wood is sourced through responsible forestry management practices—and treated

with water-based, low-VOC (Volatile Organic Compounds) finishes to avoid toxins. The skateboards are manufactured in a California factory powered entirely by solar energy.

KINGSWOOD SKIS

Kingswoodskis.com
The first modern-day, high-tech bamboo skis were handcrafted in New Zealand by Kingswood Skis—and today are shipped all over the globe. The skis feature cores made from engineered bamboo. Sure, it's an eco-aware choice, but the company was also inclined to use bamboo because it's extremely strong and shock-absorbing, ideal qualities for skis.

VENTURE SNOWBOARDS

Venturesnowboards.com
Venture handcrafts premium snowboards using only the finest materials available that also minimize the company's eco-footprint, such as FSC-certified woods for snowboard cores and hemp and organic cotton for top sheets. The company also offsets all of its energy usage through the purchase of wind energy credits.

Information/Education

OUTDOOR RETAILER

Outdoorretailer.com/or/about_us/green_steps.jsp
The Green Steps Program overseen by Outdoor Retailer provides a mechanism for outdoor industry companies to share their best environmental practices with one another. Outdoor Retailer organizes trade events for the outdoor industry and uses the proceeds of the Green Steps Program to purchase wind energy credits to offset energy used at those events. The program's website also enables consumers to quickly research eco-friendly companies and learn about their eco-initiatives.

3

THE WORLD
IS YOUR
OYSTER

Travel

Travel has become an integral part of modern life, and

whether it's for business or pleasure, we expect the experience to be easy and enjoyable. Today it's also possible to combine luxury accommodations and unforgettable experiences with environmental consciousness. Even routine necessities like auto and air travel can be merged with a newfound eco-awareness.

Bio-Beetle is pushing the car rental industry in a green direction by offering rental cars fueled by biodiesel—a clean-burning diesel gasoline made from renewable sources like vegetable oil. What began as a way for Shaun Stenshol to help green the local tourism industry on the island of Maui in Hawaii has become a smash success. 2006 saw the opening of a second location in Los Angeles, California. Car models include Volkswagen Beetles, Jettas, and Passats and even a biodiesel-powered Jeep. Rates are reasonable and run from $200 to $300 per week in Los Angeles and slightly more for a week in Hawaii.

Visitors to the West Coast can also turn to EV Rental Cars for eco-friendly car transportation. Available in major Californian cities such as San Diego, Los Angeles, Oakland, San Jose, and San Francisco, EV Rental Cars provides an auto fleet comprised exclusively of hybrid vehicles, including the Toyota Prius, Ford Escape Hybrid SUV, and the Honda Civic Hybrid. Expansion plans are under way for Las Vegas, Nevada, and the company is already up and running in Phoenix, Arizona.

If you're in need of a car service to take you to the airport, the Dodgers game, or the Academy Awards ceremony, then turn to Eco Limo, a company that operates a fleet of stylish, black Toyota

Prius vehicles. If your car service needs are on the East Coast, in New York City, then OZO Car will chauffeur you in style in its own fleet of Toyota Prius hybrid vehicles. OZO Car outfits all of its vehicles with wireless Internet access so you can be as productive as you wish while en route. If flying into Logan Airport outside of Boston, Massachusetts, then call PlanetTran to come get you in one of its eco-advanced hybrid vehicles. PlanetTran's eco-car service operates throughout the Boston area, and plans are in the works to open a second location in San Francisco.

Eco-travel agencies can help you green your transportation and provide broad expertise to let you travel in style while treading lightly on the planet. Better World Club offers a range of travel-related services including insurance, roadside assistance, and travel planning. For each trip booked online through its website the company donates $1 to environmental causes. Vouchers that offset greenhouse gas emissions associated with air travel can be easily purchased and are automatically included when booking directly through the company's travel agents. Better World Club members also benefit from eco-travel discounts through an extensive green partner network. Recent partnerships with Bio-Beetle and EV Rental Car, for example, enable members to receive eco-friendly rental car discounts of up to 15 percent off regular prices.

Manaca EcoTravel uses an extensive eco-assessment tool to select the best eco-tours and eco-lodges around the world (think Peru, Australia, Fiji, and Madagascar). The company rates each one on its commitment to the environment as seen through food, education, community, and protection of fragile sites. Upon receiving approval by Manaca's staff, eco-operators then sign the Responsible Tourism Pledge attesting to their ongoing commitment to Earth-conscious practices. Visitors to the company website can surf the database of eco-options and contact Manaca to book destinations and airfare. You could soon find yourself at far-flung destinations like the Chumbe Island Coral Park in Tanzania, a private nature reserve that includes one of the most pristine coral reef sanctuaries in the world. Nestled right on the ocean in a protected area, the resort is mandated to have zero impact on the environment, which means you'll be sleeping in a state-of-the-art eco-bungalow equipped with solar water heating and electricity, rainwater catchment systems, gray water filtration, and composting toilets.

Eco-lodging is not only for adventure seekers. Many hotels in the United States and abroad are implementing measures to green their operations. In fact, two of the most widely respected hotel operators in North America are combining stylish accommodations with eco-principles to offer guests uncompromising experiences.

The Kimpton Group is the largest boutique hotelier in the country. From the Triton Hotel in San Francisco, to the Sky Hotel in Aspen, to 70 Park Avenue in New York City, Kimpton manages forty four-star properties throughout the country. In addition to providing intimate settings, stylish decor, and high-tech conveniences like in-room MP3 players and wireless Internet, Kimpton also provides a healthy, eco-enlightened atmosphere for business or leisure. Each hotel features water conservation and recycling programs as well as nontoxic cleaning products. Travelers may give little thought to how hotel linens are washed and rooms are kept tidy, but toxin-free laundry detergent and carpet and counter cleaners give guests a safer lodging experience and the staff a healthier working environment. Kimpton's environmental commitment even extends to its corporate materials, which are printed on recycled paper with soy ink, and to its in-house beverages—guests are treated to organic coffee and tea throughout the day and an organic wine happy hour. Several Kimpton hotels also offer "eco floors," and the Triton has celebrity-designed eco-suites. Guests can stay in the Red Hot Chili Pepper suite equipped with rescued furniture, hemp textiles, and organic cotton sheets, or Woody Harrelson's "oasis" with bamboo floors and hemp linens.

Fairmont Hotels & Resorts merges luxurious ambience with eco-intelligence. The company's forty-four properties in eight countries are set amid some of the most pristine and desirable real estate, such as the Fairmont Château Lake Louise, which draws 40 percent of its energy from wind power and hydropower from free-flowing rivers and is situated in the heart of the Canadian Rockies on a UNESCO World Heritage Site. Fairmont's luxury hotels are landmarks in U.S. cities such as Boston, Chicago, Dallas, Miami, Santa Monica, San Francisco, Seattle, and Washington, DC. In 1990, the company began implementation of its Green Partnership program, which strives for improvements across all of its hotel properties in waste management, energy and water conservation, and community outreach. Since 1997, Fairmont has successfully encouraged more than 80 percent of its hotel properties to reduce paper consumption by 20 percent. Bathrooms have been retrofitted with low-flow showerheads, toilet dams, and tap aerators to conserve water. Energy-efficient lighting has been installed in many properties. And now every front desk computer in every hotel is run on certified wind energy, so checking in is done entirely off the power grid. The results have been widely recognized, and in 2006, Fairmont received the World Travel & Tourism Council's prestigious 2006 Global Tourism Business Award, recognizing Fairmont as one of the word's leading examples of environmental best practices and responsible tourism.

Other hoteliers are making eco-strides too. The Orchard Garden Hotel in San Francisco opened in October of 2006 and is the first hotel in California to be LEED (Leadership in Energy and Environmental Design) certified by the U.S. Green Building Council. Guest rooms in the luxury boutique hotel are outfitted with an LCD flat-screen television with DVD and CD player, cordless telephone, and wireless Internet access. Bath products are all organic. And each room is fitted with a key-card energy control system designed to automatically shut off all lights and electronics when you leave the room. Up the road in Napa Valley, the Gaia Napa Valley Hotel offers luxury amenities, spa services, and plenty of eco-intelligent design features. The hotel is pursuing LEED certification and features eco-innovations like solar power for energy needs and recycled gray water from showers and sinks for outdoor landscaping irrigation.

In Boston, the Saunders Group operates the historic Lenox Hotel and the Copley Square Hotel, both of which have been recognized for their award-winning environmental programs. Superior energy efficiency and reductions in greenhouse gas emissions are achieved through forward-thinking initiatives like low-E windows that provide superior insulation and energy-efficient heat pumps for heating and cooling in guest rooms. Hotel vans run on compressed natural gas to reduce pollution and emissions. Water conservation is addressed through low-flow showerheads and toilets. Waste disposal demands are minimized by donations of food scraps to a local pig farm. These are but a few of the more than ninety projects that led the EPA to label the Saunders Hotel Group "a national leader in energy efficiency and environmental innovation."

Travelers in search of vacation destinations can go in eco-style too. Snow lovers can launch into some of the deepest powder in North America at Silverton Mountain in Colorado. Silverton has been ranked by *Powder* magazine as number one in steeps and number one in powder in the U.S. It's the ultimate skiing experience, with an equally formidable environmental record. For starters, no ski runs are ever cut clear, which keeps the environment pristine and the skiing adventurous. Silverton also plants two trees for every one that is cut down to make room for a lift. You may be picturing a mountain the size of Aspen (great environmental record by the way) with lift lines to match, but this is a different skiing experience. Silverton offers access to some of the most pristine terrain in the country and manages to effectively serve its skiers with just one lift. There are no more than one hundred skiers allowed on the mountain each day, and a guide accompanies every one. Located in the San Juan Mountains, Silverton's thirteen hundred acres have been leased to owner Aaron Brill by the Bureau of Land Management with the understanding that he will preserve the land.

If big resorts are more your style, then Vail Resorts, the company that owns and operates Vail, Beaver Creek, Breckenridge, and Keystone ski resorts in Colorado, Heavenly ski resort in California and Nevada, and Grand Teton Lodge in Jackson Hole, Wyoming, will help you minimize your eco-impact with every lift you ride or cup of hot chocolate you drink. In 2006, Vail began offsetting all of its energy consumption at all of its mountains—including lifts, restaurants, and resort hotels—through purchases of wind energy. Yet you won't see wind farms towering above China Bowl or other pristine ski areas. The wind energy credits that Vail Resorts purchases through Renewable Choice Energy enable wind-generated power to enter the national power grid elsewhere, serving to reduce carbon dioxide greenhouse gas emissions by 211 million pounds per year—the equivalent of taking eighteen thousand cars off the road. In the United States, Vail is now the second largest purchaser of wind energy, behind only Whole Foods.

Not into snowcapped vacations? There's always the exploration of remote locales via a luxury small-craft ship. These boats take you to the places that the larger cruise boats simply can't access. Once you arrive at your destination, a team of seasoned guides—geologists and oceanographers—will take you along as they conduct cutting-edge research for the likes of the National Geographic Society. Lindblad Expeditions has been taking travelers and researchers around the world for thirty years. From the Galapagos to the Antarctic, founder Sven Lindblad ensures that exploration is as much about discovery as it is about environmental conservation. Lindblad's conservation programs range from the Baja Forever Campaign to partnerships with the World Wildlife Fund, the Alaska Whale Foundation, the Marine Stewardship Council, and the RARE Center for Tropical Conservation. Lindblad is also a member of the Chef's Collaborative, an organization that sources the freshest ingredients from local farmers and fisherman, so you can support the local economies you visit by enjoying a sumptuous feast.

Lindblad is a member of the Adventure Collection, a group of premier adventure travel operators as committed to creating unique and unforgettable vacations as they are to eco-conservation and responsible tourism. Buddy Bombard's Europe will take you on tours of Europe's castles and make you feel like you can reach out and touch the spires and turrets from your perch in a hot air balloon. Backroads will guide you on adventure bike treks amid North American glacier peaks. Bushtracks Expeditions sets you down in remote eco-regions through its private-air safaris. Canadian Mountain Holidays helicopters you into the pristine mountain high country accompanied by expert guides for activities ranging from skiing to climbing and mountaineering. Geographic Expeditions can lead your adventure to the East Face of Mount Everest. And these are but a few of the exploration possibilities that await you.

Car Rentals and Services

BIO-BEETLE
Bio-beetle.com
The first all-biodiesel rental car company in the world, Bio-Beetle offers its rental car services in Los Angeles and the Hawaiian island of Maui. True to its name, Bio-Beetle rents Volkswagen Beetles as well as Golfs, Jettas, Passats, and Jeeps.

ECO LIMO
Eco-limo.com
When in Los Angeles, do what the stars do and hire Eco Limo to take you around town in a stylish, eco-intelligent black Toyota Prius. National expansion plans are currently in planning. Look for Eco Limo locations soon in San Francisco, Washington, DC, and New York.

EV RENTAL CARS
Evrental.com
With locations in California, Arizona, and coming soon, Las Vegas, EV Rental offers more than 350 hybrid engine rental cars. The company's mission is to offer the most technologically and environmentally advanced cars to the public as soon as they are available. Hybrid car models available include the Toyota Prius, Toyota Highlander SUV, and the Honda Civic.

OZO CAR
Ozocar.com
A New York City car service that chauffeurs customers exclusively in hybrid vehicles, Ozo Car is committed to providing a luxury experience that won't compromise the planet. All vehicles are fitted with wireless Internet access so you can be as productive as you wish while en route.

PLANET TRAN
Planettran.com
Servicing Boston and nearby Logan Airport, Planet Tran is an eco-service that picks you up and transports you in eco-style with its fleet of hybrid vehicles. A second location is being planned for San Francisco.

Travel Agencies

BETTER WORLD CLUB

Betterworldclub.com

Better World Club offers a range of travel-related services including insurance, roadside assistance, and travel planning. For each trip booked online at its website, the company donates $1 to environmental causes. Vouchers that offset greenhouse gas emissions associated with air travel can be easily purchased and are automatically included when booking directly through the company's travel agents.

MANACA TRAVEL

Manaca.com

Manaca EcoTravel uses an extensive eco-assessment tool to select the best eco-tours and eco-lodges around the world—rating food, education, community, and protection of fragile sites. Visitors to the website can surf the database of eco-options and contact Manaca to book destinations and airfare.

Hotel Operators

FAIRMONT HOTELS & RESORTS

Fairmont.com

Fairmont's hotels and resorts merge luxurious ambience with eco-intelligence. The company's forty-four properties in eight countries implement eco-initiatives to conserve energy and water and recycle waste. All front-desk computers in every hotel are powered by wind energy from the purchase of renewable energy credits.

KIMPTON HOTELS

Kimptonhotels.com

Eco-floors and celebrity-designed eco-suites are just the beginning. Kimpton hotels also feature water conservation and recycling programs and use only nontoxic cleaning products. Stop by one of the chain's boutique hotels around the country for a free organic wine happy hour.

SAUNDERS HOTEL GROUP

Saundershotelgroup.net

The Saunders Group operates the historic Lenox Hotel and the Copley Square Hotel, both of which have been recognized for their award-winning environmental programs. The EPA has labeled the Saunders Hotel Group "a national leader in energy efficiency and environmental innovation."

CHUMBE ISLAND CORAL PARK

Chumbeisland.com

Stay at this private nature reserve in Tanzania that offers one of the most pristine choral reef sanctuaries in the world. Guests sleep in state-of-the-art eco-bungalows equipped with solar water heating and electricity, rainwater catchment systems, gray water filtration, and composting toilets.

GAIA NAPA VALLEY HOTEL

Gaiahotelnapavalley.com

The Gaia Napa Valley Hotel offers luxury amenities, spa services, and plenty of eco-intelligent design features. The hotel is pursuing LEED certification and features eco-innovations like solar power for energy needs and recycled gray water from showers and sinks for outdoor landscaping irrigation.

HOTELITO DESCONOCIDO

Hotelito.com

Perched on a wetland estuary between the Sierra Madre Mountains and the Pacific Ocean, Hotelito is run entirely on solar power—candles light the rooms and restaurant at night. The resort also sits on a major sea turtle and bird reserve.

MACHU PICCHU PUEBLO HOTEL

Inkaterra.com

Located in Machu Picchu's Historical Sanctuary in the cloud forest, Pueblo's whitewashed cottages are spread across twelve acres of streams, waterfalls, and forest. The hotel features the world's largest collection of native orchids, and the rooms are outfitted with handcrafted Andean architecture, alpaca bedspreads, and handmade organic amenities and aromatherapy products.

ORCHARD GARDEN HOTEL

Theorchardgardenhotel.com

The first hotel in California to be LEED certified by the U.S. Green Building Council, the Orchard Garden Hotel in San Francisco features guest rooms outfitted with an LCD flat-screen television with DVD and CD player, a cordless telephone, and wireless Internet access. Bath products are all organic. And each room is fitted with a key-card energy-control system designed to automatically shut off all lights and electronics when you leave the room.

WILDERNESS OUTPOST AT BEDWELL RIVER

Wildretreat.com

Inspired by late-nineteenth-century Great Camps, the Wilderness Outpost in British Columbia offers eighteen sumptuous tents equipped for luxury camping. Each tent at this eco-resort features an Adirondack-style bed, antique dressers, pressed-glass oil lamps, heirloom accessories, and a propane wood stove. Explore the natural surroundings by going on an eco-safari on horseback and by helicopter.

Adventure

ADVENTURE COLLECTION

Adventurecollection.com

The Adventure Collection is a group of premier adventure travel operators as committed to creating unique and unforgettable vacations as they are to eco-conservation and responsible tourism. Explore the corners of the Earth with award-winning tour operators by helicopter, private airplane, small cruise ship, bicycle, or hot air balloon. If you can dream it, these companies can likely make it happen.

JIMINY PEAK MOUNTAIN RESORT

Jiminypeak.com

The first ski resort in the U.S. to install its own wind turbine to generate wind power, Jiminy broke ground on the $4 million turbine in 2006, and construction is scheduled for completion in 2007. When finished, the wind turbine will create enough clean energy to supply one-third of the resort's energy needs, roughly the equivalent of powering 766 homes.

LINDBLAD EXPEDITIONS

Expeditions.com

Skip the big, impersonal cruise for a Lindblad adventure. Destinations include the Galapagos and the Antarctic, and guides are often geologists and oceanographers. Conservation is a focal point of Lindblad's mission, as is a commitment to supporting local agriculture.

SILVERTON MOUNTAIN

Silvertonmountain.com

Skiing has never looked like this. No ski run is ever cut clear, and there are less than one hundred skiers allowed on the mountain each day. Go big. Go deep. Get all the freshies your legs can take.

SUSTAINABLE ENERGY IN MOTION BICYCLE TOUR

Portlandpeace.org

Bike hundreds of miles along the beautiful Oregon coastline, study and apply the philosophies of permaculture and alternative building, and observe local economics projects and grassroots democracy movements in the places through which you travel.

VAIL SKI RESORTS

Vailresorts.com

Vail Resorts, the company that owns and operates Vail, Beaver Creek, Breckenridge, and Keystone ski resorts in Colorado, Heavenly ski resort in California and Nevada, and Grand Teton Lodge in Jackson Hole, Wyoming, offsets all of its energy consumption at all of its mountains—including lifts, restaurants, and resort hotels—through purchases of wind energy.

Ones to Watch

"1" HOTEL & RESIDENCES

Starwoodhotels.com

The first global eco-luxury hotel brand is getting set to open its doors. "1" will combine green architecture and interior design with top-flight service and comfort. The Starwood Capital Group is behind the venture and has brought in the National Resources Defense Council (NRDC) as an environmental advisor. The first hotel is slated to open in Seattle in 2008, with others to follow in Scottsdale, Arizona; Fort Lauderdale, Florida; and Mammoth ski resort in California. "1" hotels in New York, Los Angeles, and Washington, DC, are also anticipated.

ALOFT HOTELS

Starwoodhotels.com / alofthotels

Coming in 2008 are the Aloft Hotels, labeled "a vision of W Hotels." The hotels will be more accessibly priced than W Hotels but will still deliver upscale contemporary decor and super-fun atmosphere. Green features include Seventh Generation cleaning supplies and laundry detergents to rid toxins from hotel rooms and linens and even the pool. Coveted parking spaces directly outside the hotel will be reserved exclusively for hybrid cars.

BOEING

Boeing.com/news/releases/2003/q3/nr_030711p.html
The world-class leader in airplanes is working on a hydrogen fuel-cell airplane that would emit zero greenhouse gas emissions while in flight. The prototype is currently being developed at its research center in Madrid, Spain.

RICHARD BRANSON

virgin.com/subsites/virginfuels
The world-class entrepreneur behind Virgin Atlantic, Virgin Records, and lots of other Virgins is placing big bets on alternative energy. Branson has committed to investing $3 billion to develop the green fuels of the future, and word has it he's on to a fuel source that could help green all transportation, including air travel.

FRANCIS FORD COPPOLA

Blancaneauxlodge.com
Coppola bought Blancaneaux Lodge in the jungles of Belize because it reminded him of the wild beauty of the Philippine jungle where he filmed *Apocalypse Now*. The resort not only provides a luxurious escape, but it's also environmentally aware. Ninety percent of the lodge's power comes from a hydroelectric plant Coppola built to harness the water of the nearby Privassion River. With three resorts in Belize—he also owns Turtle Inn and La Lancha—Coppola has mastered the pairing of sumptuous vacationing and eco-consciousness. Where will he go next?

LEONARDO DICAPRIO

In 2005 DiCaprio purchased the 104-acre Blackadore Caye island, off the coast of Belize. Always the avid conservationist, he's rumored to have plans to turn it into an exclusive eco-luxury resort.

Information/Education

ENVIRONMENTALLY FRIENDLY HOTELS

Environmentallyfriendlyhotels.com
This website maintains a global database of hotels, resorts, lodges, inns, motels, and bed and breakfasts that are implementing green measures. The site rates properties on a scale of 1 to 7 for eco-friendly commitment, and travelers often post comments to provide additional information about the properties.

GOLF AND THE ENVIRONMENT

Golfandenvironment.org

An initiative of Audubon International, Golf and the Environment teams up with golf courses around the world to help management teams design and maintain courses in ways that support healthier ecosystems. Visit the website to find hundreds of golf courses that have been certified by Audubon International, attesting to their environmentally friendly practices.

GREEN HOTELS ASSOCIATION

GreenHotels.com

Green Hotels promotes and supports the greening of the hotel industry. The website features an extensive list of member hotels throughout the United States and internationally that are interested in implementing programs that save water, energy, and reduce solid waste. Green Hotels does not verify or certify eco-claims made by its member hotels, but the list presents a good starting point for discovering hotels, inns, and bed and breakfasts that take environmental issues seriously.

NATIONAL SKI AREAS ASSOCIATION

Nsaa.org

NSAA is the trade association for ski area owners and operators, and it maintains a database on its website of environmental practices implemented by its members. Click on "The Green Room" in the environment section of the website to view the environmental steps that specific ski mountains throughout the U.S. are taking to combat global warming.

RAINFOREST ALLIANCE

Rainforest-alliance.org

The Rainforest Alliance implements programs for ecosystems and the people and wildlife that depend on them. The organization's Eco-Index of Sustainable Tourism lists hotels, resorts, and tour operators throughout Latin America and the Caribbean that follow environmental and socially responsible principles.

RESPONSIBLETRAVEL.COM

This website offers an easily searchable database of eco-aware hotels and resorts around the globe. Tour operators listed are all carefully screened. Travelers also contribute independent reviews of the properties listed to provide an additional screen. Budget-conscious backpackers, families, and luxury destination seekers will all find useful information here.

SUSTAINABLE TRAVEL INTERNATIONAL

Sustainabletravelinternational.org

Sustainable Travel International (STI) is a nonprofit organization that provides education to travelers and outreach to the travel industry to improve the environmental conditions in tourism destinations. The website maintains a great database of eco-tour operators and accommodations around the globe.

WILD ASIA

Wildasia.net

This Malaysia-based think tank supports conservation initiatives in Asia to develop responsible tourism. The organization's website offers an easily searchable database of hotels and resorts throughout Asia that are committed to eco-conservation, respecting local cultures, and contributing to local economies.

4

Vehicular
Inspiration
CARS—TO OWN, TO RENT, TO DRIVE

When it comes to transportation, there's the eco-obvious and then there's the eco-innovative. Obviously, riding our bikes is better than driving our cars. Carpooling is better than driving alone. Keeping our tires pumped up helps fuel efficiency. So do full fuel tanks. Yet there are lots of other easy, attractive options out there to green our transportation.

Let's start with roadside assistance. If you drive a car, you probably have a roadside assistance plan, and the provider of that plan is most likely the American Automobile Association (AAA). AAA is great on service but lousy on the environment. The company is a longstanding member of the highway lobby, a business coalition that aims to put more cars on the road regardless of their toll on the environment. For roadside assistance with an environmental twist, consider Better World Club, a company that matches AAA in service without compromising the environment. Better World Club donates 3 percent of its proceeds to environmental causes, offers discounts to hybrid car drivers, taxes those who drive fuel-inefficient cars, and even offers a bicycle roadside assistance plan. It's a good, easy choice for you and the planet.

If you're ready to give up your car, but not quite ready to be 100 percent biker, check out services like Zipcar. For an hourly fee you can reserve a car whenever you need one, pick it up at convenient locations throughout your city, and drive for as long—and far—as you desire. Insurance costs and the first hundred miles of gas are included in the rental cost. Zipcar, and its close competitor Flexcar, make car sharing startlingly cool. You can cruise in a hybrid, Mini Cooper, even a BMW. And if you need more trunk space, there's the roomy Honda Element. Zipcar gives you easy access to a car without any of the expenses of actual car ownership, and reduces traffic congestion and carbon dioxide emissions in the process.

Since most car owners can't imagine life without four wheels, a hybrid model—cars whose engines run on both electric energy and gasoline—provides ample opportunity to enjoy a sweet ride while saving money at the pump and preventing greenhouse gases from harming your future grandchildren. The Toyota Prius is the most well-known hybrid model on the road. No wonder. It's got a space-age dashboard, plenty of legroom, and a surprisingly powerful engine. At 60/51 mpg on the road and highway, the Prius is best-in-class on fuel efficiency, a star performer, and a perpetual provider of sci-fi thrills with an engine that starts with the simple push of a power-on button.

The Prius is a prime example of what I would consider a *conspicuous* eco-product. Its widely recognizable, distinctive design loudly proclaims its driver's lofty intent to save the planet. As Mark Spellun, publisher of *Plenty* magazine has written, "You never see a bumper sticker on a Prius." The car already says it all.

For folks who have no desire to collect eco-inspired high-fives from parking attendants and toll collectors, yet still prefer lower fuel costs and a cleaner environment, there are other options. Hybrid car models that look identical to their conventional counterparts, like the Toyota Camry Hybrid and Honda Accord Hybrid, are now available. These cars signal the next evolution of eco-design, the introduction of what I think of as *invisible* eco products. The eco-smarts that enable the Camry Hybrid to get 25 percent better gas mileage than the standard Camry are invisibly embedded inside the car. The 2007 Camry model has been given a sleek redesign, and since it's the best-selling car in the United States, there are definitely going to be lots of satisfied lazy environmentalists on the road in the very near future. In California, hybrid drivers get to drive in the coveted carpool lane even without another passenger. How's that for a perk?

Even SUV lovers can join the ranks of the environmentally aware. No longer banished to eco-hell, SUV aficionados can opt for hybrid versions of the Ford Escape and Mercury Mariner. The EPA gives these big vehicles 37/31 mpg and 33/29 mpg respectively in the city and on the highway. But the Lexus RX 400h rules the SUV hybrid hierarchy. The hybridization of the RX 400h engine not only delivers better gas mileage but also more horsepower. This hybrid SUV gets 31/27 mpg and accelerates from zero to sixty in under seven seconds, which even has speed junkies smiling.

For the environmentally chic, invisible eco has successfully turned a diesel version of the Mercedes-Benz E Class sedan into a planet-friendly ride. Powered by BlueTec, an eco-advanced auto system that filters dirty tailpipe emissions, this car cruises smooth and clean. Though diesel-engine cars typically receive high marks for fuel efficiency, they have been strictly regulated in the United States due to noxious emissions of toxins, like sulfur, that lead to acid rain. But the luxurious Mercedes-Benz E320 BlueTec sedan delivers an EPA-rated 27/37 mpg. Look for BlueTec technology to begin appearing throughout Mercedes-Benz's lineup of luxury sedans and SUVs. Chrysler is also said to be adopting the technology from its parent company, DaimlerChrysler, to offer a more fuel-efficient version of its popular Jeep Grand Cherokee.

Okay, a bike's not enough, a hybrid isn't your thing, and BlueTec isn't intriguing. You're keeping the car you own and you want options that fit what you've already got. There's a good chance you may be one of the unsuspecting six million car drivers already behind the wheel of a flex-fuel vehicle—cars that can run on both regular gasoline and cleaner alternatives like E85. The mother of all clean fuels, E85 is a combination of 85 percent ethanol (think grain alcohol) and 15 percent conventional gasoline. Ethanol is produced in the United States principally from corn, which means your tasty corn on the cob is shaping up to be a key ally in the battle against global warming. Research is also indicating that weedy plants like switchgrass may prove even more potent in the production of ethanol, providing almost two times more energy than is needed to produce it—a key measurement of ethanol's ability to replace oil-derived gasoline on a very large scale. Switchgrass is native to North America, growing naturally from North Dakota to Louisiana, and therefore requires minimal amounts of noxious pesticides and insecticides to cultivate. Billionaire entrepreneurs like Vinod Khosla, founder of Sun Microsystems, are investing millions of dollars to explore the potential of switchgrass to become a super energy crop that could reinvent our energy landscape.

E85 is generally less expensive than gasoline, delivers slightly more horsepower (around 5 percent), and gets slightly less fuel mileage (in the range of 10 percent). E85 also reduces greenhouse gas emissions by as much as 70 percent over gasoline. Since ethanol is derived from plant crops that feed on and absorb carbon dioxide, the net effect is to reduce carbon dioxide emissions from the production of ethanol toward zero. Factor in the potential for using switchgrass and other biomass waste generated during ethanol production to actually power an ethanol-producing factory and we're looking at a self-contained, highly efficient, clean fuel-producing infrastructure, homegrown on American soil.

As for flex-fuel vehicles, their introduction en masse beginning in the late 1990s began as a low-cost program that enabled car companies to meet federal fuel efficiency requirements without truly having to raise fuel efficiency. Thankfully, what was meant to provide little more than an environmental loophole for the auto companies has turned out to be a massive opportunity for lazy environmentalists. And here's the real tire-kicker—today many of the biggest and best-selling automobiles in this country, namely Ford's F-1 Series pickup trucks and the Chevrolet Silverado pickup truck from General Motors, are being mass-produced as flex-fuel vehicles capable of running on clean E85 fuel. In 2007 most of the major car makers, including Ford, General Motors, Chrysler, Mercedes-Benz, and Nissan, will introduce flex-fuel models. Where will these cars fill up? While the numbers are still small, in 2007, E85 fuel stations will at least double, from seven hundred to one thousand four hundred, across the country. Visit E85fuel.com to find flex-fuel vehicle models and locate filling stations.

Running our cars on clean fuel presents opportunities for diesel drivers too. Biodiesel is a clean-burning, renewable diesel fuel replacement made from vegetable oils or animal fats. It can be used in any car or truck with a diesel engine, is comparable in price to conventional diesel fuel, and gets better gas mileage. And, yes, it's also biodegradable. Diesel engines can run on biodiesel that's virtually pure, though it is most commonly used as a blend of 20 percent biodiesel, 80 percent conventional diesel. Country music legend Willie Nelson is a major player in the biodiesel industry. BioWillie fuel can already be found in California, Texas, Georgia, South Carolina, Tennessee, Mississippi, and Louisiana. Actress Julia Roberts has also stepped into the clean fuel arena as a spokesperson for BioWillie's parent company, Earth BioFuels, which also develops broader initiatives like encouraging the use of biodiesel in over five hundred thousand diesel school buses.

With all of this automotive innovation under way, you'd think we all could find an eco-alternative to fit our lifestyles. There really is something for everyone—even those who drive Hummers, the most colossal of all urban assault vehicles (the one that averages a fuel economy of 14 mpg). By offsetting the carbon dioxide emissions spewing from your car's tailpipe, TerraPass offers Hummer drivers eco-salvation. Cars emit approximately ten thousand pounds of carbon dioxide into the atmosphere each year. At TerraPass.com you can calculate your vehicle's emissions and then purchase a customized TerraPass, which will offset the damage by contributing to investments in wind and solar energy and other greenhouse gas reduction initiatives. For about $75 annually, you'll get a TerraPass decal for your car certifying your participation. Carbon offsetting programs like TerraPass don't reduce your car's environmental impact, but they do provide a mechanism for all individuals to easily take responsibility for their greenhouse gas contributions.

Car Makers and Models

AC PROPULSION

Acpropulsion.com

When Tom Hanks went looking for a new electric vehicle that would produce zero greenhouse gas emissions he turned to AC Propulsion. You can too. Electric versions of the Toyota Scion, dubbed the eBox, are now available with some impressive specifications. With a top speed of 95 miles per hour and a top range of 180 miles per charge, the eBox will deliver lots of planet-saving thrills.

FORD

Ford.com

Ford is giving Toyota legitimate competition with its Mercury Mariner and Ford Escape SUV hybrids. Ford's lineup of flex-fuel vehicles create new possibilities to drive the cars we love and fill them up with cleaner, eco-friendly fuels.

GENERAL MOTORS

Generalmotors.com

GM's Saturn division offers a hybrid model of the VUE SUV. GM is also placing heavy emphasis on its fleet of flex-fuel vehicles that can run on clean-burning ethanol in the form of E85 fuel. Most notable among these models is the popular Chevrolet Silverado pickup truck (comes in a hybrid too). Yes, pickup trucks are feeling the eco-love.

HONDA

Honda.com

As if Honda wasn't already delivering high-performance gas-sippers, both the Civic and the Accord now come in hybrid models that increase fuel efficiency and save money at the pump. But that's not all. The Honda Civic GX reduces greenhouse gas emissions by 90 percent versus gasoline-powered cars, because it runs entirely on compressed natural gas—a fossil fuel that burns clean. Californians and New Yorkers can purchase the car now. Honda also has plans to make it available throughout the country.

LEXUS

Lexus.com

Luxury still reigns at Lexus, but this time supreme hybrid technology is part of the package. Check out the SUVs and luxury sedans equipped with hybrid engines that outperform on horsepower and fuel economy.

MERCEDES-BENZ

Mbusa.com

New advances in diesel technology dubbed BlueTec are putting Mercedes-Benz at the head of the eco-class. The benefits are starting to spill over to its sister division Chrysler too.

PHOENIX MOTORCARS

Phoenixmotorcars.com

The fully electric pickup truck has been parked on the South Lawn of the White House while being inspected by President Bush, and soon you'll be able to park one in your garage. This zero emission vehicle has a top speed of 95 miles per hour and range of over 100 miles per charge. A fully electric SUV is also being released starting first in California. Plug it in, charge it up, and go.

SMART CAR

Smart.com

Coming soon to a road near you may be a car so nifty and small that it can park sideways. Yet the Smart car is big on design and performance and eco-responsibility. The nimble cars are owned and manufactured by DaimlerChrysler and are already a big hit in Europe.

TANGO

Commutercars.com

George Clooney drives one, and you might too when you consider that the Tango T600 is an emission-free electric car that goes from zero to sixty in four seconds and has a top speed of 150 mph. Like the Smart car, the Tango is tiny and may help decongest our automotive highway system.

TESLA MOTORS

Teslamotors.com

Tesla is the maker of the Tesla Roadster, a 100 percent electric-powered, plug-in car, so advanced that the technological wonder boys who founded Google both drive them.

TOYOTA

Toyota.com

Maker of the immensely popular Prius, Toyota is continuing to expand its hybrid empire with the hybrid Camry and Highlander SUV. The near future promises to bring exciting new models with innovative features and killer gas mileage.

Auto Services

BETTER WORLD CLUB
Betterworldclub.com
A provider of automobile roadside assistance, Better World Club is not part of the highway lobby, supports higher fuel economy standards, donates 1 percent of its revenues to environmental cleanup and advocacy, and offers the country's only bicycle roadside assistance plan.

BIO-BEETLE
Biobeetle.com
The first all-biodiesel rental car company in the world, Bio-Beetle offers its rental car services in Los Angeles and the Hawaiian island of Maui. True to its name, Bio-Beetle rents Volkswagen Beetles as well as Golfs, Jettas, Passats, and Jeeps.

EV RENTAL CARS
Evrental.com
With locations in California, Arizona, and soon Las Vegas, EV Rental offers more than 350 hybrid-engine rental cars. The company's mission is to offer the most technologically and environmentally advanced cars to the public as soon as they are available. Hybrid car models available include the Toyota Prius, the Toyota Highlander SUV, and the Honda Civic.

FLEXCAR
Flexcar.com
You don't need to own a car to drive one. FlexCar liberates people from the cost and responsibility of car ownership by giving members access to hundreds of cars parked in cities around the country.

OZOCAR
Ozocar.com
OZOcar is New York's first car service that combines luxury and eco-responsibility. OZO's fleet of Toyota Priuses and Lexus RX 400h hybrid SUVs are equipped with satellite radio and, better still, Wi-Fi Internet connections so you can check your email and surf the web while being chauffeured to the airport, the Giants game, or Peter Luger's steakhouse. Yum.

TERRAPASS
Terrapass.com
The average car emits about ten thousand pounds of carbon dioxide pollution each year. When car owners purchase a TerraPass, the company

funds clean energy projects that reduce industrial carbon dioxide emissions, thus balancing out the effects of the car's emissions. Terrapass.com can also do the same thing for carbon emissions created from powering our homes and from traveling.

ZIPCAR
Zipcar.com
Car sharing services like Zipcar and FlexCar free drivers from vehicle responsibility, while the environment benefits from fewer car owners.

Alternative Fuels

BIOWILLIE
Biowillie.com
Willie Nelson's BioWillie outlets serve biodiesel to drivers in California, Texas, Georgia, and South Carolina.

EARTH BIOFUELS
Earthbiofuels.com
The parent company of BioWillie, Earth Biofuels is a producer, distributor, and marketer of biodiesel and ethanol. The company has attracted celebrity spokespeople such as Morgan Freeman and Julia Roberts (in addition of course to Willie) and also develops broad initiatives like encouraging the use of biodiesel in over five hundred thousand diesel school buses.

TRI-STATE BIODIESEL
Tristatebiodiesel.com
New Yorkers will soon get a chance to tap into the promise of clean, renewable energy with the introduction of biodiesel fuel thanks to Tri-State Biodiesel CEO and longtime environmental advocate Brent Baker. Tri-State Biodiesel's blend relies primarily on leftover restaurant grease that it recycles into an ultra-low-emission, nontoxic diesel fuel.

Car Maintenance

OPTIMUM POLYMER TECHNOLOGIES
Ecocarcare.net
Conserve water and reduce chemical runoff into drainage systems during car washing and waxing with Optimum Polymer Technologies' unique, ecologically safe products. Clean, restore, and protect car interiors using Protectant Plus, an advance formula that contains zero VOCs.

Check Out

AMERICAN SOLAR CHALLENGE

Americansolarchallenge.org

Competitors design, build, and race solar-powered cars from Austin, Texas, to Calgary, Alberta. The race draws teams of engineers from universities throughout North America and demonstrates the potential of solar power.

AUTOMOTIVE X PRIZE

Auto.xprize.org

Following on the heels of its successful space flight competition, X Prize turns its attention to automobile innovation with a competition designed to attract top-flight teams from around the world to create super-efficient, next-generation vehicles that people will want to buy. One-hundred-mpg cars may soon be on the horizon.

BMW HYDROGEN 7

Bmw.com (click on BMW Insights)

In 2006, BMW introduced the world's first hydrogen-drive luxury performance automobile for everyday use, capable of running either on hydrogen or on gasoline and based on the BMW 7 Series. While hydrogen offers tremendous potential as a clean fuel, the challenge is to produce it from clean, renewable energy sources instead of fossil fuel sources like coal and natural gas. Still, this is a big step in a clean direction.

INDYCAR SERIES

Indycar.com

The IndyCar Series is staking a claim to the most eco-enlightened sport in the world. In 2007 every racing car on the track will be powered by 100 percent ethanol fuel, demonstrating that eco-power can kick gasoline power's butt any day and especially on race day.

WHO KILLED THE ELECTRIC CAR?

Sonyclassics.com / whokilledtheelectriccar

This documentary directed by Chris Paine tracks the rise and demise of the electric car in the United States. It's good entertainment and also captures the story of a technology that could indeed influence our driving future. Electric cars offer the potential to reduce tailpipe greenhouse gas emissions to zero. They can be charged by plugging into the energy grid through any electric outlet, which provides a significantly cleaner energy source than conventional gasoline.

Information/Education

DEPARTMENT OF ENERGY

http://afdcmap2.nrel.gov/website/stations/viewer.htm

Offers an up-to-date list of all alternative energy fuel stations in the United States including E85 and biodiesel. Fun, interactive maps help you pinpoint fuel stations near your home or on your route.

E85FUEL.COM

Home of the National Ethanol Vehicles Coalition, this site offers comprehensive information about the performance and environmental qualities of E85 fuel and highlights flex-fuel vehicles on the road and available for purchase.

EV WORLD

Evworld.com

EV World provides in-depth information on topics pertaining to sustainable transportation including the people, policies, and technologies that are shaping the emerging green transportation landscape. The well-designed site is easily navigable, and full membership gives you total access to news, research, and analysis on green vehicles, clean energy, and green industry investing.

FUELECONOMY.GOV

Get gas mileage tips, learn about energy-efficient vehicles, and compare cars for greenhouse gas emissions, air pollution, and miles per gallon at this site sponsored by the EPA's Department of Energy Efficiency and Renewable Energy.

HYBRIDCARS.COM

Bradley Berman is the go-to guy for all things hybrid. His site has information on every aspect of hybrid cars, from gas mileage and oil dependency to cultural impact and environmental benefits.

HYDROGEN CARS

Hydrogen-cars.biz

A thoughtful, well-researched resource for information about hydrogen car models, concept cars, fuel stations, fuel cells, and other hydrogen developments.

GREENCARCONGRESS.COM

It's all about "sustainable mobility" at Mike Millikin's site, where he covers technologies, products, issues, and policies.

THE NATIONAL BIODIESEL BOARD

Biodiesel.org

The trade association website for the biodiesel industry offers fun facts and easy-to-understand information about biodiesel along with updates about its growing availability and quick links to key players in the coming biodiesel boom.

NEARBIO

Nearbio.com

Find biodiesel fueling stations throughout the United Sates and get the information delivered to you on your cell phone for free. Enter your city and state, zip code, or GPS coordinates and NearBio will provide the address, distance, directions, and phone number for the nearest biodiesel filling station. All information is also available at Nearbio.com.

PLUG IN AMERICA

Pluginamerica.com

Track developments in the electric car industry and learn about car models that plug in to the energy grid to charge and go. The founders of this website are committed to promoting plug-in vehicles as a means to deliver a driving experience powered by cleaner, cheaper, domestic energy that reduces U.S. dependence upon foreign oil and improves the global environment.

5

Two-
wheeled
Transportation

There's a lot to be said for commuting on vehicles

with just two wheels. Traffic congestion becomes a thing of the past. Parking spots are plentiful. Motorcycles and motor scooters sip gasoline and save money at the pump. Bicycles use nothing more than human power and trim waistlines in the process. Today, innovation in engineering and design is encouraging the switch from four-wheeled vehicles to two-wheeled vehicles by offering increasingly stylish and convenient options. And thanks to minimal fuel needs that reduce greenhouse gas emissions, the two-wheeled choice is also the eco-choice.

Motor scooters aren't for everyone, but for those who decide to scoot, the benefits are plentiful. Scooters, like cars, give us the independence and freedom to come and go as we please. If you haven't seen the newest lineup of Vespa motor scooters, it may be time to visit one of the sixty-five Vespa boutiques situated throughout the United States. With their rich Italian design heritage, clean lines, and sensuous curves, Vespas have a knack for turning heads. For sixty years, the engineers at Vespa have produced scooters that outperform the competition. Continuously striving for improvement, Vespa has redesigned the new lineup to improve acceleration and handling, ride quieter, and reduce tailpipe emissions. The Vespa GTS, the top-of-the-line model, can comfortably reach speeds over 75 mph and gets between 65 and 70 mpg—fuel mileage that outperforms lauded hybrid automobiles like the Toyota Prius. With a price tag under $6,000, the Vespa GTS provides an economic commuter option for urban and suburban settings. The Granturismo, LX, and PX 150 models round out the lineup and enable you to choose a model that most closely meets your commuting needs.

Vespa is currently testing the possibility of hybrid engines for its scooters, which would lend the machine an aura of eco-invincibility. But hybrid or not, Vespa motor scooters are already hovering near the top of the eco-transport pyramid. Paolo Timoni, CEO of Vespa for the Americas, is coordinating with mayors around the United States to have scooters incorporated into municipal strategies to combat global warming. Look for increased scooter/motorcycle parking around cities as the two-wheelers like Vespa play an increasingly prominent role in our transportation economy.

Vespas are sexy, sure, but there are other stylish motor scooters on the road too. The eGO Cycle 2 by eGO Vehicles presents a refined eco-solution tailored to the needs of individuals who seek a fun, zippy ride yet don't require highway speeds. The eGO is a sleek design-driven head turner combining the efficiency of a moped with space-age lines and a retro flair. It's the kind of machine that Michael J. Fox's character, Marty McFly, would have ridden in *Back to the Future* had the mad scientist, Dr. Brown, invented it. However, instead of requiring 1.21 gigowatts of energy and a flux capacitor to operate, the eGO runs on pure electricity and is easily charged by plugging directly into any wall socket. The machine is equipped with an internal battery that takes five hours to charge completely. An external fast-charger can do the job in two hours. With a driving range up to 25 miles per charge and top speed of 23 mph, the eGO makes a lot of eco-sense. And at around $1,700 for the top-of-the-line model, it provides a cost-effective mode of primary transportation that fuels up for roughly the equivalent of 10 cents per gallon. As secondary transportation, the eGO eliminates the need to fire up the SUV for short errands. Cars (except for hybrids that run on electric energy at low speeds) spew the most greenhouse gases when operating at low speeds. So switching to a fun, stylish, and clean alternative for shorter trips at lower speeds can be a better way to go. Cruising through a college campus, a suburban main street, or the busy intersections of a big city—eGO Cycles are DOT (Department of Transportation) compliant, so they can be safely driven on streets with traffic—is sheer pleasure.

Just strap on a helmet, sit back on the seat, twist the throttle, and go.

While electric vehicles like the eGO Cycle 2 generate zero tailpipe emissions and subsequently zero tailpipe-related greenhouse gases, they're not a complete environmental victory. Electric plug-in vehicles are still being powered by whatever energy sources are fueling the energy grid. Though it varies from region to region, the United States gets about 50 percent of its energy from carbon-based coal, which is one of the worse eco-offenders. However, a 2004 study by the California Air Resources Board (appointed by the governor of California) found that even when they obtain energy from the power grid, electric vehicles generate 60 percent fewer greenhouse gas emissions than gasoline-powered vehicles. Automakers may have quashed their electric vehicle programs over the past few years (see the movie *Who Killed the Electric Car?*), but options like the eGO Cycle 2 give us access to the advanced eco-IQs of electric vehicles.

For bicycle enthusiasts, key innovations are making human-powered, non-polluting transportation distinctly more conducive for commuting. The award-winning iXi Bike is one of the most forward thinking and delightfully designed commuter bicycles available. For starters, the iXi is equipped with a greaseless rubber belt drive that replaces the so-very-nineteenth-century greasy chain, eliminating the geeky necessity of tucking your pant leg into your sock to avoid grease stains or dangerous snags. Next comes a well-placed cup holder for your morning java so you can sip easily while pedaling. While the wheels are smaller than a conventional road bike, the iXi's quality four-speed gearshift provides solid performance on hills and other gradients. If it rains, you're in luck because the iXi comes with a poncho stored inside the bicycle's aluminum frame, along with a tool repair kit in case of flats. The iXi is also particularly suited to confined spaces. Both the handlebars and the pedals fold flat against the frame, creating a slim profile when stored flush against a wall. And one model of the iXi can be quickly disassembled into two parts and stowed in carrying cases—a convenience that works equally well in an elevator or an airplane.

Storability and portability are front and center—or more likely tucked away in the corner—in the line of high-performance folding bicycles from Brompton. Each bicycle is handmade at Brompton's production facility in London, England, and engineered to be easy to fold and carry, and fun and comfortable to ride. The full-size frames weigh between twenty and twenty-nine pounds and can be folded within fifteen seconds to a size that is about two feet square and less than ten inches wide. Carry it with you using the handle or stow it on a train or plane using a specially designed Brompton storage bag. However you choose to take it, the Brompton is your mega-convenient commuting option.

And it's in good company. As improved bicycling performance helps folding bikes become realistic commuting options, customers are also turning to Dahon. The world's largest manufacturer of folding bikes has been making and refining them for twenty-five years. Dahon sets its internal bar for innovation very high, demanding that its development team improve bikes by at least 15 percent per year in areas like design form, riding performance, comfort, weight, folding function, and durability. The results speak for themselves, as Dahon has sold more than 2 million folding bikes worldwide since beginning production in 1982. Reasonably priced yet performance-driven, Dahon bikes offer eight urban fold-up models, and the company also provides mountain and road-bike models.

For a fully customized folding bike designed to match your exact body dimensions, turn to BikeFriday. The company will build to order a touring, road, mountain, and commuter folding bike that is built, quite literally, just for you. And if you are on the triathlon circuit, BikeFriday will design a triathlon bike that travels with you in your standard luggage and then folds open on race day so you can conveniently compete wherever the race may lead.

For those looking to assign more heavy-duty tasks to their bicycles—like transporting kids to school, dogs to the vet, or surfboards to the beach—an Xtracycle SUB (sport utility bicycle) system may be right for you. Dubbed the Free Radical, Xtracycle's innovative attachment shifts your bicycle's rear wheel back fifteen inches and adds a long, stable platform on top of it accompanied by big, sturdy saddlebags. Rather than hitching an unwieldy trailer to your bicycle to provide additional hauling capacity, the Free Radical transforms your bicycle into an integrated SUB that's still light-weight, easy to handle, and fast. The system is designed for rapid installation with a basic set of tools and can be purchased independently to install on your current bike or purchased preassembled on name-brand bicycles directly through Xtracycle's website.

The Xtracycle can easily handle loads of up to 150 pounds. To make that kind of heavy hauling easier on your body, a company called Cleverchimp recently introduced the Stoke Monkey, an electric assist system that works seamlessly with the Xtracycle SUB to give an added boost to human pedal power. It's no longer just a bicycle—it's a bicycling lifestyle.

Two-Wheeled Brands

BIKE FRIDAY
Bikefriday.com
For a fully customized folding bike designed to match your exact body dimensions, turn to BikeFriday. The company will build to order a touring, road, mountain, or commuter folding bike that is built, quite literally, just for you. Super-specialized bikes like triathlon models are also available.

BROMPTON
Bromptonbicycle.co.uk
Brompton's full-size, foldable bicycles are lightweight, high-performance machines. The sturdy steel frame can be assembled and disassembled in about twenty seconds to take with you on public transportation or stow out of sight in the office.

BUELL
Buell.com
The sports motorcycle subsidiary of Harley-Davidson, Buell prides itself on offering some of the cleanest, most fuel-efficient motorcycles on the road. The 2007 Blast, a classically appealing model, has a 492 cc air-cooled engine that rides smoothly, accelerates comfortably at highway speeds, and averages about 70 mpg, for outstanding fuel economy and a minimal eco-impact.

DAHON

Dahon.com

The largest manufacturer of folding bikes in the world, Dahon offers bike models for convenient urban commuting and more specialized fold-up models for mountain and road biking.

EGO VEHICLES

Egovehicles.com

EGO Vehicles' eGO Cycle 2 is a quiet, 100 percent electric, zero-emission motor scooter that closely resembles a moped. The turn-throttle acceleration quickly enables the eGO to reach speeds of 23 mph. A full charge can last up to twenty-five miles before you have to temporarily plug it back into any wall socket. Great for local commutes.

IKOO

Ikoo.us

This futuristic-looking, tiny, portable electric motorcycle is made of surgical stainless steel. Cool enough for the cool kids and functional enough for intrepid commuters, the Ikoo gets up to eighteen miles per charge and tops out at 18 mph. Avoid arriving to work sweaty and then fold it up and store it in your office.

IXI BIKE

Ixibike.com

A next-generation bicycle that meets the demands of commuters and recreational enthusiasts, the iXi features a greaseless drive train, collapsible handlebars and pedals, a repair kit stowed inside the frame, and a host of other innovations that make bicycle commuting increasingly attractive and realistic.

MONTAGUE

Montagueco.com

Montague makes high-performance full-size, foldable bikes. No need to splurge on a car rack. After a solid day of mountain biking on the toughest terrain you can throw at it, Montague's military-grade mountain bikes will fold up and fit easily in your trunk or backseat.

SCHWINN

Schwinnbike.com

Schwinn bikes are as American as baseball and apple pie. And for 2007 Schwinn is offering some of the best-designed electric-assist bicycles available. The electric components are integrated into the bicycle's frame, and a battery sits unobtrusively on the cargo rack. In short, these bikes look just like any others save for the integrated power boost, which makes steep hills a cinch. When the battery gets low, just plug it into any outlet to charge it back up.

STRIDA

Strida.com

An ultra-portable, fold-up bike packaged in a space-age design, the Strida is not only fun to ride, but it's also a chick magnet. Take it with you on the subway and be prepared to hand out your phone number. Yup, it works better than a puppy.

VECTRIX

Vectrix.com

The Vectrix electric maxi-scooter is a high-performance motor scooter capable of handling the demands of everyday commuting. The motor scooter accelerates quickly and can reach speeds over 60 mph and travel up to seventy miles on a single charge. The onboard charger plugs into any standard electrical outlet, making this motor scooter the super-sleek, ultra-convenient, eco-aware choice.

VESPA

Vespa.com

This is the maker of the renowned Vespa motor scooter, the quintessential design-driven eco-alternative to automobiles. Vespa motor scooters can reach speeds of up to 80 mph and achieve gas mileage of 65 mpg. Vespa also makes the Piaggio line of motor scooters with some touring models hefty enough for long highway road trips.

Accessories

BIONX

Bionx.ca

Convert your conventional bike into an electric bike with a sleek, lightweight BionX motor, battery, and console system that mounts unobtrusively onto your bike and delivers up to sixty miles per charge. Purchasing a BionX doesn't mean you're lazy; it means you're wise.

CLEVERCHIMP

Cleverchimp.com

CleverChimp offers the StokeMonkey electric motor assist kit that works with the Xtracycle SUB (sport utility bicycle) to provide an added boost when hauling large and heavy loads. The forward-thinking folks at

CleverChimp are into hybrid human-electric technology that makes bicycles abundantly more versatile in handling the tasks of daily living.

SOY CLEAN
Soyclean.biz
When in need of a bicycle chain lubricant, look no further than the eco-friendly soy-based Bar and Chain Lubricant from Soy Clean. Soy Clean also offers a full line of soy-based, nontoxic, biodegradable cleaning supplies.

REVOPOWER
Revopower.com
The RevoPower Wheel presents an innovative way to motorize your standard bike. Swap out your old front wheel and install the RevoPower Wheel, and suddenly you'll be climbing hills with the assistance of a clean-burning gasoline-powered engine. The gas tank is the size of a water bottle and tucks in snugly against the bike frame. Due out in 2007.

XTRACYCLE
Xtracycle.com
Make the most of your transportation needs by transforming your standard bicycle into an SUB (sport utility bicycle). Transport your surfboard, dog, or a week's worth of groceries through the use of the hitch-less trailer that stretches your real wheel further back behind the seat and creates an unsurpassed bicycle cargo capacity of up to 150 pounds.

Retailers

ELECTRIC CYCLERY
Greenspeed.us
Kevin Penrose of Electric Cyclery in Laguna Beach, California, offers the most-proven, top-of-the-line electric scooters, motorcycles, bicycles, and now skateboards. Electric Cyclery also offers fold-up bikes that make storage and travel super convenient.

ELECTRIC TRANSPORTATION SOLUTIONS (ETS)
Electrictransport.net
Seth Leitman's New York–based company offers a top-flight lineup of electric bikes, motor scooters, and motorcycles. ETS also sells electric golf carts and electric conversion automobiles to customers throughout the United States. Check out the electric-powered Porsche.

SKOOTER COMMUTER

Skootercommuter.com

Providing electric scooters and bikes to the Washington, DC, region, Skooter Commuter is dedicated to offering the best possible pollution-free alternative to automobiles. The company continually tests and evaluates the many electric vehicles on the market to provide a quality selection for many different uses and price ranges.

Cool and Noteworthy

BICYTAXI

Bicytaxi.com

Bicycle taxis are a fun, eco-friendly way to commute around a city. Now BicyTaxi is bringing its fleet to American streets, starting out in New York City. What better way to gaze admiringly upon One Bryant Park—the most eco-friendly commercial skyscraper in the United States—than from the passenger seat of these stylish eco-roadsters.

BIKE 2015 PLAN

Bike2015plan.org

The city of Chicago—already one of the most bike-friendly big cities in the country—has a plan to make it a place where bicycling is easily integrated into daily life. The foundation of the plan is a vision to establish a five-hundred-mile bikeway network throughout Chicago.

CRITICAL MASS

Criticalmass.info

I first encountered Critical Mass six years ago in Paris when my taxi driver stopped at a red light and suddenly thousands of bikes went whirring through the intersection. Critical Mass is a monthly bicycle ride that takes place in cities worldwide to celebrate cycling and assert the cyclists' right to the road.

6

Real Estate

GREEN HOMES ARE HERE

One of the most exciting trends in lazy environmental living is the growth of newly constructed green homes. These homes have eco-intelligence embedded in their walls and floors and countertops, improving the quality of the air we breathe, reducing our energy consumption, and lowering our utility bills—these are the homes of our future and the future is well under way.

On the southwestern tip of Manhattan, facing the Statue of Liberty, rise the greatest testaments to our collective will and capability to lead outrageously cool lifestyles in balance with nature's capacity to sustain them. These majestic symbols of human hope are called the Verdesian, the Solaire, and Tribeca Green, and you can move into any of them today. High-rise skyscraper developers throughout New York City are on the front lines of the burgeoning green building movement. The 254 rental apartment units in the Verdesian, for example, boast Forest Stewardship Council certified sustainable wood floors, expansive floor-to-ceiling windows made of low-E glass that keep apartments cooler in the summer and warmer in the winter, and Energy Star–rated appliances, accompanied by high-efficiency lighting, that reduce energy usage and save on utility bills. The building itself draws 5 percent of its energy from solar panels built directly into its outside walls. Inside the building's lower reaches is a natural gas microturbine that helps the Verdesian efficiently generate its own energy, reduce its greenhouse gas emissions, and recapture enough waste energy to fulfill 100 percent of its residents' hot water needs. Throw in a host of forward-thinking features like low-VOC paints and finishes and eco-advanced filtration systems to eliminate toxins from the indoor air and water, and we are talking about a next-generation apartment that actually does all the heavy eco-lifting for us. To join in on the quest to be eco-aware, all you have to do is move in and enjoy the view.

Venture farther north in Manhattan and you'll encounter the Helena, a green rental apartment building, with similar eco-attributes to the Verdesian, that draws more than 50 percent of its energy from wind power. In Harlem there is 1400 on 5th and the Kalahari, both green apartment buildings. On Roosevelt Island in the East River is the Octagon, which boasts the largest array of solar panels of any building in New York City plus picturesque views of the Manhattan skyline and a two-acre ecological park landscaped with indigenous plants. New York's biggest developers are finding ways to lavish attention on their tenants while considering the planet.

This is all just to rent green. If you want to buy green in New York City, then Riverhouse at One Rockefeller Park, overlooking the Hudson River, is an ideal spot. You can also check out the Millennium Tower Residences, a thirty-five-story, 236-condominium apartment complex, built to impeccable standards by Millennium Partners, the same developers who build Ritz Carlton hotels. In addition to its luxurious green amenities, Millennium Partners relied heavily upon recycled materials during construction, including steel, wood, and concrete that were drawn from local sources to reduce transportation emissions.

While New York City is indisputably the reigning champion of high-rise green residential living, other cities are moving quickly to close the gap. Los Angeles is home to Evo South, Elleven South, and Luma South—a cluster of new green high-rise apartment buildings that will serve as the heart of a downtown revitalization project. Chicago has the Lexington Park Condos, 340 on the Park, and Emerald Chicago. On a slightly smaller scale, Beverly Hills has 9900 Wilshire, San Francisco has the Arterra, Seattle has Veer Lofts and the Alcyone Apartments, and Nashville has Morgan Park and Terrazzo—each a building that takes substantial steps to utilize green materials, conserve energy, and reduce greenhouse gas emissions. In Washington, DC, Elevation 314 pushes the eco-envelope with a geothermal heating system that modulates temperatures throughout its apartments by drawing exclusively on heat trapped below the building, deep inside the earth.

While the cities have the green apartments and condos, the suburbs also boast green living opportunities. It's no surprise that the Pacific Northwest is leading the country in green building, based around Portland and Seattle, with the regions around San Francisco, Denver, and Austin following closely on its heels. But if you want to find the state that's leading the union into a greener twenty-first century, you're going to have to follow your retired grandparents down to Florida. Residential developers inside the sunshine state are going green in a big way. Get out the map and locate Sarasota County. Its county administrators recently passed an ordinance that expedites building permits for green developments, reducing the wait period from six weeks to six days for those who are committed to building a greener future. Talk to any home builder, and he'll tell you that navigating municipal bureaucracies is the bane of a builder's existence. Fast-tracking building permits provide a major incentive to adopt green building methods.

And it's paying off. Sarasota County is home to Lakewood Ranch, a seven-thousand-acre master-planned community being built on what was once the home to the Schlitz Brewing Company's agricultural operations. Today over twenty home building companies are developing the residential villages that make up the community under green specifications. The process is regulated by the Lakewood Ranch development company, which is led by Bob Sisum, who is also the chairman of the Florida Association of Home Builders' green building committee and sits on the board of directors of the National Association of Home Builders. Sisum's influence is helping to spread the green building gospel through the nation from atop the industry's most influential trade association. At Lakewood Ranch all newly constructed houses are being built to green specifications, including energy efficiency and green building materials. So far six hundred homes have been completed, and hundreds more are in progress. As Sisum states, "The homes look just like regular, stylish houses that you'd expect to find in Florida. It's the materials, systems, and appliances that are smarter and healthier."

In addition to the residences, the entire Lakewood Ranch development treads lightly on the land. Wetlands have been restored and preserved. Water is conserved through advanced irrigation systems. And plenty of green space has been set aside for parks and nature trails. Adds Sisum, "We're building in such a way that animals and people can enjoy the best of Florida living."

Not too far from Lakewood Ranch, in Venice, Florida, is the Venetian Golf and River Club development, which boasts the "greenest" homes in Florida as certified by the Florida Green Building Coalition. Developed by WCI Communities, the Venetian offers single-family homes built to green specifications including use of eco-friendly building materials, energy and water efficiency, indoor air quality, and proper home orientation for natural cross-ventilation and sunlight.

Treading lightly on the land is a hallmark of WCI Communities' Florida-based residential developments. At the Venetian, half of the eleven hundred acres are devoted to lakes, wetlands, conservation areas, and a seventy-acre nature park. Situated throughout the development are three large preserves where wetlands have been restored from damaged pasture. The preserves are connected by wildlife corridors—at least fifty feet wide—that enable wildlife to move throughout the property for food and water. Native plants have also been introduced to increase the entire property's biodiversity.

Lest you think that all this eco-stuff exacts some toll on the quality of life for residents, consider that the Venetian is also home to an eighteen-hole championship golf course that is one of only nine courses in the world to have been certified by the International Audubon Society as a Gold Signature Sanctuary, reflecting a superior environmental commitment in course siting, design, and resource management. And of the eight residential developments in the world to receive Gold Signature Sanctuary certification, four of them were developed by WCI Communities in Florida. Three others are in North Carolina, and one is in California.

If the thought of following the lazy environmentalist path to green living by moving into a prebuilt green residence has you excited, there are two simple ways to go about finding a home. The first is to visit Moderngreenliving.com, where you'll find the most extensive directory of green residential developments throughout the United States, Canada, and overseas. Searching the directory is quick and free and will enable you to easily find green homes in your area. The directory was developed by my team at Vivavi to put all of these wonderful green residential options at the fingertips of consumers. Second, consult with a certified green realtor. You can find them through Moderngreenliving.com and by visiting Ecobroker.com, which provides a list of certified green realtors who have the eco-expertise to help you find the green home that's right for you.

Realtors and Residential Properties

340 ON THE PARK
340ontheparkchicago.com
Located along the lakefront in Chicago, 340 on the Park combines "urban chic" with environmental intelligence. Condominiums with open floor plans feature high-tech, energy-efficient heating and cooling systems, advanced air-quality systems, and a host of renewable building materials.

1400 ON 5TH
1400on5th.com
The first affordable green multifamily residential development in the Harlem neighborhood of New York City. Recycled and renewable materials played a major role during building construction, accounting for approximately 70 percent of all materials used.

9900 WILSHIRE
9900wilshire.com
Luxury green condominiums come to Beverly Hills with the introduction of 9900 Wilshire. Award-winning architect Richard Meier has designed a complex that uses 25 percent less energy, 50 percent less water, and significantly reduces greenhouse gas emissions when compared to standard residential buildings.

ALCYONE APARTMENTS

Alcyoneapartments.com

Seattle's Alcyone Apartments combine the best of contemporary urban living with a strong nod to the environment. A rooftop garden recycles rainwater to reduce the need for potable water while providing a green space for residents. Interiors benefit from low-VOC carpets and paints, and 80 percent of construction site waste was recycled.

ARTERRA

Arterrasf.com

Clean design, practical amenities, and quality finishes are what you find at the Arterra in San Francisco. Bamboo or cork flooring, Energy Star-rated appliances, energy-efficient lighting, dual-flush toilets for water conservation, and low-VOC paints and carpets are just some of the green features you'll find at these competitively priced flats and townhouses.

ELEVATION 314

Momirents.com

The Elevation 314 apartment complex in the Takoma Park neighborhood of Washington, DC, pushes the eco-envelope with a geothermal heating system that modulates temperatures throughout its apartments by drawing exclusively on heat trapped below the building, deep inside the earth. Residents also enjoy green features like bamboo flooring.

EMERALD CHICAGO

Emeraldchicago.com

Chicago's edgy sophistication is on display at Emerald Chicago where style and eco-awareness are equally celebrated. Residents sense the enlightened vibe as soon as they step into the 8,000-square-foot, two-story lobby that features recycled glass terrazzo floors and designer furniture crafted of sustainable materials with reclaimed fabrics.

GREEN KEY REAL ESTATE

Greenkeyrealestate.com

San Francisco–based Green Key Real Estate is the choice for green-minded buyers and sellers seeking a firm that shares their values. Green Key Real Estate will point you toward green homes where available and can direct you toward green professionals who can undertake green remodeling jobs in cases where green homes aren't available. The company also strives to green its own operations and offsets 100 percent of its energy use through renewable energy credits

GREEN WORKS REALTY

Greenworksrealty.com

Seattle-based Green Works Realty is one of the first full-service real estate firms in the U.S. specializing in healthy, green homes and community-focused developments. The company's realtors will help you find a green home. If none are available to your specifications, then opt for their Healthy Home Package, which informs homeowners on ways to conserve water and energy, improve indoor air quality, and make attractive, eco-aware purchasing decisions to increase their quality of life.

THE HELENA

Thehelena.com

This green rental apartment building in New York City draws more than 50 percent of its energy from wind power. Apartments feature eco-friendly materials such as FSC-certified sustainable oak plank floors and walls made from 100 percent recycled gypsum.

KALAHARI

Kalahari-nyc.com

A mixed-income green condo development in the Harlem neighborhood of New York City, the Kalahari gets more than 25 percent of its energy from wind and solar sources and circulates fresh-filtered air to its residential units.

LAKEWOOD RANCH

Lakewoodranch.com

Lakewood Ranch is a seven-thousand-acre master-planned community in Sarasota, Florida, where all newly constructed houses are being built to green specifications, including energy efficiency and green building materials. So far six hundred homes have been completed, and hundreds more are in progress.

LEXINGTON PARK CONDOS

Lexingtonparkcondos.com

Award-winning architectural design merges with superior finishes and attractive features at this high-rise condo development. Who wouldn't want a 15,000-square-foot roof deck with a large dog run that's outfitted with a special membrane to deflect heat in order to keep building cooling costs low? Or an energy-efficient heating and cooling system? How about bicycle storage and changing rooms? It's all available at Lexington Park Condos.

MILLENNIUM TOWER RESIDENCES

The-tower-residences.com

The Millennium Tower is a thirty-five-story 236-condominium apartment complex built to impeccable standards by Millennium Partners, the same developers who build Ritz Carlton hotels. In addition to the tower's luxurious green amenities, Millennium Partners relied heavily upon recycled materials during construction, including steel, wood, and concrete that were drawn from local sources to reduce transportation emissions.

MORGAN PARK

Morganparkplace.com

Located in Nashville's historic Germantown, Morgan Park brings eco-awareness to urban living. Luxury features like granite countertops and freestanding air jet tubs merge with green features including bamboo floors, Energy Star–rated appliances, compact fluorescent lights, and organic lawn care, all of which is designed to promote health and reduce energy consumption.

RIVERHOUSE AT ONE ROCKEFELLER PARK

Oneriverterrace.com

A luxury green condo building in the Battery Park City neighborhood of Manhattan in New York City, Riverhouse features renewable energy systems and residents benefit from advanced air and water filtration systems, Energy Star–rated appliances, and triple-layered windows for increased insulation.

THE SOLAIRE

Thesolaire.com

The first environmentally advanced residential tower built in the United States, the Solaire in New York City was designed to be extremely resource efficient, requiring 35 percent less energy and 50 percent less potable water than a conventional residential high-rise building. Apartment residents also benefit from a host of green and healthy living features including advanced air and water filtration systems.

THE SOUTH GROUP

Exploresouthgroup.com

South is a new neighborhood in downtown Los Angeles led by the real estate development firm The South Group. The project is anchored by three environmentally smart high-rise apartment buildings: Elleven South, Evo South, and Luma South.

TERRAZZO

Terrazzonashville.com

Slated to be Nashville's first LEED certified green residential building, Terrazzo features 109 condominiums with a choice of 26 different floor plans. Green features include low-flow water fixtures and dual-flush toilets to conserve water and Energy Star–rated appliances. Over 50 percent of the building's construction site waste is being recycled. Enjoy panoramic views of Nashville's skyline through floor-to-ceiling windows.

THE OCTAGON

Octagonnyc.com

The Octagon Apartment development on Roosevelt Island in New York City was conceived as an eco-friendly "green building" from the outset. It features numerous energy-efficient and renewable energy systems including the largest solar panel system of any building in New York City. Residents also benefit from a two-acre park landscaped with indigenous plants.

TRIBECA GREEN

Tribecagreen.com

A luxury condominium high-rise in the Tribeca neighborhood of Manhattan, the building features rooftop solar panels and rainwater recycling for landscaping. Individual units feature Energy Star–rated appliances, airtight wall systems for better insulation, and advanced air filtration systems for healthy, fresh air.

VEER LOFTS

Veerlofts.com

Seattle's Veer Lofts offers bright open loft spaces each accompanied by a wall that is almost entirely made of glass to maximize daylight. Green features include low-VOC paints, water conserving fixtures, energy-efficient Whirlpool appliances, and countertops made from recycled banana leaf fibers.

VENETIAN GOLF AND RIVER CLUB

Venetiangolfandriverclub.com

Located in Venice, Florida, and developed by WCI Communities, the Venetian offers single-family homes built to green specifications, including use of eco-friendly building materials, energy and water efficiency, indoor air quality, and proper home orientation for natural cross-ventilation and sunlight. The Venetian also boasts an eighteen-hole championship golf course certified by the International Audubon Society as a Gold Signature Sanctuary.

THE VERDESIAN

Theverdesian.com

A twenty-six-story environmentally advanced apartment building located in Battery Park in New York City, the Verdesian boasts FSC-certified sustainable wood floors, expansive floor-to-ceiling windows made of low-E glass that keeps apartments cooler in the summer and warmer in the winter, and Energy Star–rated appliances, accompanied by high-efficiency lighting, that reduce energy usage and save on utility bills. The building itself draws 5 percent of its energy from solar panels built directly into its outside walls.

Information / Education

ECOBROKER

Ecobroker.com

EcoBroker provides a green certification program for realtors throughout the United States. EcoBroker-certified realtors can help clients purchase green homes and help homeowners effectively market the green features of their properties. Use the website's directory to locate an EcoBroker-certified realtor near you.

ENERGY STAR

Energystar.gov

When purchasing your next home, look for the Energy Star label (or ask the developer or realtor to show it to you). Over five hundred thousand new homes in the U.S. have qualified for the Energy Star program, attesting to their superior energy-efficient performance. Visit Energystar.gov and click on "Find Local Homebuilders" to view a list of builders of energy-efficient homes in your area.

GOLF AND THE ENVIRONMENT

Golfandenvironment.org

An initiative of Audubon International, Golf and the Environment teams up with golf courses around the world to help management teams design and maintain courses in ways that support healthier ecosystems. Visit the website to find hundreds of golf courses that have been certified by Audubon International, attesting to their environmentally friendly practices. Many of the courses are located amid private residential communities.

MODERN GREEN LIVING

Moderngreenliving.com

At Moderngreenliving.com you'll find the most extensive directory of green residential developments available in the United States, Canada, and overseas. You'll also find information and links to green professionals like architects, builders, interior designers, landscape architects, renewable energy specialists, and realtors, who can you help you easily design, build, furnish, remodel, or find a green home.

U.S. GREEN BUILDING COUNCIL

USGBC.org

The U.S. Green Building Council is one of the principal organizations driving the growth of green building in the United States. The organization created and oversees the Leadership in Environmental and Energy Design (LEED) building framework—a series of green design initiatives that buildings must satisfy in order to receive green certification. What started as a program focused on commercial buildings has expanded to include residential high-rises and individual houses. LEED certification is also available to building professionals and attests to their green expertise.

7

Architecture and Construction

Whether we're building the home of our dreams,

adding an extension, or taking on a few remodeling projects, eco-intelligent options are rapidly becoming the performance-driven, cost-competitive, and super-stylish choice. The shift is being driven by forward-thinking materials, new technologies, and a lot of common sense. When it comes to the place we call home, the logic is back in "ecological."

Building a home is a big deal. Despite our best efforts, complications arise and cost overruns and time delays can drive us to the very limits of sanity. To address these challenges, visionary architects and developers are partnering with manufacturers to build homes inside factories where quality can be closely monitored, economies of scale can lower prices, and excess material and waste can be easily collected and reused. The components—like roofs and walls—of these "prefab" or modular homes are shipped to home sites for quick assembly. In some instances, entire homes are shipped preassembled for the ultimate in instant gratification and cost reduction.

Prefab homes have been around for years, but the difference is that today's practitioners include some of the best architects and visionary developers, who are as committed to great design as they are to a greener future. LivingHomes, based in Santa Monica, is run by Steve Glenn, a former dot-com guru turned green developer. Glenn has recruited world-class architects like Ray Kappe, founder of the Southern California Institute of Architecture (Sci-Arc), and David Hertz—whom I first discovered while watching an ABC-TV architecture special filmed in his own home—to design and build prefabricated houses that are stylish and gadget-ized enough to appeal to Generation iPod, and green enough to entice hippie anarchists living under bridges in Santa Cruz to invest in a place of their own. Green touches include FSC-certified sustainable and reclaimed woods, low-VOC paints and finishes, formaldehyde-free millwork, and energy-efficient heating and cooling systems. Rooftop gardens capture water runoff and reduce urban heat-island effect to help lower urban temperatures by replacing dark, hard surfaces with vegetation. Solar panels are an easily integrated option. Glenn currently lives in his company's showcase home in Santa Monica and is overseeing the first LivingHomes community near Joshua Tree National Park.

Delving into prefab is but one way to construct a contemporary eco-dream home. You can also opt for life-size Legos—components that fit seamlessly together to form a tight, well-insulated wall or roof. They're called insulated concrete forms (ICFs) and structural insulated panels (SIPs), and they are giving wood-framed homes a run for homeowners' money. ICFs and SIPS are made primarily of polystyrene, which is basically a foam-based plastic also known as Styrofoam. Think of an Oreo cookie with Styrofoam on the outside and concrete on the inside and you've basically got ICFs. Because ICFs are fireproof, mold-resistant, sound-resistant, and strong enough to withstand hurricane winds, they make excellent walls. Now surround the Styrofoam with engineered wood boards called OSBs (oriented strand boards) and you've essentially got SIPs. Lightweight yet durable, SIPs can be good for both walls and roofs. Companies like Amvic produce ICF blocks made of polystyrene with 100 percent recycled content. Companies like Enercept produce SIP panels using polystyrene with up to 80 percent recycled content. Shifting home construction to these life-size Legos can save eight to ten trees per home. The walls are so well insulated that energy consumption for heating and cooling is typically reduced between 40 and 50 percent per month, which translates into reduced greenhouse gas emissions and direct savings on your energy bills.

For new wood-framed homes and drafty homes in need of

an insulation upgrade, high-performance all-natural, recycled, and plant-based insulation materials will knock your socks off— though now your toes will be nice and toasty. New Zealand–based Latitude Insulation offers all-natural home insulation made from, you guessed it, sheep's wool. While fiberglass insulation contains some recycled content, most varieties also contain formaldehyde, a known carcinogen that should have no place in a home. Some insulation companies, like Bonded Logic, offer recycled cotton denim insulation, which is a fashionable idea and a much better thing to do with jeans than tossing them in a landfill. BioBased Insulation touts a next-generation spray-foam insulation derived from annually renewable soybean oil. But what truly distinguishes Latitude's natural wool insulation is wool's innate capacity to absorb and store carcinogenic formaldehyde particulates already present inside our homes. Since your furniture, rugs, and wallpaper are likely off-gassing formaldehyde as you read this, natural wool insulation comes out on top.

Now that the structure of our homes is in place, it's time to make them look pretty. Low-VOC and zero-VOC—short for volatile organic compounds, many of which are known carcinogens—paints look great and improve the quality of the indoor air we breathe. EPA studies routinely indicate that indoor air quality in the United States is significantly worse—on the order of two to five times worse—than outdoor quality. Painting with low-VOC and zero-VOC paints is an excellent means of correcting this situation. Both big companies and more specialized companies offer exciting options. Benjamin Moore has a low-VOC EcoSpec line. Anna Sova offers zero-VOC paints made with 99 percent food-grade ingredients that can even be scent-enhanced to provide long-lasting aromatherapy. Olympic's Premium Interior Paint is a zero-VOC option, available in over a thousand color shades, that you can purchase at Lowe's.

When thinking about a beautiful, sensuous wall surface that is healthier for you, your family, and the planet, the natural choice is American Clay's eco-aware plasters. Made from natural clay and available in thirty-two colors thanks to coloring agents derived from natural oxides and ocher mineral pigments, American Clay plasters are the zero-VOC, nontoxic choice that is also highly recommended for babies' and kids' rooms. American Clay plasters also restore energy balance to indoor environments. Granted this concept is a bit "New Agey," but American Clay plasters have been found to emit negative ions, which counteract the positive ions emitted from electronics like televisions, radios, and appliances such as microwaves. So it's not only the eco-choice, but the Zen choice too.

You've found an eco-friendy option for your walls and ceilings. Now what about your floors? The options are vast and exciting. Amorim Revestimentos, based in Portugal, is going "old school" with its Wicanders Collection of cork flooring made in the same time-honored Portuguese tradition since 1868. The bark of the cork tree is shorn by hand every nine years without damaging the tree, which can live to between 150 and 200 years. It's a highly efficient, continually renewable process that produces a warm, inviting flooring surface. Cork floors provide thermal and sound insulation and are soft, comfortable, and antibacterial. New advances make cork flooring easier to install, and now varying texture patterns and colors are available too.

Design fans will appreciate the modular linoleum flooring tiles offered by Forbo, called Marmoleum Click. The tiles easily snap together and are made from natural ingredients like flax, rosins, wood flour, and jute. Eighteen color options are available, which can be mixed and matched in a limitless number of patterns. So lay down some flooring, and if you don't like the way it looks, change it anytime you want.

Fast-growing, rapidly renewable, and eco-ubiquitous, bamboo makes its flooring presence felt through Smith & Fong's gorgeous line of bamboo flooring marketed under the name Plyboo. EcoTimber will satisfy a homeowner's hankering for wood with its beautiful hardwood flooring made from a variety of reclaimed and FSC-certified sustainable woods.

Rugs are also undergoing an eco-facelift. Interface Flors offers modular rug tiles that are easy to install, come in an amazing assortment of colors, and contain both recycled and renewable materials. Create wall-to-wall carpeting or accent rugs in any pattern choice you can imagine. And no longer worry about permanent stains; damaged tiles can be easily replaced while the rest of your rug remains intact.

For eco-aware rugs in patterns with a designer edge, check out the New Zealand wool collection offered by Angela Adams and available in a broad range of contemporary patterns. The backing is made from conventional cotton—insecticides and pesticides make cotton a questionable eco-option—but the glues are formaldehyde-free. All things considered, the Angela Adams collection is a substantial step in an eco-direction and a great choice for a warm evening by the fire.

Showcase the beauty of the materials covering your walls and floors with terrific lighting. The healthiest and most energy-efficient way to light a home is through natural sunlight. So if you're ready to be bathed in UV-protected sunlight from dawn till dusk and in every room in your home including your basement, then say hello to tubular skylights from Solatube. The only visible components of a tubular skylight are the small circular head that protrudes outward from your roof about six inches to capture sunlight from all directions and the ten- or fourteen-inch-diameter ceiling fixture that shines natural sunlight into your room. In between the head and fixture is a state-of-the art tube encased in high-tech mirrors. Whenever there is daylight, the head collects the light and channels it down the tube and into your home. A ten-inch fixture provides enough daylight for a room fifteen feet by fifteen feet. The fourteen-inch fixture effectively lights rooms up to twenty feet by twenty feet. The tubes can come in lengths of up to twenty feet, giving you flexibility to decide where you want your sunlight to go. Tubular skylights are affordable—about $300 per unit. Installation is straightforward and requires no structural adjustments.

At night compact fluorescent lightbulbs (CFLs) are the planet-friendly and long-term wallet-friendly alternative to conventional incandescent bulbs. It used to be that light emitted from CFL bulbs was harsh and cold and evoked nightmarish visions of being back in middle school classrooms and gymnasiums. But in a few short years, CFL bulbs have made great strides and now emit a luminescent glow equivalent to that of incandescent bulbs. A typical CFL bulb uses almost 75 percent less energy than an incandescent bulb to produce the same amount of light. Because CFL bulbs are much more efficient at turning energy into light instead of heat, they are 70 percent cooler than incandescent bulbs when operating, making them both the safe and the energy-saving choice. Do CFL bulbs cost more? Of course they do. They cost more up front because they last ten times longer, use less energy, and ultimately save you money. Ccrane.com carries a wide selection. So does Wal-Mart. In fact, the world's largest retailer is on a mission to sell 100 million compact fluorescent lightbulbs—one for each of its regular customers—to flip the switch on global warming solutions.

Similar eco-logic can apply to how we choose to heat our homes. Radiant heat heats a home by running hot water pipes below the floors. Geothermal heat is a great option if you're willing to invest in running pipes beneath the earth to tap heat trapped there and funnel it up to your home, and space heaters are a highly efficient means of delivering warmth to the areas in your home where you most prefer to be. Certain types of solar panels can be installed to help heat water. All are good options. Yet as a lazy environmentalist, I am most enamored of the energy-efficient tankless water heaters offered by Takagi, which help limit the eco-impact of marvelously pleasurable luxuries like really long showers. Heating water for household activities—like showers, dishwashing, clothes washing—is an energy-intensive chore. The Takagi tankless water heater handles it admirably through an advanced compact design that is about the size of a suitcase, weighs about sixty pounds, and installs flat against a wall surface. The Takagi replaces your home's conventional water boiler, which is always on even when hot water isn't running. The Takagi goes to work within five seconds of a hot water tap being turned on and, by relying upon a state-of-the-art heat coil system, instantly provides hot water on the order of between 180 and 300 gallons every hour. The system is so efficient that it will generate savings of up to 50 percent on water utility bills. Other companies make tankless water heaters, but the Takagi is one of the most energy efficient and is the only one of its kind to receive SCAQMD (Southern California Air Quality Management District) approval for its low emissions of noxious gases like carbon monoxide and nitrous oxide.

Prefab Housing

LIVINGHOMES

Livinghomes.us

Developer Steve Glenn partners with world-class architects to offer semi-custom, factory-built homes that combine the best of contemporary living with green amenities like FSC-certified sustainable and reclaimed woods, low-VOC paints and finishes, living rooftop gardens, and optional solar panel systems. The first LivingHomes development is under way near Joshua Tree National Park.

MARMOL RADZINER PREFAB

Marmolradzinerprefab.com

Highly customizable, premanufactured homes delivered directly to your home site. Marmol Radziner Prefab homes combine modern aesthetics with expansive living details like floor-to-ceiling windows and wide decks that enable indoor and outdoor living. These quality, recycled steel-frame homes include eco-attributes like FSC-certified sustainable woods, low-VOC paints, and solar panels.

MICHELLE KAUFMANN DESIGNS

Mkd-arc.com

One of the emerging leaders of the contemporary sustainable prefab movement, Michelle Kaufmann strives to make thoughtful, eco-aware living accessible to a wide audience. Her prefab models—Glidehouse, Sunset Breezehouse, and mkSolaire—integrate quality construction and high-performance systems with green building principles and offer a range of design possibilities suitable for both the countryside and the urban landscape.

OFFICE OF MOBILE DESIGN

Designmobile.com

Architect Jennifer Siegal advances contemporary, clean aesthetics and modern manufacturing techniques to create her affordable, eco-advanced prefab homes. Siegal's newest offering, the Portable House, is manufactured and assembled inside a factory and delivered directly to home sites.

Notable Green Architects

DAVID BERGMAN
Cyberg.com
Bergman runs a multidisciplinary design studio that emphasizes sustainable design principles in architecture, interior design, and product design. His award-winning Fire & Water lighting is one of the only contemporary eco-lighting collections available today. Bergman also teaches sustainable design courses at the Parsons School of Design in New York City.

NEIL CHAMBERS
Greengroundzero.org
The green architect who never sleeps, Chambers is the sustainable director of Timbes Architectural Group, with offices in New York, South Carolina, and Michigan. He is also the executive producer and host of *re:Form*, a television show, airing throughout New York City, featuring prominent environmental thinkers and visionaries like Governor Brian Schweitzer of Montana and *Metropolis* editor in chief Susan S. Szenasy. Students can take Chambers's courses in green design and environmental policy at NYU, where he is an adjunct professor.

ERIC COREY FREED
Organicarchitect.com
Freed is the principal of Organic Architect, a design practice committed to designing award-winning buildings that are organic and environmentally friendly. He has been named "Best Green Architect" by *San Francisco* magazine. Freed also teaches sustainable architecture at the University of California, Berkeley, and the Academy of Arty University. His forthcoming book—*The Inevitable Architect: A Phase By Phase Guide to Green Building*—will be published in 2007.

KELLY LERNER
One-world-design.com
Lerner is the principal of One World Design, an architectural firm specializing in sustainable natural building. She is one of the foremost experts on straw bale construction—the process of stacking straw bales to create exterior walls, a technique that is exploding in popularity. Lerner is also the coauthor with Carol Venolia of *Natural Remodeling for the Not-So-Green House*.

WILLIAM MCDONOUGH

Mcdonough.com

A leader of the green architecture movement and one of the most influential architects practicing today, William McDonough is the founding principal of William McDonough + Partners, Architecture and Community Design. He is also the co-founder principal of McDonough Braungart Design Chemistry (MBDC), a sustainable product design and certification firm that emphasizes Cradle to Cradle product lifecycle principles. McDonough is the coauthor of *Cradle to Cradle: Remaking the Way We Make Things*, which has become something of a bible for the green design and business community.

Walls and Roofs

AMVIC

Amvicsystem.com

A Lego-like building material comprised of recycled polystyrene foam and concrete. Amvic blocks are insulated concrete forms (ICFs) that are stacked on top of one another to build walls and can be easily cut into different shapes to fit the needs and desires of homeowners. They provide an extremely durable, fireproofed, sound-insulated, and weather-insulated barrier that creates extremely energy-efficient homes.

ENERCEPT

Enercept.com

Another Lego-like building material comprised of up to 80 percent recycled polystyrene foam sandwiched between engineered wood boards. Enercept blocks are known as structural insulated panels (SIPs), which are suitable for walls, flooring, and roofs due to their light weight. New advances in SIPs enable them also to be cut into numerous shapes and easily assembled on home sites, saving time and therefore saving cost. SIPs like Enercept can also save you up to 40 to 60 percent on heating and cooling bills.

RASTRA

Rastra.com

Yet another Lego-like ICF comprised of recycled polystyrene foam and concrete, Rastra was first developed in Europe over thirty years ago, has been continuously improved ever since, and is currently in major demand throughout the United States.

Insulation

LATITUDE INSULATION

Latitudeinsulation.com

Latitude Insulation offers natural wool insulation that utilizes wool's innate heating and cooling properties. Wool also naturally absorbs formaldehyde—a known carcinogen present in conventional flooring, rugs, furniture, paints, and wallpaper—and stores it in the insulation's fibers, helping to improve air quality inside the home.

BIOBASED INSULATION

Biobased.net

A soy-based foam made from annually renewable soybean oil. It quickly expands to one hundred times its original size to fill air pockets and create an airtight sealed envelope, making a healthy, energy-efficient home.

BONDED LOGIC

Bondedlogic.com

Bonded Logic's Ultra Touch insulation relies upon recycled cotton denim. Energy efficient in its manufacturing, safe to handle during installation, and significantly healthier than conventional insulation products in its elimination of nasty chemicals like formaldehyde, Ultra Touch is a very solid performer.

Decks

CHOICEDEK

Choicedek.com

Where do all those milk jugs go when we're done with the milk? Why, into our outdoor decking, of course. Available exclusively from Lowe's, ChoiceDek is an engineered wood comprised of recycled wood and recycled milk jugs. It's extremely durable, resistant to insect and moisture damage, and very easy to install.

TREX

Trex.com

Trex offers superior outdoor decking and railing products made of a unique combination of recycled plastic and reclaimed wood. The decks will last for years without the need for staining or repairing, are suitable for virtually all climates, and are available in numerous colors to match any home style.

Paints and Plasters

AFM

Safecoatpaint.com

Safecoat's zero-VOC paints perform exceptionally well while eliminating all toxins and off-gassing agents that can degrade air quality. AFM also offers wood finishes, sealers, and cleaners that are nontoxic and never tested on animals.

AGLAIA

www.aglaiapaint.com

Aglaia is a highly regarded German maker of natural plant-based paints for over one hundred years. Aglaia paints smell good, look good, and are easy to apply. In addition to paints, natural oil and wax wood finishes are also available.

AMERICAN CLAY

Americanclay.com

Made from natural clay and available in thirty-two colors thanks to coloring agents derived from natural oxides and ocher mineral pigments, American Clay plasters are the zero-VOC, nontoxic choice.

AMERICAN PRIDE PAINT

Americanpridepaint.com

American Pride offers eco-responsible high-performance paints that contain no known toxic materials or carcinogens. American Pride paints were originally developed by scientists at the University of Southern Mississippi to provide a healthy alternative to latex paints for use by the U.S. Department of Defense.

ANNA SOVA

Annasova.com

Anna Sova is devoted to luxury, premium-quality products made with pure and renewable materials. Anna Sova paints are milk-based, with up to 99 percent other food-based ingredients—as in yogurts, milkshakes, and chocolates—to eliminate nasty chemicals and ingredients found in traditional latex paints. Aromatherapy oils may be blended into the paint during application for a long-lasting, mood-enhancing lift.

AURO

Aurousa.com

Auro offers natural paints and finishes derived from plants and minerals. Indoor and outdoor varieties are easy to work with and available in an attractive palette of natural colors.

BENJAMIN MOORE

Benjaminmoore.com

Benjamin Moore dips its brush into low-VOC options with its Eco Spec line. Available in thousands of colors, Eco Spec paint is a good, cost-effective option.

BIOSHIELD

Bioshieldpaint.com

BioShield offers top-quality healthy, eco-aware paints. Our Vivavi showroom was painted using BioShield's natural clay paints. They are very efficient to apply and help create rich, luxurious interiors. BioShield also offers eco-smart stains, finishes, and household cleaners.

KELLY MOORE

Kellymoore.com

Kelly Moore's Enviro Cote line of paints is a low-VOC option available in a multitude of colors. The E coat paint line is made from recycled paint—at least 50 percent—and is suitable for both indoor and outdoor applications. Kelly Moore is the largest employee-owned paint company in the United States, with more than 160 retail stores and approximately two thousand employees.

OLYMPIC PREMIUM INTERIOR PAINT

Lowes.com / Olympic

Olympic's zero-VOC interior paint comes in more than a thousand different colors and is available exclusively from Lowe's.

YOLO COLORHOUSE

Yolocolorhouse.com

YOLO offers premium, zero-VOC paints in 40 warm, earthy colors. Not one to skimp, YOLO offers potential customers large, poster-size color swatches with which to gauge how its paint will look once applied.

Paint Remover

SILENT PAINT REMOVER

Silentpaintremover.com

Remove paint and varnish without the need for any chemicals. The Silent Paint Remover utilizes infrared heat to handle the task. The handheld device is safe and easy to use.

SOY CLEAN

Soyclean.biz

Soy Clean celebrates the power of soy to do just about anything, including pant stripping. The soy-based Paint Stripper uses 100 percent all-natural ingredients and works on latex, oil-based, lead-based, and spray paints. Soy Clean also offers a full line of nontoxic, biodegradable cleaning supplies.

Flooring

AMORIM REVESTIMENTOS

Wicanders.com

Based in Portugal, Amorim Revestimentos offers its Wicanders Collection of elegant, practical, and distinctive cork floors. Cork floors provide thermal and sound insulation and are soft, comfortable, and antibacterial. The Wicanders Collection cork tiles can be easily sealed, making them impenetrable to moisture and insects.

BAMBOO MOUNTAIN

Bamboomountain.com

Since 1997 Bamboo Mountain has been supplying high-quality bamboo flooring from its own factory, where it is kiln-dried, precision-milled, and factory-finished using advanced technology. Bamboo Mountain was one of the first companies to introduce formaldehyde-free bamboo boards to create a zero-VOC flooring surface and a healthier home.

DURO-DESIGN

Duro-design.com

Beautiful, sumptuous cork and bamboo flooring can be yours thanks to Duro-Design, a leading manufacturer of eco-aware flooring products. Colors and styles are available to complement any home decor.

ECO FRIENDLY FLOORING

Ecofriendlyflooring.com

From its headquarters in Madison, Wisconsin, Eco-Friendly Flooring ships quality flooring products throughout the United States. The broad selection features lots of material choices, including recycled aluminum and glass tiles, bamboo, cork, linoleum, and reclaimed and sustainable woods.

ECOTIMBER

Ecotimber.com

Hardwood floors look just how you hoped they would when you work with EcoTimber. Only now your floor is also healthier for the planet. Choose from beautiful reclaimed woods and FSC-certified woods. Bamboo flooring is also available.

EXPANKO

Expanko.com

Combining traditional craftsmanship with advanced production, Expanko is the master of multiple cork flooring aesthetics. There's even a product line that blends cork with recycled rubber for a truly unique look.

FORBO MARMOLEUM

Themarmoleumstore.com

Marmoleum Click modular tiles easily snap together and are made from natural ingredients like flax, rosins, wood flour, and jute. Eighteen color options are available, which can be mixed and matched in a limitless number of patterns.

GLOBUS CORK

Corkfloor.com

Design takes center stage in this inspiring cork flooring collection from Globus Cork. Sure it's eco-friendly, but the colors and styles will wow design fans entirely on their own.

SMITH & FONG

Plyboo.com

Smith & Fong produces high-quality, formaldehyde-free bamboo flooring and bamboo panels that it markets under the name Plyboo. Continuous innovation is a hallmark of this company. In addition to Plyboo, Smith & Fong also offers Durapalm—an engineered palmwood board made from coconut palms. Both Plyboo and Durapalm are great for flooring, cabinets, paneling, and furniture.

TERAGREN

Teragren.com

Teragren offers premium-quality bamboo flooring. Deeply involved in the manufacturing process from harvest to finished product, Teragren ensures that its products are made to the highest standards. Teragren's bamboo boards are great for cabinets, furniture, and paneling.

TERRAMAI

Terramai.com

Lazy environmentalists can enjoy exotic hardwoods thanks to Terramai's gorgeous selection of reclaimed woods from around the world. Terramai flooring comes in a wide range of colors and distinctive visual patterns to create exceptional beauty combined with old-growth quality.

Rugs

ANGELA ADAMS

Angelaadams.com

For eco-aware rugs in patterns with a designer edge, check out the New Zealand wool collection offered by Angela Adams and available in a broad range of contemporary patterns.

DOLMA RUGS

Dolmarugs.com

Hand-spun in Nepal using the finest Tibetan wool and time-honored techniques, Dolma Rugs come in both traditional and contemporary patterns to match virtually any interior decor. The colorful patterns are achieved using natural, chemical-free dyes.

EMMA GARDNER DESIGN

Emmagardnerdesign.com

Artist and designer Emma Gardner is renowned for the sophisticated contemporary patterns that inform her company's rug collection. With manufacturing partners in both India and Nepal, Gardner relies upon traditional techniques and materials to produce rugs made of alpaca, wool, and silk.

GLEN EDEN WOOL CARPET

Glen-eden.com

Sophisticated, timeless design is what you'll get with Glen Eden wool carpets. Made in the United States from 100 percent pure New Zealand wool, Glen Eden carpets grace the floors of such rarefied addresses as the White House, Buckingham Palace, and the home of Bruce Willis.

GODFREY HIRST
Godfreyhirst.com
This Australian company offers premium carpets, including a 100 percent natural wool selection suitable for all climates, stain-resistant, and eco-certified for low VOC emissions.

INTERFACE FLOR
Florcatalog.com
Transform your rooms with modular tiles from Interface FLOR that are available in a multitude of colors and present nearly infinite design possibilities. The low-VOC tiles are made of wool, hemp, or nylon, with backings made of recycled materials.

NATURAL ELEMENTS
Natural-elements.net
Subtle woven patterns are on display in the Natural Elements line of rugs. Materials come from all over the world and include coir (a fiber derived from coconut husks), seagrass (from marshlands in Southern Asia), sisal (from plants grown in East Africa), mountaingrass (otherwise known as hemp and grown in the mountainous regions of Asia), and fine New Zealand wool.

URBAN LINE
Urban-line.net
Designed by Colin Campbell, Urban Line offers a selection of fine-quality natural wool carpets made by manufacturers in Australia, New Zealand, and Greece. The line was developed to make affordable wool carpets of high quality accessible to a broad audience.

Lighting

C. CRANE
Ccrane.com
For thirty years C. Crane has been providing consumers with quality electronics and home products. Find here a wide selection of eco-advanced LED lightbulbs that will help create an energy-efficient home.

SOLATUBE
Solatube.com
Solatube tubular skylights bring natural, healthy sunlight into your home by channeling it through a state-of-the art tube encased in high-tech mirrors, from your roof into any room you choose. Unlike standard skylights, installation of tubular skylights requires no structural changes.

WAL-MART
Walmart.com
The world's largest retailer is on a mission to sell 100 million compact fluorescent lightbulbs—one for each of its regular customers—to flip the switch on global warming solutions.

Heating

TAKAGI
Takagi.com
The Takagi tankless water heater is a compact design about the size of a suitcase that replaces your home's conventional water boiler. A state-of-the-art heat coil system provides between 180 and 300 gallons of hot water every hour. The efficient system generates savings of up to 50 percent on water utility bills.

Home Improvement Retailers

Many of the options discussed here are available through an increasing number of eco-home improvement stores opening throughout the United States. Here's a list to get you started:

BETTENCOURT GREEN BUILDING SUPPLIES
Bettencourtwood.com
Brooklyn, New York

BUILDING FOR HEALTH MATERIALS CENTER
Buildingforhealth.com
Carbondale, Colorado

ECO-GREEN LIVING
Eco-greenliving.com
Washington, DC

ECO HOME IMPROVEMENT
Ecohomeimprovement.com
Berkeley, California

ENVIRONMENTAL BUILDING SUPPLIES
Ecohaus.com
Portland and Bend, Oregon

ENVIRONMENTAL CONSTRUCTION OUTFITTERS (ECO) OF NEW YORK
Environproducts.com
Bronx, New York

ENVIRONMENTAL HOME CENTER
Environmentalhomecenter.com
Seattle, Washington

THE GREEN BUILDING CENTER
Greenbuildingcenter.net
Salt Lake City, Utah

GREEN FUSION DESIGN CENTER
Greenfusiondesigncenter.com
Marin County, California

GREENMAKER BUILDING SUPPLY
Greenmakersupply.com
Chicago, Illinois

LIVINGREEN
Livinggreen.com
Los Angeles and Santa Barbara, California

MEASURE FOR MEASURE
Measureformeasurehome.com
Bridgeport, Connecticut

PLANETARY SOLUTIONS
Planetearth.com
Boulder, Colorado

SAFE BUILDING SOLUTIONS
Safebuildingsolutions.com
Waukesha, Wisconsin

TERRA BUILDING SUPPLY
Terrabuildingsupply.com
McCall, Idaho

YOUR HOME YOUR WORLD
Yourhomeyourworld.com
Concord, New Hampshire

Information/Education

BUILDINGGREEN
Buildinggreen.com
BuildingGreen is an independent company that evaluates and verifies the claims of green building products and publishes those that pass its criteria online via its GreenSpec Directory and through its book, *Green Building Products,* making more than 1,600 products available to homebuilders and homeowners.

GREEN BUILDING BLOCKS
Greenbuildingblocks.com
Green Building Blocks offers an extensive directory for residential customers seeking green professionals to help them green their homes.

From electricians to landscape architects, if you can think of an area in your home that you want to make more eco-aware Green Building Blocks likely lists a professional who can help.

GREEN HOME GUIDE

Greenhomeguide.com

Green Home Guide is a community-based website providing extensive resources for consumers who want to green their homes. Green home experts from fields like architecture and interior design evaluate the merits of individual green products. Visitors to the website can search for green home professionals in their area who can help with green projects, and find green retailers that stock the latest green goods.

MODERN GREEN LIVING

Moderngreenliving.com

At Moderngreenliving.com you'll find the most extensive directory of green residential developments available in the United States, Canada, and overseas. You'll also find information and links to green professionals like architects, builders, interior designers, landscape architects, renewable energy specialists, and realtors who can you help you easily design, build, furnish, remodel, or find a green home.

8

MORE THAN
ONE WAY
TO HEAT A
HOME

Energy
Alternatives

The U.S. power grid—which connects to each of our homes—relies upon fossil fuels like coal, natural gas, and oil for about two-thirds of its energy. Because they are carbon-based, fossil fuels emit carbon dioxide greenhouse gases into the atmosphere, creating a situation that is far from eco-optimal. Thankfully, fossil fuels are not the only option. Today new technology, new designs, and new services are available that make it easy, convenient, and attractive to tap into limitless, nonpolluting energy sources like wind and solar. In many instances, these clean, green energy solutions are just a few mouse clicks away from powering your home and dramatically reducing your carbon footprint.

In the United Sates more than six hundred power utilities in thirty-six states offer green energy options to their residential customers. The choices are vast and range from 100 percent wind energy to combinations of green energy like wind, solar, small river hydropower, and landfill methane gas—a potent greenhouse gas that is created from the decomposition of landfill garbage. You do not need to live directly underneath a windmill or next to a landfill to receive residential energy from green energy sources. Often all that is required to get the green energy flowing is a quick visit to your utility company's website, where you enter your customer ID number, check a few boxes, and click "submit."

As it's still in its early stages, green energy is a little more expensive than traditional energy sources. But not much more. Look at Alabama, where customers of the Alabama Electric Cooperative can select landfill gas to power their homes for just 2 cents more per kilowatt hour (kWh). According to the Department of Energy,

U.S. homes on average use about 900 kWh of energy per month. Multiplying 2 cents times 900 kWh equals $18 in additional costs per month to switch to clean green energy and reduce your home's greenhouse gas emissions toward zero.

In New York and parts of Massachusetts residents can select 100 percent wind energy or a combination of 35 percent wind energy and 65 percent hydropower from free-flowing rivers through ConEdison Solutions. Both options carry a small price premium, but a quick visit to Conedsolutions.com can have your home running on green energy in no time. For a typical apartment in New York City, the cost of switching to 100 percent wind power would be about $10 extra per month. The cost of switching to a combination of wind and hydropower would be about $4 extra per month.

When ConEdison Solutions began offering green energy options in 2001, only a handful of customers made the switch. Today thousands of customers are using wind energy or a combination of wind and hydropower. Demand is so high that ConEdison Solutions has outgrown in-state green energy suppliers and has begun purchasing green energy from suppliers throughout New England. It is exactly this type of market demand that encourages new investments in wind energy and hydropower technology and propels us toward a greener future.

And the strategy is working. In Boulder, Colorado, and Austin, Texas, green energy choices offered by utility companies actually cost less than the standard choices. Prices for green energy in other parts of the country are quickly becoming competitive too. To check whether a utility in your area offers green energy choices, visit the Green Power Network website of the Department of Energy.

For residents who want the benefits of green energy, but don't have a green energy utility provider nearby, Renewable Energy Certificates (RECs), also known as green tags and tradable renewable certificates, make it possible and can be purchased from a number of providers. A REC is often described as the environmental attributes associated with green energy, which can be a little hard to grasp. So here's a simple example of how it works. Today, when a utility company wants to buy the lowest-priced energy available, it often chooses coal because it is cheapest. If a wind energy company—or another type of green energy company—lowers its prices to match coal, it will go out of business. So to be competitive with coal, the wind energy company creates a renewable energy certificate—a.k.a. REC—equivalent to the price difference between the two energy sources. When you buy RECs you enable green energy companies to remain in business by keeping their prices low enough for utility companies to purchase their green energy. Doing so actively increases the use of green energy throughout the United States. One of the leading REC providers is Renewable Choice Energy which provides RECs to consumers and corporations. The company helps Vail Ski Resorts offset 100 percent of its energy use with wind energy purchased through RECs—enough wind energy to power more than fourteen thousand homes a year.

Consumers often purchase RECs in blocks equivalent to the amount of monthly energy that they use in their homes, thereby offsetting the "bad" energy with the "good" energy and moving toward a carbon-neutral lifestyle. Companies known as "green energy marketers" sell RECs, which tend to cost as much as the premium that utility companies charge their customers per month for green energy. In addition to Renewable Choice Energy, other prominent marketers include Community Energy, Bonneville Environmental Foundation, and Native Energy. Purchasing RECs that have been Green-e certified ensures that the green energy claims made by marketers of these green energy products have been verified and are accurate. See Green-e.org for a list of REC providers by state.

There's another attractive way to bring green energy into your home: opt for your own windmill. The Skystream 3.7 brings the latest innovations in wind energy technology directly to your doorstep. Developed and manufactured by Southwest Windpower in Flagstaff, Arizona, the Skystream 3.7 looks like a tall basketball pole topped with rotating blades. The sleek, compact model extends a minimum of forty-two feet into the air and connects easily to your home and to the power grid. This "plug and play" capability enables the Skystream 3.7 to rely upon the power grid to store extra wind energy that your home doesn't use. But don't worry about other people taking advantage of your wind energy, because on its way back to the grid, your wind energy spins your energy meter backwards, effectively paying you for the energy that your wind turbine generated by lowering your energy bill. Whenever you need to draw power from the grid to compensate the power from your Skystream 3.7, your energy meter spins forward. Such "net metering" enables you to enjoy all the energy generated by your Skystream 3.7 without requiring expensive battery storage equipment. Instead, the power grid acts as a twenty-four-hour storage tank.

According to the U.S. Census Bureau, approximately 17 million U.S. households are suitably situated for residential wind energy, which requires at least half an acre of unobstructed land and average wind speeds of at least 10 mph. If those conditions are met, your local zoning permits the construction of a structure at least forty-two feet tall, and your utility company offers an interconnection agreement—most do—then the Skystream 3.7 may be right for you. Skystreamenergy.com features extensive information about financial incentives, wind maps to determine the wind-generating capacity of your home, and links to dealers throughout North America who can help with installation. For between $6,000 and $8,000—including full installation (subsidies are available in many states)—one Skystream 3.7 can fulfill approximately half the annual energy consumption needs of the typical home. Pair two together, attach a couple of hoops, and you can drop off the grid completely while enjoying a full-court basketball game.

The same attributes that make the Skystream 3.7 so appealing—aesthetically pleasing design, ease of use, and cost-effective price—are also emerging in the residential solar industry. Deciphering the costs associated with installing solar panels on your home can be frustrating. It's often difficult to get from a solar installer a price quote that separates the price of the panels from the overall cost of installation. Many installers are hesitant to divulge the truth—approximately half the cost of a residential solar system goes to labor and installation equipment. But it's hard to blame installers. Installing solar panel systems is cumbersome, often requiring customization and specific training and skill. So it stands to reason that if solar panels were available in pre-configured, easy-to-install modules that could fit any home, labor and equipments costs would dramatically drop and solar power would become a more accessible option.

Enter Ready Solar. Based in Portola Valley, California, this entrepreneurial company is determined to transform how we think about solar power. No longer limited to nutty, off-the-reservation survivalists, solar power now fits into a new category called "energy appliances," which are as easy to purchase and use as a dishwasher or toaster oven. Ready Solar builds standardized, pre-configured solar systems that lie close to the roof and look more like skylights than the clunky solar installations of the past. The modular system comes in a variety of frame colors and allows you to start small, with a solar configuration that will provide about 20 percent of your home's energy, and add on as you desire for solar power increases (or go for a larger configuration all at once). Better still, Ready Solar's modules are portable, so your solar systems can move with you. The company provides financing and factors in all available rebates and tax credits to simplify the purchasing process—which can be done through its website. The compact, all-in-one design that houses the panels requires fewer holes to be drilled in the roof, cutting down on installation time and generating savings that Ready Solar passes on to the customer.

If you're seeking complete control over your household energy, turn to Gridpoint. The Washington, DC–based company has created appliances that master energy management. The device looks like a sleek refrigerator, but "acts like Tivo for the energy needs of your home," explains CEO Peter Corsell. Gridpoint appliances automatically purchase and store energy from the power grid when energy costs are low (usually during the middle of the day while most people are at work) and feed that energy to your home at times when energy costs are high (in the evenings when everyone is home). Gridpoint appliances also monitor the energy usage of each appliance in your home and allow you to monitor that data in real time via your personal electricity dashboard, which is available online. You will instantly know how much electricity you use to light your bedroom, how efficient your Energy Star dishwasher really is, and how severely your husband's Xbox habit is draining the children's college fund. The Gridpoint energy management appliance gives you the information necessary to take full control of your home's energy consumption and can save you up to 25 percent on your monthly bills. The appliance also connects with personal wind or solar energy systems to maximize your home's energy efficiency, and its high-performance batteries double as a clean backup generator which can store enough energy to power your home for up to three days in case of blackouts. At a cost of approximately $10,000, Gridpoint is not cheap, but it costs less than the average home generator and eventually pays for itself with energy savings.

Utility Green Energy

ALABAMA ELECTRIC COOPERATIVE
Powersouth.com
Alabama Electric Cooperative offers Alabama residents the opportunity to switch from conventional fossil fuel–derived energy sources to recaptured landfill gas, a convenient solution for reducing greenhouse gas emissions without altering our lifestyle. The program carries a small premium.

AUSTIN ENERGY
Austinenergy.com
Austin Energy's Green Choice renewable energy program is the most successful in the United States. Austin, Texas, residents who have signed up for the energy utility's program pay lower monthly energy bills while eliminating greenhouse gas emissions.

CONEDISON SOLUTIONS
ConEdisonsolutions.com
In New York and parts of Massachusetts, through ConEdison Solutions residents can select 100 percent wind energy or a combination of 35 percent wind energy and 65 percent hydropower from free-flowing rivers. Customers can visit the website to easily sign up. Though the program carries a small premium, demand is so high that ConEdison Solutions has

outgrown in-state green energy suppliers and has begun purchasing green energy from suppliers throughout New England.

XCEL ENERGY
Xcelenergy.com
Colorado customers who have signed up for Xcel Energy's Windsource program not only receive 100 percent wind energy, but also pay less per month than customers who receive "regular" energy. The program's success has led to a long waiting list as the appeal of green energy grows. To help meet demand, Xcel Energy is currently building the largest solar energy power plant in the United States, located in south central Colorado.

Renewable Energy Certificates (RECs)

BONNEVILLE ENVIRONMENTAL FOUNDATION
B-e-f.org
A nonprofit organization that promotes watershed restoration programs and the development of new sources of renewable energy, Bonneville Environmental Foundation (BEF) funds its initiatives through the sale of RECs and is considered one of the most reputable marketers of these green energy credits. Eco-fashion retailer the Green Loop offsets all greenhouse gas emissions resulting from product shipments to consumers by purchasing green energy credits made available by BEF.

COMMUNITY ENERGY
Newwindenergy.com
Community Energy enables people throughout the U.S. to move toward carbon-neutral lifestyles by purchasing wind energy credits from new, state-of-the-art wind farms. This green energy marketer also helps develop new wind farms, including one located just on the outskirts of Atlantic City.

NATIVE ENERGY
Nativeenergy.com
Native Energy enables you to offset the greenhouse gas emissions associated with your energy use by purchasing RECs. Unlike other green energy marketers, Native Energy invests funds in new green energy sources, helping to increase green energy supplies. The company is off to a strong start. In addition to residential customers, Native Energy also works with companies like Stonyfield Farm and Ben & Jerry's. The film company Participant Productions turned to Native Energy to offset the carbon emissions created during the filming of *Syriana* starring George Clooney. Native Energy is 100 percent Native American–owned.

RENEWABLE CHOICE ENERGY

Renewablechoice.com

Renewable Choice Energy helps individuals and businesses offset their carbon footprint and helps promote renewable energy development around the country. One of the oldest and most respected renewable energy marketers, Renewable Choice is the exclusive wind power partner of Whole Foods Market, the first and only Fortune 500 company to go 100 percent wind power. Renewable Choice is also the leading renewable energy provider to green building projects nationwide. The publisher of this book turned to Renewable Choice to offset the electricity consumed in the manufacturing and production of *The Lazy Environmentalist*.

Residential Systems

CITIZENRE RENU

Renu.citizenre.com

If purchasing a solar energy system for your home seems cost-prohibitive, then eliminate the up-front costs by turning to Citizenre's REnU program that lets homeowners rent solar panels for their homes and lock in long-term electricity rates that are the same as or lower than utility rates. It's quite simple and straightforward. You agree to purchase the solar energy created by the panels for a period of up to twenty-five years, and Citizenre handles all the expenses of installation on your roof along with ongoing maintenance.

EVERGREEN SOLAR

Evergreensolar.com

Evergreen Solar is a manufacturer of lower-cost thin-film solar panels that require less silicon than conventional solar panels and deliver reliable, clean electric power to homes. Thin-film solar panels can easily do double duty as roof shingles, lowering roof construction costs and integrating solar directly into a home's structure.

GRIDPOINT

Gridpoint.com

"A TiVo for the energy needs of your home," says Gridpoint CEO Peter Corsell. Gridpoint appliances intelligently manage your home's energy consumption, effectively increasing energy efficiency and reducing energy purchase costs. The intelligent all-in-one system can save you 25 percent on your energy bills.

HOME DEPOT

Homedepot.com

Home Depot is partnering with BP Solar to provide solar power systems to residential customers throughout the United States. The straightforward process starts with a free in-home consultation. Home Depot completes all paperwork on your behalf, including permits, tax credits, and coordination with the power utility. Your system gets installed by screened professionals and comes with a twenty-five-year warranty.

READY SOLAR

Readysolar.com

A next-generation residential solar energy company that is spearheading a new movement to make solar power easy to buy, install, and use. Preconfigured, modular systems help lower costs and enable consumers to expand their solar power systems at their own convenience.

SHARP CORPORATION

Solar.sharpusa.com

The world's largest producer of solar cells is using its huge economies of scale to help drive down solar costs, and predicts that by 2010, the cost of solar power generation will be cut in half. Sharp solar systems can be integrated into all rooftop types and can generate up to six times more power than conventional solar systems.

SKYSTREAM 3.7

Skystreamenergy.com

Southwest Windpower, the leader in small wind turbines, introduces the Skystream 3.7 residential wind generator, making wind power accessible and economically viable for millions of homes in the United States. The sleek, plug-and-play design connects directly to your home and the power grid.

SUNPOWER

Sunpower.com

SunPower offers some of the most efficient solar panels available today. Its SPR-315 generates up to 50 percent more power per square foot of roof area, with half as many panels, than conventional solar panels.

Cool and Unique

GO SOLAR CALIFORNIA

Gosolarcalifornia.ca.gov
In 2006, delivering on his campaign promise to make the environment
a central focus of his administration, Governor Schwarzenegger signed
Senate Bill 1 into law. The bill allocates funds for a plan to create a million
solar-powered homes in California by 2017. It's the biggest solar initiative
in the U.S., and in the world it is second only to the initiative under way
throughout the entire country of Germany.

INTERNATIONAL SPACE STATION (ISS)

Shuttlepresskit.com/ISS_OVR
The International Space Station—home to astronauts—is the largest and
most complex international scientific project in history and now receives
25 percent of its energy from its two arrays of 240-foot-wide solar panel
systems.

Information/Education

AMERICAN SOLAR ENERGY SOCIETY (ASES)

Ases.org
ASES strives to accelerate the adoption of solar and other renewable energy
throughout the United States. Stay up-to-date on solar and renewable
energy news and trends through the organization's *Solar Today* magazine
and its free bimonthly newsletter, *Sunbeam*. ASES also organizes the
National Solar Conference, the largest conference in the U.S. for solar
and other renewable energy sources, as well as the National Solar Tour,
which enables individuals throughout the U.S. to visit and experience
buildings that utilize solar and wind energy, daylighting, and green building
technologies.

AMERICAN WIND ENERGY ASSOCIATION (AWEA)

Awea.org
The hub of the wind energy industry, the AWEA website offers up-to-date
information about wind energy projects around the world, wind energy
companies, technology developments pushing wind energy forward, and
policy developments that are changing the broader wind and renewable
energy landscape.

ENERGY QUEST

Energyquest.ca.gov/story/index.html

The award-winning energy education website of the California Energy Commission, Energy Quest is geared principally toward kids, to provide an energy primer and cultivate conservation awareness. The website offers concise, well-written information about all types of energy sources, including renewable energy and fossil fuels.

GREEN-E

Green-e.org

When purchasing renewable energy certificates (RECs) for your home, look for the Green-e logo to ensure that the green energy credits have been verified for accuracy and certified for quality. A program of the Center for Resource Solutions, Green-e provides an easily searchable database on its website to help customers locate Green-e certified renewable energy marketers in each state.

THE GREEN POWER NETWORK

Eere.energy.gov/greenpower

A program of the U.S. Department of Energy, the Green Power Network provides information about the green energy options available from more than six hundred power utility companies situated throughout the United States. Check to see what options are available to you in your area. The website also provides a thorough yet easy-to-understand overview of the green power options that are increasingly available to consumers.

RENEWABLE ENERGY ACCESS

Renewableenergyaccess.com

A top-flight resource for news and information about renewable energy products, technologies, events, and jobs, Renewable Energy Access was started in 1998 by a group of energy professionals who wanted their work to relate to their passion for renewable energy.

9

YOU ARE
WHAT YOU
SIT ON

Furniture
and Home Decor

One of the easiest ways to reverse global deforestation and tropical forest devastation is to give quick consideration to the chair you choose to sit on, the bed you sleep in, and the table you eat on. Opting for eco-intelligent furniture choices provides far-reaching benefits for your health and the health of the planet.

Scrapile combines high style with eco-intelligence to redefine not only what furniture looks like but also what it's made from. As the name implies, this Brooklyn-based company builds furniture using scraps of wood. Thousands of perfectly good scraps that would otherwise be discarded into landfills are gathered from construction sites, furniture studios, and factories throughout New York City. With its unique production process, Scrapile layers the pieces of wood atop one another and transforms them into colorful, striated boards that are used to create coffee and dining tables, benches, chairs, and shelves. The presence of varying wood types creates a strong connection to nature and is rendered thoroughly modern by the collection's clean, contemporary lines.

Scrapile designers Bart Bettencourt and Carlos Salgado met while working at the Guggenheim Museum in New York City, and they merge a love for sculpture with a mission to reuse the massive amounts of leftover quality materials available to municipalities. "Green to me is just being responsible," says Salgado. "Scrapile shows people that there are ways to reuse even the smallest amounts of what you would consider trash."

Scrapile's eco-conscious approach extends to its selection of nontoxic adhesives and finishes that keep unwelcome toxic carcinogens, like formaldehyde, out of the environment and away from homes. The presence of formaldehyde and other hazardous volatile organic compounds (VOCs)—which off-gas into indoor air from sources such as furniture, flooring, rugs, paints, and wallpaper—has led the EPA to conclude that indoor air quality throughout the United States is typically two to five times worse than outdoor air quality. Options like Scrapile furniture present an easy and stylish way to create a healthier home while conserving forests.

Acronym Designs makes sleek, contemporary benches, tables, low stools, counter stools, and bar stools from reclaimed hardwoods coupled with brushed stainless steel or concrete legs and bases. Most of the wood that Acronym relies upon for its elegant and sturdy designs is actually twice reclaimed. The Kansas City–based company sources its wood from reclaimed flooring. Yet pushing eco-conservation one step further, Acronym utilizes only the manufacturing cutoffs—wood that is ordinarily destined for the dump or burned for heating. The innovative approach enables customers to enjoy the beauty of these materials as quality indoor/outdoor furniture.

Opting for furniture that utilizes reclaimed materials is an excellent way to bring the warm, inviting qualities of wood into your home. But you don't have to avoid the forest altogether to select wood furniture. Certifying organizations supported by the Forest Stewardship Council (FSC) have established forestry management guidelines for growing and harvesting trees responsibly around the globe. Since the creation of the FSC in 1993, more than 280,000 square miles of forests in more than seventy-two countries have received FSC certification—a land size that would encompass every state in New England as well as all of Pennsylvania, Maryland, Virginia, and West Virginia. An easy way to ensure the eco-integrity of your furniture is to check for the FSC label when purchasing.

Managing forests responsibly is essential for rolling back global warming. Young, growing trees feed on carbon dioxide. Mature trees store massive amounts of carbon dioxide below the ground in their extensive root systems. The more trees we have around to do this, the less carbon dioxide is released into the atmosphere. You don't have to physically hug trees to do your part. Selecting

FSC-certified furniture is the virtual equivalent of a really big hug.

Portland, Oregon–based designer Christopher Douglas creates FSC-certified wood furniture with a nod to the early modernists yet with a futuristic flavor all his own. The Material Furniture collection includes benches, tables, chairs, and platform beds that ship flat and are easily assembled by slotting one piece of wood into the next. Minimalist, sleek, and abundantly practical, Material Furniture products are easy to assemble and take apart. They're ideal for those wanting a stowable designer dining table or for "urban nomads" for whom apartment-hopping seems hardwired into their DNA.

Seattle, Washington–based Greener Lifestyles creates eco-aware furniture that is durable and comfortable enough for extended periods of extreme couch potato-ing. The company utilizes FSC-certified wood for the frames of its sofas, love seats, and chaise lounges, and natural rubber latex foam for the cushioning—a healthy alternative to conventional polyurethane-based cushioning made with hazardous chemicals. Furniture items are upholstered in a range of stylish, eco-aware fabrics made from materials such as hemp and organic cotton. Color choices extend well beyond the earthy, natural palette of twentieth-century eco-living. Greener Lifestyles offers a range of color selections to match virtually any interior decor.

Legare Furniture brings FSC-certified wood to the home office with a delightful line of innovative furniture that requires absolutely no screws or glues to assemble. The knock-down furniture assembles quickly by slotting one piece into the next, locking them into place to form contemporary, super-functional desks, bookcases, and file carts. The modular design enables additional products to be easily integrated with others over time as needs increase, transforming single desks into entire office systems. Modular media centers are also available and are great for supporting flat-screen, LCD, or plasma televisions.

Eco-aware furniture is also informed by natural materials that have been engineered to outperform their conventional competition. The ever-versatile bamboo grass is rapidly becoming the material of choice for forward-thinking furniture designers. The stalks of bamboo can be spun into luxurious yarn for bedding and also engineered into super-strong boards for furniture making. Bamboo stalks can reach heights of up to one hundred feet in just six years. When harvested, the stalks are cut down but the root systems remain intact, enabling the bamboo to regenerate extremely quickly. With the tensile strength of steel and a unique aesthetic, bamboo presents a terrific alternative to wood—and plastics and anything else used for furniture.

Brave Space Design utilizes bamboo for much of its contemporary furniture collection. The Brooklyn, New York–based design trio of Sam Kragiel, Nikki Frazier, and Jesse James Arnold create furniture that is as aesthetically exciting as it is extremely practical. The Hollow Series of streamlined bamboo coffee, console, and side tables are "hollowed" out to offer hidden interior storage spaces—perfect for stashing books, magazines, multiple remote controls, and gaming consoles. The Bamboo Stagger is a stunning wall-size shelving unit designed to accommodate an assortment of objects by integrating shelves of varying widths and heights. The Bamboo Slide is an innovative kitchen island designed with a built-in wine rack, all sorts of storage compartments, and retractable surfaces that can expand to provide more space when serving or preparing meals. Brave Space Design's emphasis on logical solutions informs much of its green thinking too. Says Kragiel, "When you're making furniture, you don't want toxic dust coming off of the materials that you are cutting. You don't want to use finishes that are hazardous for yourself and the consumer and for the environment as a whole. That's what has led us toward using environmentally sustainable materials. It just makes sense."

The pursuit of eco-logic is the inspiration behind the Logic Lounge series of bamboo-framed lounge chairs designed by Chuck Heckman of Delano Collection for Vivavi. Heckman infuses eco-awareness into clean lines and minimalist curves and complements the bamboo frame's contemporary aesthetic with comfortable cushions made of pure, natural latex, and colorful upholstery created from recycled and organic fabrics. Glues and finishes are both nontoxic. The approach reflects Heckman's and Vivavi's ongoing commitment to offer comfortable, design-driven furniture that promotes healthier indoor air and a cleaner global environment.

You can also find bamboo in the sleek, asymmetrical coffee tables designed by Todd Laby of Rhubarb Decor, the Asian-inspired contemporary wall and freestanding shelving units designed by Steve Hessler of Iola Design, and the customizable sliding shelving units designed by Mark Righter of Cambium Studio. Michael Iannone brings bamboo to consoles and storage cabinets. ModernLink relies exclusively upon bamboo to produce its entire furniture collection, which includes streamlined office desks, sideboards, coffee tables, platform beds, and bedroom dressers.

Most of the bamboo in use today for contemporary furniture is imported from China. Critics contend that bamboo companies are cutting down forests to make way for bamboo plantations, in itself a counterproductive eco-practice. While it's hard to verify or refute these claims, credible American companies like Smith & Fong ensure that their bamboo, trademarked under the term Plyboo, is grown and harvested responsibly and that the workers on their bamboo plantations receive living wages.

Critics also contend that bamboo is not a viable eco-alternative because it's shipped from China and therefore requires burning massive amounts of oil in the form of shipping fuel to bring it to the United States. It's a good point. Yet what distinguishes lazy environmentalists is our willingness to recognize that perfect eco-solutions rarely exist. Bamboo is an excellent eco-alternative to conventional wood furniture—and toxic, composite board furniture—and when placed in the hands of a quality designer, it becomes one that we can readily integrate into our lives.

And bamboo is merely one of a number of eco-innovations spurring on the green furniture industry. Loll Designs recently introduced an outdoor furniture collection made of 100 percent recycled plastic. The fun, casual furniture line is extremely durable and includes benches, picnic tables, and several contemporary versions of the traditional Adirondack chair.

Peter Danko has been designing super-efficient, eco-aware furniture for more than twenty years and his line is offered by J. Persing. Danko utilizes ply-bending, a furniture-making technique that is nine times more efficient than conventional furniture making, and he is known for innovations like the Bodyform chair, which is made of a single sheet of wood, resulting in no excess waste, and the Arbor chair, which fashions seat and back support out of post-industrial seat belts—excess seat-belt material from manufacturing that would otherwise be thrown away. Danko's striking furniture can be found in the permanent collections of numerous museums, including the Smithsonian Institution and the Museum of Modern Art.

Q Collection is making eco-believers out of many home furnishings fans with its broad collection of sofas, club chairs, benches, dining chairs, and tables and home accessories like sensuously curved bookends and serving trays. Cofounders Jesse Johnson and Anthony Cochran conduct extensive research to incorporate only the purest and most responsibly sourced materials available today, including FSC-certified woods and vegetable-tanned leather.

Wiggers Furniture utilizes FSC-certified woods for its line of contemporary and art deco furniture and has been known to add a spiritual dimension by crafting furniture according to the holistic design principles of feng shui and the vastu shastra of the ancient Vedic tradition. Designer and craftsman John Wiggers also considers the therapeutic potential of furniture by integrating details like desk compartments made of sassafras and hawthorn—woods that possess healing aromatherapy properties. The scents accumulate inside drawers when closed and are released into the air when the drawers are opened.

Furniture Labels

ACRONYM DESIGNS

Acronymdesigns.com

Acronym Designs provides sleek, contemporary benches, tables, low stools, counter stools, and bar stools from reclaimed hardwoods coupled with brushed stainless steel or concrete legs and bases. Most of the wood that Acronym relies upon for its elegant and sturdy designs is actually twice reclaimed, for a double eco-bonus.

BETTENCOURT DESIGN

Bettencourtwood.com

Bart Bettencourt's signature line of sustainable furniture features contemporary chairs, ottomans, tables, and media centers constructed of bamboo. Bettencourt is a leader of the sustainable design movement and a major force behind Brooklyn's emergence as a major center for sustainable furniture design.

BRAVE SPACE DESIGN

Bravespacedesign.com

A Brooklyn-based design trio that works with bamboo and FSC-certified wood to make contemporary furniture that is as aesthetically exciting as it is extremely practical. Brave Space emphasizes modular design, shelving, and versatile tables that can serve many roles.

CAMBIUM STUDIO

Cambiumstudio.com

Cambium Studio works with reclaimed and certified sustainable woods and renewable materials like bamboo to craft innovative, contemporary furniture. The Slippery Shelves collection features wall-mounted shelving units made of bamboo that can be easily adjusted into multiple configurations by sliding the shelves into different positions.

DELANO COLLECTION

Delanocollection.com

Designer Chuck Heckman designed Delano's Logic line of furniture, which offers high style and eco-awareness at accessible prices. The Logic Lounge Chair, the signature piece in the line, is constructed of bamboo, zero-VOC natural latex cushions, and low-VOC recycled and organic fabrics. The Logic series is available exclusively through Vivavi at Vivavi.com.

EL: ENVIRONMENTAL LANGUAGE

El-furniture.com

A leader in the "eco-smart" furnishings market, el offers furniture that is both aesthetically elegant and environmentally sound. The company emphasizes high-end, high-style furniture and furnishings and has recently moved into office designs to complement its residential furniture.

FIRE & WATER

Cyberg.com

David Bergman's line of eco-advanced lighting integrates recycled and recyclable materials along with compact fluorescent lighting. Bergman is also an architect, interior designer, and lecturer, on sustainable design, at the Parsons School of Design.

HENRYBUILT FURNITURE

Henrybuilt.com

Dedicated to providing well-built, intelligently engineered, modern furniture and custom kitchens that respect the planet, Henrybuilt works with FSC-certified woods to create tables, seating, and storage units that are built to last for generations. Kitchens combine classically modern aesthetics with premium-quality sustainable materials.

IANNONE:SANDERSON

I-sdesign.com

Committed to designing and creating good modern furniture, designer Michael Iannone works with a range of eco-advanced materials like certified sustainable woods, bamboo, and Kirei Board to realize his vision. The rapidly expanding collection includes coffee tables, consoles, cabinets, and dressers.

IF GREEN

ifgreen.com

This Portland, Oregon, furniture design company creates accessibly priced, contemporary furniture using only sustainable or recycled materials. The simple, elegant lines of the company's Sling Back chair make it great for the dining room or the office. *Sunset* magazine awarded the Sling Back "Best New Chair" for 2006.

IOLA DESIGN

Ioladesign.com

Iola Design is a design and manufacturing company specializing in innovative display shelving and cabinet units. Designer, craftsman, and cofounder Steve Hessler works with bamboo to bring personality, grace, and a connection to the natural world into any space.

J. PERSING

Jpersing.com

J. Persing offers eco-modern furniture with many of the pieces designed by eco-visionary Peter Danko. Post-industrial seat belts serve as seats and backing for chairs. Frames are made from bent-ply wood, a production process that is up to eight times more efficient than conventional wood furniture.

LAUREL HOOVER DESIGNS

Laurelhoover.com

A timeless collection of handcrafted furniture made of FSC-certified solid woods, Laurel Hoover's products are signature pieces that will last for generations. Check out the Golden Section Coffee Table, which features a stained glass top by Llorens, one of the oldest family-run glass studios in the U.S.

LEGARE FURNITURE

Legarefurniture.com

Legare Furniture brings FSC-certified wood to the home office with its innovative furniture that requires no screws or glues to assemble. The modular, easily expandable collection includes desks, bookcases, and file carts. Modular media centers are also available and are great for supporting flat-screen, LCD, or plasma televisions.

LOLL DESIGNS

Lolldesigns.com

The perfect outdoor furniture series for lollygaggers, Loll's 100 percent recycled plastic furniture offers a contemporary interpretation of Adirondack chairs and other traditional bench and table styles. All furniture is made in Minnesota. Also available through Vivavi.com.

MATERIAL FURNITURE

Materialfurniture.com

Based in Portland, Oregon, Material Furniture founder Christopher Douglas creates contemporary furniture with a nod to the early modernists yet with a futuristic flavor all his own. All wood furniture is FSC-certified sustainable. Douglas also works with Meddite II, a sturdy material made from 100 percent recovered and recycled paper fiber.

MIO CULTURE

Mioculture.com

Mio Culture's forward-thinking designers create eco-friendly lighting, wallpaper, flooring, seating, and accessories with a whimsical touch. Their products often emphasize "customerization"—they design it, but you get to shape it to your own whims.

MODERN LINK

Modernlink.com

Sleek, contemporary bamboo furniture that places equal emphasis on aesthetics and functionality, Modernlink's credenzas, bookshelves, dressers, beds, and desks are as enjoyable to gaze upon as they are to use.

MOE DESIGN STUDIO

Studiomoe.com

Designer Andrew Moe unites twenty-first-century design with traditional handcrafted quality to offer a broad range of aesthetics using reclaimed lumber. The Musashi Coffee Table is an Asian-contemporary fusion of curves and wide storage spaces. The Olathe Coffee table is a study in refined elegance. Bring Moe your plans and ideas and he'll create whatever you like.

NICHE DESIGN

Design-niche.com

The SHAPE furniture series by Niche Design is created from locally sourced, reclaimed materials and features coffee tables, side tables, consoles, bar stools, and benches. Wood tops are sculpted from salvaged wood and rest upon reclaimed wrought iron frames. The effect is to create a contemporary, minimalist design that draws a connection to the outdoor landscape.

PIE (PROJECT IMPORT EXPORT)

Projectimportexport.com

Handcrafting products from natural materials like water hyacinth, liana, bamboo, and rattan, PIE offers a broad collection of sensuous, rounded lounge chairs that are designed to imitate nature. The Tonecoon and Sushi Daybed are designed for extreme leisure and are suitable for both indoor and outdoor covered use.

Q COLLECTION

Qcollection.com

Founded by Anthony Cochran and Jesse Johnson, Q Collection offers high-end, stylish design with the purest and most environmentally friendly materials available. Extensive research is undertaken to ensure that Q Collection's furniture meets the highest standards for environmental stewardship.

REFORM

Reform.biz

Reform creates functional, contemporary furniture using eco-advanced materials that are biodegradable and/or fit within a continuous cycle of use so that no materials need end up in the landfill. With the company's ultra-modern coffee tables and chairs crafted from single sheets of aluminum, and functionally unique, double-tiered coffee tables made of bamboo, probably nothing ever will.

RHUBARB DECOR

Rhubarbdecor.com

Designer Todd Laby works with bamboo to create furniture that marries a unique aesthetic with supreme functionality. The Slant series of coffee tables features useful shelving spaces underneath for books to lean on their sides, reducing spine fatigue.

SCRAPILE

Scrapile.com

Brooklyn-based designers Bart Bettencourt and Carlos Salgado create contemporary, minimalist benches, tables, and shelving in unique patterns by collecting wood scraps and laminating them together using nontoxic glues. The result is a beautiful and unique striped aesthetic that epitomizes the potential of eco-aware furniture to enhance our lives.

URBAN TREE SALVAGE

Urbantreesalvage.com

Toronto-based Urban Tree Salvage recovers and treats fine-quality lumber that would otherwise end up in landfills. Founder and designer Sean Gorham creates contemporary furniture that allows the beauty of the recovered wood to speak for itself.

WIGGERS FURNITURE

Wiggersfurniture.com

John Wiggers is a studio furniture maker who specializes in contemporary and art deco–inspired designs. His holistic approach to furniture making often integrates exotic veneers and ayurvedic principles with deep respect for the environment. In 1998, John was one of the first furniture makers in the world to be certified to the rigorous standards of the FSC.

Retailers

2MODERN

2modern.com

2Modern features a wide selection of talented contemporary furniture designers from the United States and abroad. The company recently made a concerted effort to identify and carry eco-friendly collections and is steadily building an exciting eco lineup in addition to its more conventional designers.

ABC CARPET & HOME

Abchome.com

This trendsetting Manhattan department store offers a unique retail experience renowned around the world. Paulette Cole, CEO and creative director, has made sustainability a top priority, reflected in the sumptuous eco-friendly furniture and furnishings on display.

GREENER LIFESTYLES

Greenerlifestyles.com

A Seattle-based provider of contemporary, eco-friendly furniture, Greener Lifestyles also makes its own line of stylish, sustainable, and affordable sofas, chairs, and loveseats constructed with FSC-certified woods, natural latex cushioning, and nontoxic glues.

VIVAVI

Vivavi.com

The company I founded in 2003, Vivavi represents many of today's most forward-thinking furniture and home furnishings designers, who combine cutting-edge aesthetics with pure, renewable, and recycled materials. Many of the furniture collections presented in this chapter are available through our retail website and Brooklyn showroom. Our motto is "Live Modern + Tread Lightly," which also reflects our commitment to green business practices. Our headquarters and showroom are powered by 100 percent wind energy.

Information/Education

HAUTE GREEN

Hautegreen.com

A New York City–based exhibition of the best in sustainable home design that takes place each May. Furniture, lighting, and accessories designers from around the globe submit their eco-advanced products in hopes of having them showcased to a discerning and increasingly broad audience.

INHABITAT.COM

Founded by then Columbia University architectural graduate student Jill Fehrenbacher, this site offers in-depth coverage of green design and architecture. Explore how our homes and buildings can integrate new technologies, materials, and aesthetics that enhance our lifestyles while bringing them into greater balance with the planet.

SUSTAINABLE STYLE FOUNDATION

Sustainablestyle.org
If it's stylish and green, you'll probably find it here. The daily showcase features green products. The daily spotlight covers sustainable style information and resources. The online sourcebook provides yet another resource for great products and services to plug into your eco-lifestyle. SSF also publishes a quarterly online magazine called *SASS* and hosts the annual Outstanding Style Achievement Awards.

TREEHUGGER.COM

The top green destination on the web, this fast-paced blog is dedicated to everything that's green with a modern aesthetic. Get the latest updates on green trends and search more than ten thousand categorized posts. Check out TreehuggerTV for quality green video programming.

10

SLICE IT,
DICE IT,
SERVE IT

The Kitchen
and Dining Room

Great kitchens enable us to do more than cook great meals. The kitchen is the gathering place, the comfortable haven inside a home where we can more casually connect with friends and loved ones over a glass of wine, cup of tea, or bowl of mac and cheese. Creating a comfortable, contemporary, eco-advanced kitchen is a breeze.

Innovation is the driving force behind many of today's eco-aware contemporary kitchens. I'm not just referring to whiz-bang gadgets and gizmos like super-sleek microwaves, ovens, and refrigerators. That part is simple. To decrease the energy consumption of your kitchen appliances without sacrificing performance, simply opt for products that carry the Energy Star label. Visit Energystar.gov to view full lists of all energy-efficient product models available. Most major manufactures—from GE to Bosch—offer Energy Star–rated models across virtually all appliance categories.

It's in the eco-intelligent materials being created for cabinets and countertops—the core of the kitchen—that we encounter a startling array of new possibilities. Fast-growing, rapidly renewable natural materials like bamboo, sorghum plants, and palm trees are joining forces with recycled materials like aluminum, glass, steel, and copper to enable visually exciting, high-performance kitchens.

Bamboo is rapidly becoming the poster child for eco-intelligence, and it presents a great choice for kitchen cabinetry. Products made of this fast-growing grass are alleviating our appetite for trees. Turning bamboo into a contemporary material that is both durable and attractive requires a bit of engineering. Forward-thinking companies like Smith & Fong and Teragren have spent a lot of time figuring it out. The process involves harvesting bamboo stalks, cross-layering them atop one another, and then pressing them together into boards that resemble plywood but are stronger and more durable and possess a unique striated surface pattern. Both Smith & Fong and Teragren utilize nontoxic adhesives throughout the production process, resulting in cabinets that are healthy for humans and for the planet.

Next-generation eco-cabinetry options also include Kirei—a Japanese word that translates roughly as "that which embodies clean and beautiful"—Board. Closely mirroring the production process of bamboo boards, Kirei Board relies upon the harvested stalks of fast-growing sorghum plants commonly grown throughout the world for food (think molasses). In China, where Kirei Board is manufactured by San Diego–based Kirei USA, the sorghum stalks remaining after harvest are pressed together and glued with nontoxic adhesives to create the lightweight and durable material that offers a distinctive nutty texture. Not only does Kirei Board present a great substitute for wood, it also presents a great reuse for plant waste that would otherwise be burned or dumped.

For coconut fans, Smith & Fong turns plantation-grown coconut palm trees into cabinetry material marketed under the label Durapalm. Once the palm trees have completed their useful life as coconut producers—usually after about eighty years—Smith & Fong gathers the trees, layers multiple strands of palm wood atop one another, and transforms them into beautiful, stable ply boards. The process creates an additional use for the tree and alleviates the global demand for timber from rain forests. All of the big three—bamboo, Kirei, and Durapalm—can be used for flooring, furniture, and paneling.

Moving into composite materials—those made from a mixture of different materials—eco-possibilities for cabinetry include Wheatboard, a material created from wheat stalks and straw; MDF, a material made from wood manufacturing waste; and Meddite II, a material made from recycled paper products. Some of these materials, like MDF, have been around for a while. The difference today is that in many instances they are now being produced without carcinogenic chemicals like formaldehyde.

For homeowners who prefer wood, Citilogs helps us enjoy wood cabinets in eco-aware style. The New Jersey–based company provides homeowners with custom wood cabinetry at comparable prices to standard, mass-produced cabinetry. The magic is in the salvaging of trees that have been toppled by storms or that must be taken down due to age or to make way for new construction. If you need to clear space in your backyard for a swimming pool or deck, Citilogs will haul out your trees and deliver them back to you in the form of custom-milled cabinets, flooring, doors, furniture, or whatever else you desire. Quality is assured by partnerships with sawmills and skilled Amish craftsmen in Pennsylvania. As Stubby Warmbold, founder of Citilogs, puts it, "It's a seventeenth-century business model updated to meet the needs of the twenty-first century. We offer people the ability to have the highest quality craftsmanship while conserving virgin resources and developing a closer connection to their own land."

The same kind of material innovation evident in cabinetry is also driving a veritable revolution in kitchen countertops. IceStone is a Brooklyn-based manufacturer of surfaces that resemble the beauty of granite but are made of 100 percent recycled glass mixed with concrete. Perfect for countertops and backsplashes, IceStone surfaces are also VOC-free, making them a healthy, safe choice. Starbucks is one of the company's numerous clients and is relying upon the versatile material for hundreds of tabletops inside its shops. KlipTech Composites offers a durable, sleek countertop surface called PaperStone Certified, created from 100 percent recycled paper. Eleek, based in Portland, Oregon, offers fabulous sleek countertops and backsplash tiles made from 100 percent recycled aluminum. Bamboo also makes an attractive and functional countertop choice under the able hands of the team at Totally Bamboo.

Coming back for a moment to appliances like ovens, stoves, and microwaves, my strongest advice is to not get overly concerned about the decision and just make sure whatever model you choose is Energy Star–rated for energy efficiency. Refrigerators, however, present a unique case. While they are much more energy efficient today than they were just ten or fifteen years ago, they still consume massive amounts of energy. If energy were beer, refrigerators would be the appliances doing keg stands all night long. But it's not so much the refrigerator in your kitchen that you have to worry about. It's the older one that's been relegated to the garage or basement that is melting the polar ice caps. Retiring the "old-timer" and upgrading to a newer Energy Star–rated refrigerator model is an easy way to conserve energy and lower electrical bills.

When it's time to dine, design-conscious, eco-friendly options are plentiful. Once again, it's bamboo to the rescue. Bambu Home offers a beautiful bamboo tableware collection that includes hand-coiled lacquered bowls and plates. Vibrant colors and quality craftsmanship bring bamboo artistry to everyday dining, and the bamboo construction is better for the planet. Bambu Home also offers serving trays, serving and food prep utensils, and cutting utensils that combine bamboo handles with the cutting precision of stainless steel blades. Complement your Bambu Home collection with additional bamboo tabletop selections from Ekobo. The company's plates, bowls, and serving trays offer a very clean, contemporary look, and the line now extends into vases, bathroom cups, and even low stools.

Transglass, a U.K.–based design house, has designed a gorgeous line of tumblers, carafes and vases made from recycled glass. TwoKH, a New York City–based retailer of contemporary eco-aware home furnishings, also carries tumblers made of recycled glass by Mexican artisans. The best place to find these eco-options and others like them is through the stores and websites of leading eco–home furnishings retailers. In addition to TwoKH, these include 3R Living in Brooklyn and, exclusively on the web, both Branch and VivaTerra. All of these retailers have buyers with terrific taste and a knack for discovering the best eco-furnishings available.

For food preparation, check out the cutting boards from Epicurean Cutting Surfaces that are made of Richlite, an eco-aware paper-based product harvested from sustainably managed forests. Richlite cutting surfaces have been the preferred choice of chefs in commercial kitchens for over forty years. Epicurean Cutting Surfaces' cutting boards are extremely durable, dishwasher safe, and maintenance free. Epicurean's parent company, TrueRide, uses Richlite to make municipal skateboard parks. If skateboarders who are continually trying to destroy the sturdy, eco-aware surface can't put a dent in it, odds are neither will you. Find the cutting boards at Williams-Sonoma, Sur La Table, Whole Foods, Crate & Barrel, and more than nineteen hundred specialty gourmet retailers.

Bamboo cutting boards are available from Totally Bamboo in several styles and sizes and also make great serving trays. Find just the right size for serving cheese and crackers or even an entire turkey. Bread cutting boards come in a checkered grid pattern with cutout holes for catching crumbs. A quick visit to Macy's website will also yield rich bamboo finds. Elegant modern bamboo cutting boards are crafted by Kershaw Shun, as is a bamboo knife block that houses a stunning set of stainless steel Japanese knives. Bamboo serving trays crafted by Arthur Court feature ornately decorated handles made of aluminum. William Bounds's eight-inch and twelve-inch bamboo standing peppermills are perfect for housing salt and pepper and come with patented technology for grinding in any direction.

Food storage can be eco-optimized as well. Get rid of the plastic that can leech nasty chemicals into your food and try To-Go Ware's stainless steel containers. They are leech-free and great for storing leftovers in the refrigerator, and they also make for an ideal picnic or lunch box. Together the containers form a two-tier food carrier with integrated carrying handle, so bringing hot and cold food with you while keeping them separated is easy. A steel dish is also integrated seamlessly into the design.

For quality kitchen and dining furniture, check out selections at Vivavi—tell them Josh sent you—where you'll find contemporary eco-aware tables, chairs, and bar and counter stools. Choices include the Peter Danko–designed collection of recycled seat-belt chairs made by J. Persing, Scrapile's dining tables made from reclaimed woods, Material Furniture's knockdown dining tables from FSC-certified sustainable wood, and Allan Witt's bar and counter stools fashioned out of certified sustainable wood with cushions made of pure, natural latex from rubber tress and fabric from 100 percent organic wool. You'll also see options from Brave Space Design, including a bamboo kitchen island that has a built-in wine rack, all sorts of secret storage compartments, and retractable surfaces that can expand to provide more space when you're serving or preparing meals.

When dealing with the trash, next-generation appliances are making disposal and recycling almost pleasant. The Ecopod is a space-saving home recycling center that makes compacting cans and plastic containers as easy as dropping them in a chamber and stepping on a foot pedal. BMW Designworks, the same company that developed the BMW X5 and Z4 automobiles, developed the super-sleek Ecopod as a means to easily stow and keep cans and containers out of the way until recycling pickup day rolls around. It's available from Williams-Sonoma.

For taking out the trash, try Bio Bags, tall plastic kitchen bags. They're made from next-generation plastic derived from corn—as in corn on the cob—and are biodegradable so they won't still be here long after you're not. Seventh Generation offers kitchen bags made from recycled plastic, providing another eco-sensible option.

Gardeners will appreciate the clean, compact design of the automated, electric Naturermill Composter, which can be stowed in your closet, under the sink, or unobtrusively on the floor. Just drop in your food waste, wait a few days, and presto, you've got terrific fertilizer for growing plants. It's the easy, fun, rewarding way to recycle your garbage. Best of all, it doesn't stink.

Kitchen Construction

ALTERECO

Bamboocabinets.com

AlterECO, based in Northern California, creates custom contemporary bamboo cabinets using healthy finishes. The designers also work with other eco-aware materials, like certified sustainable woods and a range of eco-advanced composites.

BEDROCK INDUSTRIES

Bedrockindustries.com

Bedrock makes all of its 100 percent recycled-glass ties by hand inside its own local facility. The company, based in Seattle, also utilizes 100 percent recyclable materials for product packaging and shipping and operates a local community bottle drive to collect much of its glass and help ensure that bottles earmarked for recycling actually do get recycled.

BERKELEY MILLS

Berkeleymills.com

Berkeley Mills offers premium-quality custom cabinetry and full custom kitchens. Berkeley Mills was one of the first furniture companies to be certified to the rigorous chain-of-custody standards—certifying the use of eco-responsible practices throughout its entire supply chain—of the Forest Stewardship Council, and today most of the wood used by the company is FSC-certified sustainable. Berkeley Mills also offers an elegant line of Asian-inspired wood furniture.

CITILOGS

Citilogs.com

By salvaging trees destined for the dump or the incinerator, New Jersey-based Citilogs provides homeowners with custom wood cabinetry at comparable prices to standard, mass-produced cabinets. Citilogs partners with expert sawmills and Amish craftsmen in Pennsylvania to produce reclaimed wood products of the highest quality.

COVERINGS ETC.

Coveringsetc.com

The Coverings collection of eco-aware surfaces is great for countertops, tabletops, and wall surfaces. Eco-Terr is a terrazzo composed of 75 percent recycled materials, including granite, marble, and glass, that is bound with cement and available in over thirty-four colors. Eco-Cem is a gorgeous cementlike product that includes 20 percent wood pulp from recycled paper. Eco-Gres is a super-sleek tile made of 100 percent recycled porcelain.

DURAT

Durat.com

Durat was founded in 1990 with a mission to unite design with recycling. A polyester-based material made of approximately 50 percent recycled plastics, Durat offers a bold aesthetic and durable surface for kitchen countertops. The company's signature collection of minimalist-designed bathtubs, shower trays, and washbasins are constructed with the same material, which is available in forty colors.

ELEEK

Eleekinc.com

Eleek is a design-fabrication company based in Portland, Oregon, that has a very strong commitment to eco-aware products and business practices. The company's 100 percent recycled aluminum tiles present a super-sleek material choice for backsplashes and countertops. Sinks are also available and are made from 100 percent recycled cast aluminum and 90 percent recycled sand-cast bronze. And don't miss the selection of lighting that similarly incorporates recycled materials.

ENVIROGLAS

Enviroglasproducts.com

EnviroGLAS is a terrazzo made with 100 percent recycled glass and porcelain, which offers a polished surface with inviting depth. EnviroSLAB is the countertop version. EnviroPLANK can be used for flooring. These long-lasting surfaces come in a variety of colors and make a tremendous design statement.

GREENWAY CABINETRY

Breatheasycabinetry.com

New York–based Greenway Cabinetry offers its collection of Breathe Easy cabinetry designed to provide numerous style choices and match many budgets. The cabinet boxes are constructed of FSC-certified plywood with doors made of either FSC-certified wood or bamboo. All cabinets are formaldehyde-free and treated with nontoxic finishes.

HENRYBUILT FURNITURE

Henrybuilt.com

Dedicated to providing well-built, intelligently engineered, modern furniture and custom kitchens that respect the planet, Henrybuilt works with FSC-certified woods to create tables, seating, and storage units that are built to last for generations. The company's kitchens combine classically modern aesthetics with premium-quality sustainable materials.

ICESTONE

Icestone.biz

IceStone surfaces are made from 100 percent recycled glass and concrete. The surface slabs rival the strength of quarried stone, possess similar aesthetic qualities as granite, and are great for kitchen countertops and backsplashes, bathroom vanities and shower walls, tabletops and flooring. The products are manufactured at the company's 55,000-square-foot facility in Brooklyn, New York.

KIREI USA

Kireiusa.com

Kirei Board is a richly textured panel created from the waste stalks of fast-growing sorghum plants. This eco-advanced material is great for cabinetry, flooring, and furniture.

KLIPTECH COMPOSITES

Kliptech.com

In 2006 KlipTech introduced PaperStone Certified, the next generation of its advanced surface composite, made of 100 percent recycled paper and FSC-certified sustainable. PaperStone Certified resembles the beauty of stone but has the strength of steel. Available in seven colors.

NEIL KELLY

Neilkellycabinets.com

A maker of cabinetry using nontoxic glues, stains, and finishes to promote healthy indoor air, Neil Kelly makes its cabinet doors and veneers from FSC-certified sustainable wood. Cabinet cores are made of wheatboard, a product created from post-harvest wheat stalks and straw.

OCEANSIDE GLASSTILE

Glasstile.com

Oceanside Glasstile has been creating beautiful, luxury glass tiles from recycled bottles and raw sand since 1992. Today the company uses one thousand tons of recycled glass each year. The tiles can be made with up to 85 percent recycled glass content. Mosaic glass and innovative glass tile designs are what you'll find at the more than three hundred showrooms around the globe that carry these products.

RENEWED MATERIALS

Renewedmaterials.com

Renewed materials makes countertop surfaces, called Alkemi, that combine polyester resin with 35 percent recycled aluminum scraps from industrial manufacturing. The end result is a hard, durable surface with a beautiful and very unique look.

RICHLITE
Richlite.com

Richlite offers a very clean-looking, durable countertop surface made from wood pulp (a by-product of lumber) from certified sustainably managed forests. This attractive, natural-feeling paper-based product is so tough and resilient that it's also used in airplanes and skateboard parks. Available in seven colors, including the very enticing slate black.

SANDHILL INDUSTRIES
Sandhillind.com

Sandhill tiles are made of 100 percent recycled glass and come in thirty-six vibrant colors. Tiles can be selected individually, in pre-designed blends or custom-designed to your tastes.

SMITH & FONG
Plyboo.com

Smith & Fong produces high-quality, formaldehyde-free bamboo boards for cabinetry, furniture, and flooring, marketed under the name Plyboo. A constant innovator, the company is also the originator of Durapalm—an engineered palm-wood board that, like Plyboo, is great for flooring, cabinets, and furniture.

SQUAK MOUNTAIN STONE
Squakmountainstone.com

What began as the project for a master's thesis is now a stunning, locally sourced, cementlike surface made from a mixture of recycled paper, recycled glass, coal fly ash (a by-product of coal production that would otherwise become waste), and Portland cement. The composite slabs bear a close resemblance to soapstone or limestone.

SYNDECRETE
Syndecrete.com

Bringing warmth to concrete surfaces is now possible. Syndecrete is a lightweight concrete composite made from 41 percent recycled materials, including waste from carpet mills and fly ash. The award-winning product was developed by award-winning architect David Hertz and comes in a range of inviting colors. In addition to countertops, Syndecrete is also great for sinks, flooring, and even furniture.

TERAGREN

Teragren.com

Teragren offers premium-quality bamboo flooring. The company oversees the manufacturing process, from harvest to final product, with its partner facilities in China and Malaysia, to ensure that all Teragren bamboo products are made to the highest standards. Teragren also makes bamboo boards, which are great for cabinets, furniture, and paneling.

TOTALLY BAMBOO

Totallybamboo.com

Totally Bamboo offers high-quality kitchen countertops, cutting boards, bowls and plates, serving trays, tools and utensils, and many more products, all made from versatile bamboo. You could outfit an entire kitchen here in eco-friendly style.

VALCUCINE

Valcucinena.com

Valcucine merges advanced technology with eco-intelligence to create sleek, ultramodern kitchens that rely upon minimal but extremely strong materials, including sturdy aluminum frames. All materials are completely recyclable and are treated with natural oil- and wax-based surface finishes to eliminate VOCs. Valcucine has also implemented a bioforest reforestation program to replenish the materials it uses in its designs.

VETRAZZO

Vetrazzo.com

Vetrazzo, based in California, transforms recycled glass into stunning terrazzo surfaces. Composed of 85 percent recycled class combined with concrete, Vetrazzo countertops are created using more than 550 pounds of recycled glass, sources of which include traffic lights, windshields, and beverage bottles. In 2006, the California Department of Conservation awarded Vertrazzo a $1.285 million grant for creating viable uses for California residents' curbside glass.

WOODSHANTI

Woodshanti.com

Woodshanti provides beautiful custom cabinetry and furniture made with FSC-certified sustainable wood and nontoxic finishes. The versatile design team of this worker-owned cooperative in San Francisco can create aesthetics ranging from traditional to contemporary.

Kitchen Tabletop

BAMBU HOME

Bambuhome.com

Bambu Home's tableware collection features hand-coiled lacquered bowls and plates. The vibrant colors and quality craftsmanship bring artistry to everyday dining. Also available are serving trays, serving and dining utensils, and cutting utensils that combine bamboo handles with stainless steel blades.

ECO KETTLE

Ecokettle.com

It looks likes a normal electric kettle, but the Eco Kettle is equipped with a special feature that enables you to fill it all the way up but then specify the exact number of cups you wish to boil. Considered practically revolutionary in the U.K.—where tea is an everyday staple—the Eco Kettle will enable you to enjoy a cup of tea while reducing your eco-impact too. Check the website for purchasing availability in the U.S.

EKOBO

ekobo.org

Ekobo offers an entire kitchen product collection made of bamboo. The company's plates, bowls, and serving trays feature rich, vibrant colors combined with hand-coiled techniques to provide a clean, Asian-inspired contemporary style. Also look for vases, bathroom cups, and low stools.

EPICUREAN CUTTING SURFACES

Epicureancs.com

Epicurean makes premium cutting boards using Richlite, an eco-aware paper-based product harvested from sustainably managed forests. The cuttings boards are extremely durable, dishwasher safe, and maintenance free.

MACY'S

Macys.com

Bamboo is abundant in Macy's kitchenware collections. Look for cutting boards and knife blocks from Kershaw Shun, serving trays from Arthur Court, and standing peppermills from William Bounds.

MANGO LEAF

Mangoleaf.com

Hand-coiled bamboo tableware and vases are great for serving or displaying food or faux arrangements. Mango Leaf relies on natural, food-safe dyes and quality construction to create the unique aesthetic of its stylish collection.

PRESERVE

Recycline.com

Select the Preserve line of tableware by Recycline to opt for quality constructed plates, cups, and cutlery made from 100 percent recycled plastic, most of which comes from Stonyfield Farm yogurt cups. At the end of your products' useful life, send them back to Recycline and they'll be recycled again.

RIVERSIDE DESIGNS

Riversidedesigns.com

Make recycled glass an everyday part of your life with dishware collections offered by Riverside Designs. The Seaglass collection features playful, organic shapes. The Architect series offers clean, elegant designs that work for both traditional and contemporary settings.

SARAH CIHAT

Sarahcihat.com

To insert a little art into your dining pleasure, check out the dishware collections designed by Sarah Cihat of Rehabilitated Dishware. Cihat collects used and unwanted dishes from secondhand stores and re-glazes and re-fires them after applying her funky, urban designs.

TO-GO WARE

To-goware.com

Store your leftovers or pack a lunch using To-Go Ware's stainless steel containers. The two-tier food carrier includes a steel dish and carrying handle. It's an elegant, stylish solution for keeping your food fresh.

TRANSGLASS

Artecnicainc.com

Manufactured by Artecnica, the TranSglass collection transforms recycled wine and beer bottles into sensuous, elegantly designed tumblers, carafes, and vases. Visually stimulating and abundantly practical, TranSglass makes you feel as though you're drinking from a work of art.

Kitchenware Retailers

Many of the kitchenware options discussed here are available through an increasing number of eco-furnishings retail stores and online stores opening throughout the United States. Here's a list to get you started.

3R LIVING

3rliving.com
Brooklyn, New York
A home decor and lifestyle store dedicated to "future friendly" products, 3R Living carefully selects products according to the principles of reducing waste, reusing unwanted or discarded materials, and recycling. Co-founder and product buyer Samantha Delman-Caserta has a sharp eye for design.

BLUE HOUSE

Shopbluehouse.com
Baltimore, Maryland
Bluehouse offers a strong collection of eco-aware furnishings, housewares, accessories, and gifts. Bluehouse's 7,000-square-foot retail store near Baltimore's Inner Harbor was built to green specifications and features a café serving natural and organic food and drinks.

EQUITA

Shopequita.com
Pittsburgh, Pennsylvania
Located in an historic ice factory, Equita assembles many of the best eco-furnishings and accessory collections. You'll find recycled glassware by Riverside Designs complemented by organic cotton tablecloths, placemats, and napkins made by artisans in North Carolina. Bath and bedding products feature LOOP Organic. Rugs are available courtesy of Angela Adams.

ORGANIC AVENUE

Organicavenue.com
New York, New York
Get your raw food and your organic denim jeans all at once by visiting this Lower East Side store in Manhattan. Del Forte and Natural High Lifestyle are just two of the featured labels in this eco-lifestyle store, where you'll also find stylish collections of tabletop and bath and bedding products.

SPRING

Astorecalledspring.com
San Francisco, California
Step into Spring to find eco-aware products to create a healthier home and

planet. Kitchenware, bath and bedding, and baby products are just a few of the categories in which you'll find better ideas for your home and loved ones.

TWOKH

Twokh.com
New York, New York
An upscale eco-home store located in the Chelsea neighborhood of Manhattan, TwoKH offers contemporary organic collections of furnishings for most rooms in the home as well as several outstanding lines of natural and organic skin-care products.

VIVAVI

Vivavi.com
Brooklyn, New York
The company I founded in 2003, Vivavi represents many of today's most forward-thinking furniture and home furnishings designers, who combine cutting-edge aesthetics with pure, renewable, and recycled materials. Our motto is "Live Modern + Tread Lightly," which also reflects our commitment to green business practices. Our headquarters and showroom are powered by 100 percent wind energy.

Online-Only Retailers

BRANCH

Branchhome.com
If the MoMA Store carried only sustainably designed products, it would be Branch. Superbly designed modern and contemporary products demonstrate how fine attention to detail and aesthetics can easily align with environmental awareness. Branch offers furnishings for nearly the entire home, as well as outstanding gifts for men, women, and children.

RE:MODERN

Re-modern.com
Re-modern emphasizes a modern aesthetic across numerous product categories and offers fun, stylish, eco-aware products. The website features tabletop collections from leading brands like Bambu Home and TranSglass. You'll also find bamboo cutting boards from Vessel and a host of other innovative products.

VIVATERRA

Vivaterra.com

This premier eco-retailer of home furnishings provides high-quality kitchen and dining products as well as organic bath and bedding products. In addition to bamboo and organic cotton towels, you'll find organic cotton damask duvets and shams; pure silk sheets, duvets, shams, and pillows; and natural merino lambswool comforters—everything you need to be nice and cozy.

Trash Disposal

BIOBAG

Biobagusa.com

Biobag's plastic kitchen bags are fully biodegradable and compostable because they are made from GMO (Genetically Modified Organism)-free corn. The forward-thinking production process uses renewable materials in place of oil-based synthetics. Choose from three-, thirteen-, or thirty-three-gallon bags.

ECOPOD

Ecopod.org

The Ecopod is a space-saving home recycling center that makes compacting cans and plastic containers as easy as dropping them in a chamber and stepping on a foot pedal. BMW Designworks developed Ecopod for easily stowing cans and containers until disposed of. It's available from Williams-Sonoma.

NATUREMILL

Naturemill.com

Recycling your garbage into compost is super-convenient with the clean, compact design of the automated, electric composter by NatureMill. Drop in your food waste (and your paper too) anytime you want, and in a few days you'll get terrific fertilizer for growing plants.

SEVENTH GENERATION

Seventhgeneration.com

Seventh Generation is an industry leader in providing products that make your home healthier. Renowned for its nontoxic cleaning products, Seventh Generation also offers tall kitchen bags and heavy-duty garbage bags made from recycled plastics. And spills can be quickly wiped up using its paper towels made from recycled paper.

11

SLEEP RIGHT

The Bedroom

The bedroom is where we dream, and with any luck, it's also where dreams come true. So whether you're sleeping or entertaining a guest, creating a healthy, eco-aware bedroom is the surest way to achieve personal contentment and induce planetary afterglow.

What better way to get started than by sliding into a set of plush, decadent organic cotton sheets by Anna Sova. Start with a minimum 325 thread count. Eliminate all hazardous and carcinogenic pesticides—25 percent of all pesticides in the world are used on cotton, and those pesticides remain in the cotton for the life of the fiber. Utilize heavy metal–free dyes to achieve vibrant colors. Then ditch your clothes and hop into bed. Bring someone with you if you like. You are both in for a treat. Anna Sova's luxury organic bedding is heavenly, and it's designed to fit your lifestyle. The organic sheet collections are complemented by organic cotton duvets, pillow shams, and bed skirts.

For chilly weather, Anna Sova offers alpaca wool—from a Peruvian cousin of the llama—in blankets and pillow shams. Alpaca wool is almost seven times warmer than a sheep's and is extremely soft and silky. The brown and charcoal gray colors are 100 percent natural, and the honey yellow color is achieved through low-impact dyes. The pillow shams alone are so pure and delicious they could make wonderful baby blankets. Anna Sova's line of bedding is eco-aware to its core, yet there is nothing crunchy or hippie about it. As company founder Anna Walker says, "We love granola, but just for breakfast." Round out your luxurious Anna Sova organic bedroom with eco-silk drapery and accompanying bamboo hardware, as well as scented, clean-burning soy candles.

Organic cotton also plays a starring role in the bedroom collection of LOOP Organic. This elegant, sophisticated bedding line features 250-thread-count organic sateen sheets that have a soft, subtle sheen. The modern, minimalist collection includes sheet sets and textured woven blankets made of organic cotton. Accent pillows are made of linen-like hemp fabric, with subtle nature-inspired screen printings, and filled with kapok, a light, fluffy eco-aware fiber from the seeds of Asian ceiba trees.

Gaiam, one of the leading eco-lifestyle retailers in the United States, utilizes organic cotton to fine effect with its expanding line of bedding. Stripes and floral patterns are prominent features of the collection—great for both kids and adults. And colorful, contemporary sheet sets are also available in a range of colors, such as persimmon, raspberry, mulberry, natural, blue, dried sage, and honey. While the choices vary by style, Gaiam offers organic cotton sheets in super-soft jersey knit, sateen, percale, and flannel.

Bamboo, the versatile, rapidly renewable grass, appears in several bedding collections. Extremely soft with a sheen similar to silk or cashmere, bamboo fiber is both breathable and thermal-regulating. Grown without pesticides or insecticides and naturally antimicrobial, bamboo fiber delivers a healthier night's sleep too. You can find 100 percent bamboo bedding at specialty providers like Elegant Linens by Anna Rose. You can also find it at premier eco-retailers like Vivaterra.com, at specialty product retailers such as Hammacher Schlemmer, and even at Bed Bath & Beyond.

Healthy, eco-aware pillows and mattresses are the next step in creating a truly green bedroom. The Natural Bedroom collection by Vivetique, a third-generation family-run bedding manufacturer based in Los Angeles, California, is a great place to start. Pillows with your choice of firmness are made of soft, organic cotton fabric and are available with a wide choice of eco-aware fillings, including organic wool, organic cotton, natural rubber latex, and kapok. Pillows filled with organic buckwheat hulls—the hulls of the buckwheat fruit have been used in pillows throughout Asia for centuries—are also available and come wrapped in organic wool. To produce its organic wool, Vivetique uses no pesticides on the pasture, no chemicals in the animal feed, biodegradable soaps for lanolin removal, and low-environmental-impact land management systems. It's part of Vivetique's strong commitment to eco-practices that are healthier for consumers and for the planet. Vivetique's organic wool is featured prominently in its all-season comforters, quilts, and blankets and throughout its lineup of eco-aware mattresses.

The Natural Bedroom collection by Vivetique skips conventional mattress materials like polyurethane foam—the ingredients of which include hazardous volatile organic compounds (VOCs) like toluene, chlorine, phosgene, benzene, sulfuric acid, nitric acid, and formaldehyde—for mattresses that utilize organic cotton, organic wool, hemp, and natural rubber latex—taken from the sap of rubber trees. Whether you're a back, stomach, or side sleeper, and whether you prefer your mattress soft or firm, Vivetique has an option for you. As Scott Carwile, Vivetique's owner, says, "Before we get into a conversation about what the materials are, we tell you to lie on our beds and choose the one that feels the best. All of them are made with natural, healthy materials, so any choice you make is going to be the right choice."

Lifekind also offers a versatile lineup of high-quality organic mattresses. In addition to its innerspring and natural latex soft-core mattresses, other highlights include futons that feature a two-inch core of natural rubber surrounded by layers of organic cotton and naturally treated wool. A pull-out sofa mattress made of four-inch-thick natural rubber covered in organic cotton delivers a great night's sleep and is compatible with most sofa models. Lifekind is the first mattress maker in the United States to receive Greenguard certification for its mattresses, certifying that they meet rigorous low-VOC emissions standards. Greenguard is an independent program, administered by the Greenguard Environmental Institute, that tests and certifies products that meet healthy indoor air-quality standards.

If you're not yet ready to swap out your conventional mattress for an organic mattress, you can still increase your comfort and health by opting for a natural or organic pillowtop or mattress pad that rests on top of your mattress. Pillowtops provide an added layer of plush softness and put distance between your body and the carcinogenic chemicals in the mattress underneath. Lifekind offers them in chemical-free wool and natural latex. Vivetique offers three varieties: organic wool, an organic wool and organic cotton blend, and hemp—a wonder fiber that is three times stronger than cotton.

Green Sleep, another top-tier eco-bedding company, offers natural rubber latex mattress pads that allow you to sink down into safe, comfortable sleep. Green Sleep, Vivetique, and Lifekind all offer whole-bed organic sleep systems. Organic mattresses can be purchased with nontoxic wood foundations that avoid synthetic glues, dyes, or harmful finishing sprays, to fully support a comfortable, healthy night's sleep.

Organic mattresses can also be paired with eco-aware platform beds for a clean, contemporary look and additional firm support. Modernlink offers minimalist bamboo bedroom furniture, which includes platform beds, night tables, and dressers. Crate & Barrel also provides a bamboo bedroom furniture option with its Bento line of platform beds, chests, and dressers. And Material Furniture offers a knockdown platform bed with a wraparound shelf made of FSC-certified sustainable wood. For sleigh-like platform beds made of FSC-certified sustainable wood, turn to If Green. And the ultimate in eco-beds can be found in John Wiggers's Irenic platform bed, also made of FSC-certified sustainable wood. Ever attentive to detail, Wiggers has added a section of Shiva Lingam, a sacred quartz stone, from the Narmada River in India, known to encourage healing and meditation, to the bed's side rails. It is believed that to have the stone in one's possession is akin to touching the pure male/female energy of Creation.

For light reading before bed, turn to directional LED lamps that shine bright, focused beams that will enable you to read comfortably without disturbing your partner. LED bulbs are the eco-champions of lighting, lasting up to sixty times longer than incandescent bulbs and in many cases using less than 5 percent of the energy that incandescent bulbs require. Gaiam offers its Gooseneck LED lamp with an adjustable, flexible neck (also great for desks—see Chapter 18), and the Herman Miller Leaf Light LED lamp designed by Yves Behar has continued to dazzle design fans since its introduction in 2006. You can also find adjustable LED lamps through Koncept. In 2006, the Z-Bar LED Desk Lamp received the prestigious "best in category" award by *I.D.* magazine. The Koncept line also features one of the first LED floor lamps. And if you're looking for a cool gift for someone who likes to read under the covers, check out Sharper Image's Personal LED Headlamp, which wraps around your ear like a wireless headset and projects a beam of light wherever you need one.

Mattresses, Comforters, and Pillows

GREEN SLEEP
Greensleep.com
Founder Georges Lambrecht has spent thirty years working to design a bed that disturbs a healthy sleep as little as possible. Green Sleep offers organic mattresses, pillows, and mattress beds, as well as whole-bed organic sleep systems.

LIFEKIND
Lifekind.com
Lifekind is the first mattress maker in the United States to receive Greenguard certification for its mattresses, certifying that they meet rigorous low-VOC emissions standards. The extensive catalog features organic mattresses, mattress pads, pillow shams, blankets, throws, and more.

NATURA
Naturaworld.com
Natura is a family-run business that strives to bring a better night's sleep to its customers using superior and healthy sleep systems. Natura's product line includes pure wool bedding, natural rubber latex mattresses and pillows, and its patented Double Slat Mattress technology.

ROYAL-PEDIC

Based in California, Royal-Pedic's line of products includes handcrafted, organic Foxfibre cotton mattresses made with 100 percent organic cotton and no pesticides or chemical fertilization. Organic box springs, pillowtop pads, and natural latex mattresses are also available.

VIVETIQUE

Vivetique.com

Vivetique is a third-generation family-run company specializing in crafting extraordinary mattresses, comforters, pillows, and more using the cleanest and purest natural fibers available. The Natural Bedroom collection offers everything you need for a healthy, eco-aware night's sleep.

Bedding

AMENITY

Amenityhome.com

This highly regarded design studio offers an organic bedding collection featuring broad botanical silhouettes. The textile patterns reflect nature and are simultaneously both bold and striking and calming and meditative.

ANNA SOVA

Annasova.com

Wrap yourself in deep, plush organic cotton towels and bedding from Anna Sova's luxurious collections. Anna Sova's collections feature rich colors created from low-impact dyes for uncompromising style and a luxurious experience.

BED BATH & BEYOND

Bedbathandbeyond.com

Bed Bath & Beyond has moved into bamboo bath and bedding. Opt for sheets made from 100 percent bamboo fiber and towels made of 75 percent bamboo, 20 percent cotton, and 5 percent polyester.

COYUCHI

Coyuchi.com

Coyuchi offers a full line of luxury organic cotton bedding that includes sheets, pillowcases, duvet covers, pillow shams, bed skirts, throws, blankets, baby bedding, towels, and robes.

ELEGANT LINENS BY ANNA ROSE

Elegantlinensbyannarose.com

Specialty retailer Elegant Linens by Anna Rose carries luxury linens from well-known European brands, and now offers a luxury bedding line made of 100 percent bamboo.

GAIAM

Gaiam.com

One of the leading eco-lifestyle retailers in the United States, Gaiam utilizes organic cotton to fine effect with its expanding line of bedding. Sheets are available in super-soft jersey knit, sateen, percale, and flannel.

HAMMACHER SCHLEMMER

Hammacher.com

Hammacher Schlemmer, a provider of unique products since 1848, presents a line of bedroom items made of 100 percent bamboo, including linens, robes, and pajamas.

LOOP ORGANIC

Looporganic.com

The LOOP Organic collection features deep-absorbing, terry-cloth, organic cotton towels in a range of natural colors that are derived from organic, low-impact dyes. Designer Carmel Campos also offers a sophisticated bedding line featuring 250-thread-count organic sateen sheets, textured woven blankets, and accent pillows.

Bedroom Furniture

CRATE & BARREL

Crateandbarrel.com

Crate & Barrel's foray into eco-aware furniture begins with its Bento line of platform beds, chests, and dressers made of bamboo.

IF GREEN

This Portland, Oregon, furniture design company creates accessibly priced, contemporary furniture using only sustainable or recycled materials. The Platform Sleigh Bed is a masterful combination of the traditional sleigh and the comfortable platform bed and is made of FSC-certified wood.

MODERNLINK

Modernlink.com

ModernLink offers sleek, contemporary bamboo furniture that places equal emphasis on aesthetics and functionality. ModernLink's platform bed is as enjoyable to gaze upon as it is to sleep upon.

WIGGERS FURNITURE

Wiggersfurniture.com

John Wiggers is a studio furniture maker who specializes in contemporary and art deco–inspired designs. His holistic approach to furniture-making often integrates exotic veneers and ayurvedic principles with deep respect for the environment. For bedrooms he offers the Irenic Bed made of FSC-certified wood.

Accessories

ADRIFT MOBILES

Adriftmobiles.com

Adrift offers unique, decorative mobiles that are quietly captivating, designed and handcrafted by founder Brian Schmitt. The mobiles are constructed using eco-aware materials like bamboo.

KONCEPT

konceptech.com

Koncept offers a range of sleek, adjustable LED lamps that are perfect for bedrooms or offices. In 2006, the Z-Bar LED Desk Lamp received the prestigious "best in category" award by *I.D.* magazine. The Koncept line also features one of the first LED floor lamps.

LOOOLO

Looolo.ca

Looola features a full line of products made with certified organic materials, including pillows and blankets that are hand- and machine-knit, with biodegradable materials. Pillows are filled with kapok, a light, fluffy eco-aware fiber from the seeds of Asian ceiba trees. Blankets are made of Climatex Lifecycle yarns—certified organic wool/ramie, treated with toxin-free dyes—from Switzerland.

OFFI

Offi.com

This provider of adult and children's furniture offers ply-bent furniture—a technique that is nine times more efficient than conventional furniture making. The birch line is treated with a nontoxic, water-based finish. The Overlap Tray is perfect for lazy Sunday mornings in bed.

REFORM

Reform.biz

Reform creates functional, contemporary furniture using eco-advanced materials that are biodegradable and/or fit within a continuous cycle. The Bedworks tray is made of bamboo. It contains a storage compartment for files or magazines and is perfect for those who like to read or do work while in bed.

Retailers

Many of the bedding options discussed here are available through an increasing number of eco-furnishings retail stores and online stores opening throughout the United States. Here's a list to get you started.

3R LIVING

3rliving.com

Brooklyn, New York

A home decor and lifestyle store dedicated to "future friendly" products. 3R Living carefully selects products according to the principles of reducing waste, reusing unwanted or discarded materials, and recycling. Co-founder and product buyer Samantha Delman-Caserta has a sharp eye for design.

ABC CARPET & HOME

Abchome.com

New York, New York

ABC Carpet & Home offers a wide and distinctive collection of organic bath and bedding, organic beds, and decorative items. The trendsetting Manhattan department store offers a unique retail experience renowned across the world and is fully committed to environmental and social responsibility.

BLUE HOUSE

Shopbluehouse.com

Baltimore, Maryland

Bluehouse offers a strong collection of eco-aware furnishings, housewares, accessories, and gifts. Bluehouse's 7,000-square-foot retail store near Baltimore's Inner Harbor was built to green specifications and features a café serving natural and organic food and drinks.

EARTHSAKE

Earthsake.com

Berkeley, California

One of the early pioneers of eco-retailing, Earthsake got its start in 1990 and now offers high-quality organic and natural beds, bedding and bath products, and body care products. Choices are plentiful and feature materials like organic cotton, bamboo, and legna, a silky fiber made from tree cellulose.

ECO-GREEN LIVING

Eco-greenliving.com

Washington, DC

Eco-Green Living pulls together quality collections for home furnishing, redecorating, and renovation projects. At this Washington, DC, store, you'll find products like Vivetique natural and organic beds as well as the luxurous line of Anna Sova bedding and bath products.

EQUITA

Shopequita.com

Pittsburgh, Pennsylvania

Located in an historic ice factory, Equita assembles many of the best eco-furnishings and accessory collections. You'll find recycled glassware by Riverside Designs complemented by organic cotton tablecloths, placemats, and napkins made by artisans in North Carolina. Bath and bedding products feature LOOP Organic. Rugs are available courtesy of Angela Adams.

GREEN FUSION DESIGN CENTER

Greenfusiondesigncenter.com

Marin County, California

A giant eco-home superstore, Green Fusion Design Center offers quality green products for home improvement projects and stylish green living. You'll find natural and organic beds from Vivetique and Green Sleep and bath and bedding products from Coyuchi and Anna Sova.

GREENER LIFESTYLES

Greenerlifestyles.com

Seattle, Washinton

A Seattle-based provider of contemporary, eco-friendly furniture, Greener Lifestyles also makes its own line of stylish, sustainable, and affordable sofas, chairs, and loveseats constructed with FSC-certified woods, natural latex cushioning, and nontoxic glues. The company also offers luxury organic bedding and bath products from Anna Sova.

ORGANIC AVENUE

Organicavenue.com

New York, New York

Get your raw food and your organic denim jeans all at once by visiting this Lower East Side store in Manhattan. Del Forte and Natural High Lifestyle are just two of the featured labels in this eco-lifestyle store, where you'll also find stylish collections of tabletop, bath, and bedding products.

ORGANIC INTERIOR DESIGN

Organicinteriordesign.com

Venice, California

This company offers quality natural and organic mattresses as well as luxury organic bedding and bath products by Anna Sova. Principal designer Kelly Laplante is also available to work with clients to design interiors using today's most cutting-edge sustainable products.

ORGANIC MATTRESS STORE

Theorganicmattressstore.com

Hellertown, Pennsylvania

The first and largest organic mattress store in Pennsylvania and in the U.S., this company's goal is to keep it "clean and green," by constructing its mattresses from natural substances free of harsh chemicals, including natural rubber, pure wool, and certified organic cotton. You'll also find natural wood foundations, pillowtops, comforters, and linens. Featured brands include Green Sleep, Natura, Royal-Pedic, and Vivetique.

SPRING

Astorecalledspring.com

San Francisco, California

Step into Spring to find eco-aware products to create a healthier home and planet. Kitchenware, bath and bedding, and baby products are just a few of the categories in which you'll find better ideas for your home and loved ones.

TWOKH

Twokh.com

New York, New York

An upscale eco-home store located in the Chelsea neighborhood of Manhattan, TwoKH offers contemporary organic collections of furnishings for most rooms in the home, as well as several outstanding lines of natural and organic skin care products.

VIVAVI

Vivavi.com

Brooklyn, New York

The company I founded in 2003, Vivavi represents many of today's most forward-thinking furniture and home furnishings designers, who combine cutting-edge aesthetics with pure, renewable, and recycled materials. Our motto is "Live Modern + Tread Lightly," which also reflects our commitment to green business practices. Our headquarters and showroom are powered by 100 percent wind energy.

WHITE LOTUS

Whitelotus.net

New Brunswick, New Jersey

White Lotus has been making quality organic and natural mattresses, futons, and bedding products for twenty-five years. Experience the entire collection at the company's New Brunswick, New Jersey location.

Online-Only Retailers

VIVATERRA

Vivaterra.com

This premier eco-retailer of home furnishings provides high-quality kitchen and dining products as well as organic bath and bedding products. In addition to bamboo and organic cotton towels, you'll find organic cotton damask duvets and shams; pure silk sheets, duvets, shams, and pillows; and natural merino lambswool comforters—everything you need to be nice and cozy.

Information / Education

GREENGUARD ENVIRONMENTAL INSTITUTE

Greenguard.org

Greenguard is an industry-independent, nonprofit organization that oversees the Greenguard Certification Program to help improve indoor air quality and establish healthy standards. The program certifies products that are tested to meet its rigorous standards.

12

TOILETS, TUBS, AND
TOOTHBRUSHES

The Bathroom

For some the bathroom is a place to relax and rejuvenate. For others it's where they get their best reading done. However you use your bathroom—for a quick shower, a soak in the tub, or the routines of daily hygiene—there are numerous eco-solutions that will transform even the most mundane tasks into planet-saving success stories.

If innovation in the toilet arena can serve as a barometer of our ability to trade outmoded eco-behavior for easy, smart solutions, then we are in for a clean green future. Sustainable Solutions International, a Canadian-based distributor of forward-thinking eco-friendly products, recently introduced to the United States the Caroma line of dual-flush toilets. Originally developed in Australia, the toilets are equipped with two water chambers, one to flush down "number ones" and a larger chamber to sufficiently flush down "number twos." The simple push-button flush action makes it easy to select the appropriate chamber. The forward-thinking design conserves up to 80 percent of the annual water usage of a typical toilet, and as an added bonus, the wider, four-inch trap-way eliminates unpleasant blockages and ensures that one flush is always enough.

The AQUS toilet system by Water Saver Technologies is a water conservation solution that is so elegant you'll hardly know it's there. Conceived some twenty-five years ago in the childhood imagination of founder Mark Sanders, the AQUS is an instantaneous water recycling solution for the bathroom. Used water from the sink is channeled to the toilet for flushing via a water storage chamber installed inside the sink vanity. The chamber captures and filters water from the drainpipe and then channels it to the toilet through a hidden tube to reduce or altogether eliminate—depending upon how often you go—the use of fresh water for toilet flushes. It's a simple, elegant conservation solution that requires absolutely no effort on anyone's part, save for the plumber, who will need about an hour to install it. For two people using a bathroom under normal conditions, the system will save about five thousand gallons of fresh water per year, which translates to savings of roughly $60 a year. With a retail price of around $200, the AQUS is an eco-conservation dream that pays for itself in cost savings within four years.

For the ultimate in an eco-luxury bathroom experience, try pairing an AQUS toilet system with a Toto Washlet. The Washlet is a super-smart toilet seat fixture that can be retrofitted to most toilets and comes equipped with a heated seat and retractable water-spray arm that provides bidetlike action. As if that weren't exciting and hygienic enough, the Washlet's integrated dryer air-dries your bottom after it's been washed. Good-bye toilet paper, hello pleasurable sensations. Toto Washlets are hugely popular in Japan, where the company is headquartered. More than fifteen hundred engineers are working hard to help Toto, the world's largest plumbing products manufacturer, deliver unprecedented performance and conservation. Spas around the United States are jumping on the clean-butt bandwagon, and homeowners can too.

If you still rely on toilet paper, there are several recycled options to choose from. Seventh Generation's absorbent toilet paper is made from a minimum of 80 percent recycled content. And the aptly named Shitbegone offers toilet paper made from 100 percent recycled content that is also exceptionally soft. At Shitbegone.com you'll get lessons on the art of toilet paper conservation—it's still paper after all—and learn what it takes to become a true toilet paper connoisseur.

Over in the shower, it's possible to combine water pressure with water conservation with the Oxygenics line of water-efficient showerheads. Thanks to patented technology that accelerates the pace of water flow through the showerhead—where the water is also injected with oxygen—Oxygenics showerheads deliver a powerful, healthy spray that simultaneously conserves water and oxygenates your body's skin cells. While the EPA mandates that showerheads use no more than 2.5 gallons of water per minute, Oygenics showerheads reduce that amount by up to 40 percent. And since heating water is super energy-intensive, opting for a water-efficient showerhead will save you money on both your water bill and your energy bill. For a typical family of four—each taking a ten-minute shower per day—the savings could be up to $600 per year. Oxygenics products are so powerful and efficient that the MGM Grand in Las Vegas installed them in all 4,500 guest rooms of its massive hotel, injecting a bit of eco-enlightenment into the Vegas strip.

Eco-awareness extends to the tub as well. There may be no better-designed bathtub on earth than a Durat from Finland. Each tub is deep and luxurious, and reclining against its contoured walls, as hot, steaming water envelops your body, just feels so right. The planet thinks so too. Durat was founded in 1990 with a mission to unite design with recycling. Its bold yet minimalist-designed bathtubs, shower trays, and washbasins are constructed with a solid polyester-based material made of approximately 50 percent recycled plastics, and the entire collection is available in forty colors.

When you're finished playing with your all-natural, sustainably harvested rubber ducky from Grassrootsstore.com, give yourself a good scrub with the world's only certified organic loofah sponge produced by Loofah S.A., a Paraguay-based company that works in collaboration with nongovernmental organizations to ensure that the local field farmers who cultivate the loofah fruit receive fair wages for their labor. Loofah sponges rejuvenate the body, exfoliate the skin, reactivate circulation, and now they protect the planet too. See Loofah-art.com for a list of retailers.

Toweling off in eco-style presents many possibilities. LOOP Organic offers highly absorbent, organic cotton terry-cloth towels (organic cotton has none of the toxic pesticides and insecticides sprayed on conventional cotton), while Anna Sova towels are made from luxurious Turkish organic cotton and come in a variety of rich colors. Ana Sova's deep, plush towel collection can be monogrammed for a personalized touch or coordinated with a bath mat so you can pamper your feet too. Nandina's Heavenly Bamboo towel collection includes hand towels, bath towels, enormous pool towels, and even bathrobes made from a patented blend of organic cotton, bamboo—the renewable, rapidly growing grass—and other natural fibers. The Heavenly Bamboo collection is available in a dizzying array of colors and is certified free of harmful substances by Oeko-Tex, a Swiss-based international association that has established extensive guidelines for approving ecologically sound products. At Branch you'll find the Millennium towel collection made by Bonjour in Switzerland. Each towel is made from an eco-aware beechwood microfiber that's sustainably harvested from tree farms in Scandinavia. They're made of beechwood, but they feel like cashmere—luxuriously soft and decadent. The Millennium collection is available in a wide range of colors made with nontoxic, colorfast dyes.

On an island off the coast of Japan, a wind-powered factory is making towels from a blend of organic cotton and bamboo. You can find them at Vivaterra.com. Yes, the ever versatile bamboo grass is gunning for Bathroom Eco-MVP. It can also be found in bath accessories collections from West Elm, Brookstone, and Target. The three collections offer varying aesthetics and include products such as toothbrush holders, tissue and lotion dispensers, trays, and wastebaskets. West Elm also extends its bamboo theme into a stunning line of towel bars, shelves, hoops, and toilet paper holders. They're only available online, so check them out at Westelm.com.

As for personal hygiene, when it's time to brush your teeth, check out Preserve toothbrushes, specially crafted out of 100 percent recycled plastic—primarily from Stonyfield Farm yogurt cups. The advanced design was developed with dental professionals over a two-year period and is exceptionally strong and flexible. Sure, it's just a toothbrush, but it's great to know that the products we use daily can be designed to perform flawlessly while respecting the planet. Preserve also offers ergonomically designed razors made of 100 percent recycled plastics. Like the company's toothbrushes, the razor plastic is mostly created from Stonyfield Farm yogurt cups. The toothbrushes and razors are also recyclable. At the end of their useful life, simply send them back to the company in the provided postage-paid envelope, and the entire toothbrush or razor—save for the blades—will be recycled yet again, this time into plastic lumber for outdoor uses.

For a sumptuous skin care experience, check out Pangea Organics. The company not only creates decadent natural soaps, shower gels, lotions, and toners, but also packages them in boxes that are made with a unique Zero Waste process that combines 100 percent post-consumer paper with organic seeds. Soak the box in water, plant it in the earth, and your packaging will soon transform into organic herbs, like sweet basil, for an entirely new take on recycling. As for the products, they boast a superb lineup of internationally harvested ingredients—think Egyptian calendula, Nigerian ginger, Argentinean tangerine, and French chamomile—that balance and cleanse the skin without irritating or overstimulating.

Toilets, Showers, and Baths

AQUS TOILET SYSTEM
Watersavertech.com
The AQUS is your instantaneous water recycling solution for the bathroom. Used water from the sink is channeled to the toilet for flushing via a water storage chamber installed inside the sink vanity.

CAROMA
Caromausa.com
The Caroma dual-flush toilets are equipped with two water chambers, one to flush down "number ones" and a larger chamber to sufficiently flush down "number twos." The simple push-button flush action makes it easy to select the appropriate chamber. The forward-thinking design can conserve up to 80 percent of the annual water usage of a typical toilet.

DELTA FAUCET

Deltafaucet.com

Several of Delta's water-efficient showerheads are equipped with "H2Okinetic Technology" to provide a satisfying spray while reducing water flow to just 1.6 gallons per minute compared to 2.5 gallons per minute for standard showerheads. It's a low-flow choice that still feels like high-flow.

DURAT

Durat.com

Durat was founded in 1990 with a mission to unite design with recycling. Durat is also the name of a polyester-based material made of approximately 50 percent recycled plastics, which offers a bold aesthetic and durable surface for countertops and is the material choice that informs the company's signature collection of minimalist-designed bathtubs, shower trays, and washbasins.

OXYGENICS

Oxygenics.com

The Oxygenics line of water-efficient showerheads deliver a powerful, healthy spray that simultaneously conserves water and oxygenates your body's skin cells. While the EPA mandates that showerheads use no more than 2.5 gallons of water per minute, Oygenics showerheads reduce that amount by up to 40 percent.

TOTO WASHLET

Washlet.com

The Washlet toilet seat fixture can be retrofitted to most toilets and features a heated seat and retractable water-spray arm that provides bidetlike action for gently cleansing both front and back. The hygienic system incorporates an air-drier for your bottom that eliminates the need for toilet paper—a tree conservation solution.

Towels and Hardware

ANNA SOVA

Annasova.com

Wrap yourself in deep, plush organic cotton towels and bedding from Anna Sova's collections, which feature rich colors created from low-impact dyes, for uncompromising style and a luxurious experience.

LOOP ORGANIC

Looporganic.com

The LOOP Organic collection features deep-absorbing, terry-cloth, organic cotton towels in a range of natural colors that are derived from organic, low-impact dyes. Designer Carmel Campos also offers a sophisticated bedding line featuring 250-thread-count organic sateen sheets, textured woven blankets, and accent pillows.

MILLENNIUM

Branchhome.com

The Millennium towel collection by Bonjour is made of a cashmere-like, eco-aware beechwood microfiber that is sustainably harvested from tree farms in Scandinavia. Available through Branch.

NANDINA

Nandina.info

The Heavenly Bamboo towel collection offered by Nandina includes hand towels, bath towels, enormous pool towels, and bathrobes made from a patented blend of organic cotton, bamboo, and other natural fibers. The rich, woven textures are available in a wide range of colors.

VIVATERRA

Vivaterra.com

This premier eco-retailer of home furnishings provides lovely bamboo-fiber towels and sturdy bamboo board hampers in which to toss them when they need to be washed.

WEST ELM

Westelm.com

West Elm has gotten bamboo fever and now offers lustrous bamboo towels and sturdy bamboo cups.

Hygiene and Skin Care

AVALON ORGANICS

Avalonorganics.com

Avalon Organics offers all-natural, nontoxic skin care. And the company announces its pledge to organic body care clearly on the label of each product. Whether it's wild yam deodorant or lavender facial wash, you can be guaranteed that there will be no artificial colors, synthetic fragrances, or parabens—chemical preservatives. And though the herbs may sound feminine, the lightly scented products are unquestionably unisex.

BURT'S BEES

Burtsbees.com

Burt of Burt's Bees started out as a beekeeper in rural Maine and has upheld the same simple, eco-friendly values ever since. Expanding beyond beeswax candles and lip balm, Burt's Bees offers a comprehensive line of all-natural face, body, hair, and makeup products made of all-natural ingredients and packaged in containers that either contain recycled content or are designed for reuse.

DR. HAUSCHKA

Drhauschka.com

Those willing to invest in a highly effective beauty regimen should not miss Dr. Hauschka's line of body and face cleansers and moisturizers. The German skin-care line, which been around for more than thirty-five years, has started to gain significant attention in the U.S. for its unique blend of ingredients that are organic and biodynamically harvested—a method of farming that considers numerous outside factors, including the cycles of the stars and moon.

LOOFAH S.A.

Loofashop.com

Loofah sponges rejuvenate the body, exfoliate the skin, reactivate circulation, and now they protect the planet too. Loofah S.A., a Paraguay-based company, offers the world's only certified organic loofah sponge.

PANGEA ORGANICS

Pangeaorganics.com

Pangea creates decadent natural soaps, shower gels, lotions, and toners, but also packages them in boxes that are made with a unique Zero Waste process that combines 100 percent post-consumer paper with organic seeds.

PRESERVE

Recycline.com

Quality, ergonomic Preserve toothbrushes and razors by Recycline are crafted out of 100 percent recycled plastic, most of which comes from Stonyfield Farm yogurt cups. At the end of your products' useful life, send them back to Recycline and they'll be recycled again.

SEVENTH GENERATION

Seventhgeneration.com

Seventh Generation is an industry leader in providing products that make your home healthier. Renowned for its nontoxic cleaning products, Seventh Generation also offers toilet and tissue paper made from 100 percent recycled content.

SHITBEGONE

Shitbegone.com

Shitbegone offers toilet paper made from 100 percent recycled content that is also exceptionally soft. At Shitbegone.com you'll get lessons on the art of toilet paper conservation—it's still paper after all—and learn what it takes to become a true toilet paper connoisseur.

TOM'S OF MAINE

Tomsofmaine.com

Famous for its all-natural peppermint toothpaste, Tom's of Maine has expanded to include spearmint, cinnamint, gingermint, and wintermint, as well as bold non-minty flavors like fennel, apricot, orange-mango, and lemon-lime.

Retailers

Many of the bath products discussed here are available through an increasing number of eco-furnishings retail stores and online stores opening throughout the United States. Here's a list to get you started.

3R LIVING

3rliving.com

Brooklyn, New York

A home decor and lifestyle store dedicated to "future friendly" products. 3R Living carefully selects products according to the principles of reducing waste, reusing unwanted or discarded materials, and recycling. Co-founder and product buyer Samantha Delman-Caserta has a sharp eye for design.

ABC CARPET & HOME

Abchome.com

New York, New York

ABC Carpet & Home offers a wide and distinctive collection of organic bath and bedding, organic beds, and decorative items. The trendsetting Manhattan department store offers a unique retail experience renowned around the world and is fully committed to environmental and social responsibility.

BLUE HOUSE

Shopbluehouse.com

Baltimore, Maryland

Bluehouse offers a strong collection of eco-aware furnishings, housewares, accessories, and gifts. Bluehouse's 7,000-square-foot retail store near Baltimore's Inner Harbor was built to green specifications and features a café serving natural and organic food and drinks.

EARTHSAKE

Earthsake.com

Berkeley, California

One of the early pioneers of eco-retailing, Earthsake got its start in 1990 and now offers high-quality organic and natural beds, bedding and bath products, and body care products. Choices are plentiful and feature materials like organic cotton, bamboo, and legna, a silky fiber made from tree cellulose.

ECO-GREEN LIVING

Eco-greenliving.com

Washington, DC

Eco-Green Living pulls together quality collections for home furnishing, redecorating, and renovation projects. At this Washington, DC, store, you'll find products like Vivetique natural and organic beds, as well as a luxurious line of Anna Sova bedding and bath products.

EQUITA

Shopequita.com

Pittsburgh, Pennsylvania

Located in an historic ice factory, Equita assembles many of the best eco-furnishings and accessory collections. You'll find recycled glassware by Riverside Designs complemented by organic cotton tablecloths, placemats, and napkins made by artisans in North Carolina. Bath and bedding products feature LOOP Organic. Rugs are available courtesy of Angela Adams.

GREEN FUSION DESIGN CENTER

Greenfusiondesigncenter.com

Marin County, California

A giant eco-home superstore, Green Fusion Design Center offers quality green products for home improvement projects and stylish green living. You'll find natural and organic beds from Vivetique and Green Sleep and bath and bedding products from Coyuchi and Anna Sova.

GREENER LIFESTYLES

Greenerlifestyles.com
Seattle, Washington
A Seattle-based provider of contemporary, eco-friendly furniture, Greener Lifestyles also makes its own line of stylish, sustainable, and affordable sofas, chairs, and loveseats constructed with FSC-certified woods, natural latex cushioning, and nontoxic glues. The company also offers luxury organic bedding and bath products from Anna Sova.

ORGANIC AVENUE

Organicavenue.com
New York, New York
Get your raw food and your organic denim jeans all at once by visiting this Lower East Side store in Manhattan. Del Forte and Natural High Lifestyle are just two of the featured labels in this eco-lifestyle store, where you'll also find stylish collections of tabletop, bath, and bedding products.

ORGANIC INTERIOR DESIGN

Organicinteriordesign.com
Venice, California
This company offers quality natural and organic mattresses as well as luxury organic bedding and bath products by Anna Sova. Principal designer Kelly Laplante is also available to work with clients to design interiors using today's most cutting-edge sustainable products.

SPRING

Astorecalledspring.com
San Francisco, California
Step into Spring to find eco-aware products to create a healthier home and planet. Kitchenware, bath and bedding, and baby products are just a few of the categories in which you'll find better ideas for your home and loved ones.

TWOKH

Twokh.com
New York, New York
An upscale eco-home store located in the Chelsea neighborhood of Manhattan, TwoKH offers contemporary organic collections of furnishings for most rooms in the home, as well as several outstanding lines of natural and organic skin care products.

VIVAVI

Vivavi.com
Brooklyn, New York
The company I founded in 2003, Vivavi represents many of today's most forward-thinking furniture and home furnishings designers, who combine cutting-edge aesthetics with pure, renewable, and recycled materials. Our motto is "Live Modern + Tread Lightly," which also reflects our commitment to green business practices. Our headquarters and showroom are powered by 100 percent wind energy.

Online-Only Retailers

BRANCH

Branchhome.com
If the MoMA Store carried only sustainably designed products, it would be Branch. Superbly designed modern and contemporary products demonstrate how fine attention to detail and aesthetics can easily align with environmental awareness. Branch offers furnishings for nearly the entire home, as well as outstanding gifts for men, women, and children.

VIVATERRA

Vivaterra.com
This premier eco-retailer of home furnishings provides high-quality kitchen and dining products as well as organic bath and bedding products. In addition to bamboo and organic cotton towels, you'll find organic cotton damask duvets and shams; pure silk sheets, duvets, shams, and pillows; and natural merino lambswool comforters—everything you need to be nice and cozy.

Information / Education

WATERSENSE

Epa.gov / watersense
A program sponsored by the Environmental Protection Agency patterned after the Energy Star program. WaterSense is the EPA's rating system designed to promote highly efficient home products such as toilets and sink faucets that help conserve water without sacrificing performance. Visit the website to find products that have earned the WaterSense designation.

13

SCRUB,
DUST,
AND
MOP

House cleaning

We use cleaning products to create a clean and healthy home, but sometimes we get more than we bargained for. Conventional products may remove mold, fight germs, and keep glass shiny and streak free, but they often use toxins and synthetic chemicals to do so. Today there are better housecleaning options. Gone are the days when eco-friendly cleaning meant beakers of vinegar and lemon juice, a can-do spirit, and a healthy dose of elbow grease. Today's green cleaning solutions work just like their conventional counterparts, but deliver on the double promise of creating clean *and* healthy spaces.

Method's nontoxic cleaning products look as good as they act. So good in fact that many people refuse to stow them under the sink. The company's all-star lineup of products includes all-purpose and specialty surface cleaners, dishwashing and laundry detergents, air fresheners, and hand and body washes. The biodegradable, nontoxic formulas are developed by a team led by cofounder Adam Lowry, a chemical engineer from Stanford University and an environmental scientist. The attractive, playfully designed bottles are drawn from the creative mind of Karim Rashid, whose other works are featured in more than seventy permanent collections of museums around the world. The products are never tested on animals, and they smell delightful, with scents like cucumber, lavender, grapefruit, green tea, and magnolia.

If Method is the design-driven nontoxic cleaning upstart, Seventh Generation is the wise elder statesman of healthy cleaning and, for now, the industry leader. Led by President and CEO Jeffrey Hollender, Seventh Generation has been developing and refining its line of biodegradable, nontoxic cleaning products for more than fifteen years. The line includes all-purpose household cleaners and laundry and dishwashing products. Seventh Generation also offers recycled paper products, including paper towels, facial tissue, toilet paper, napkins, and paper plates. So once you've cleaned your home, Seventh Generation products will help you enjoy an eco-aware picnic. Personal care products include healthy chlorine-free diapers and baby wipes, and feminine care products for women.

Most eco-cleaners perform just as well as their conventional counterparts without using hazardous ingredients. The EPA estimates that anywhere from three to twenty-five gallons of toxic materials—mostly in cleaners—are present in the average U.S. household, so the situation can pose risks and be highly corrosive. With so many nontoxic cleaning choices available, identifying which work best for you can be a question of sampling a few until you find the right fit. Other brands that consistently receive praise are Citra-Solv, Ecover, and Mrs. Meyers. Actor and environmental activist extraordinaire Ed Begley offers his Begley's Best line of biodegradable, nontoxic cleaning products. The products are derived from plant-based ingredients like pine, citrus fruits, palm, maize, fermented sugar, and olive seeds. Some call that dinner, but Begley calls it all-purpose household cleaners, surface cleansers, and carpet stain removers.

Throughout the Midwest, a nontoxic cleaning revolution is spreading thanks to entrepreneur Laurie Brown and her line of Restore cleaning products. Sold in big supermarkets—including Whole Foods—and in smaller stores, Restore features all-purpose cleaners and laundry and kitchen cleaning products. Specialty products include nontoxic toilet bowl and oven cleaners. And look for the toxin-free bath wash that is gentle enough for humans and pets. Restore gets extra points for its patented automated Restore Filling Station, which enables customers to use the same bottle over and over again by bringing it back to the store and refilling it. To encourage such planet-friendly behavior, the filling station automatically dispenses a $1 coupon for each bottle refill, making it cheaper to refill than to buy new.

For those who want the benefits of a healthy, clean home but don't have time or the inclination to do it themselves, help is on the way. Eco-friendly cleaning services are sprouting up around the country. Portland has Eco Clean. Charlotte and New York City each have a Green Clean. In Chicago and Atlanta it's Green & Clean. Green Clean Planet is in Phoenix. Green Home Cleaning Services is in Washington, DC. And Green Friendly Cleaning can be found in Ann Arbor. But the cleaning service Brooklynites turn to, first because it's local and second because they put an organic chocolate bar on your bed, is Zen Home Cleaning.

Zen Home Cleaning is like your standard cleaning service, but a hundred times better. For starters, like all eco-friendly cleaning services, Zen Home relies exclusively upon nontoxic cleaning products to clear away dirt, grime, and grease. But the service is about more than cleaning. It's about making your home feel like a luxurious hotel room at an exclusive spa getaway. Perhaps it's the burning during cleaning of essential oils like lavender, citrus, and jasmine. Or maybe it's the turn-down service in the bedroom and the fragrant sachet of potpourri left on your bed. Or the organic chocolate bar. As if that's not enough, Zen Home will even organize your closets and home office—a lazy environmentalist's dream come true.

All-Purpose Cleaners

BEGLEY'S BEST
Begleysbest.com
Actor and eco-activist Ed Begley offers a line of biodegradable, nontoxic cleaning products derived from plant-based ingredients like pine, citrus fruits, palm, maize, fermented sugar, and olive seeds.

BI-O-KLEEN
Bi-o-kleen.com
Manufacturing quality nontoxic products for your home is top priority at Bi-O-Kleen. The full line of cleaning products is complemented by a special soy-based line that includes toilet and surface cleaners. The laundry detergents also routinely receive high marks.

BIOSHIELD

Bioshieldpaints.com

This manufacturer of top-quality, healthy, eco-aware paints is expanding into cleaning products and offers nontoxic dishwasher soaps, glass cleaners, toilet bowl cleaners, and an all-purpose vinegar-based cleaner for refrigerators, sinks, stoves, tiles, bathrooms, and more.

CITRA-SOLV

Citra-solv.com

Dedicated to the idea that people should enjoy performance-driven, high-quality cleaning and personal care products that respect the planet, Citra-Solv offers a full lineup of nontoxic cleaning products that avoid harsh chemicals and petroleum distillates. Check out the highly regarded all-purpose Cleaner & Degreaser, which relies upon orange extractives to get the job done.

ECOVER

Ecover.com

Ecover's biodegradable, nontoxic cleaners are derived principally from plant-based ingredients and produced in Belgium at the company's eco-factory, which is powered by green energy (through the purchase of green energy certificates) and features eco-innovations like a 10,000-square-foot grass roof for natural insulation and soccer games. Choose from high-performing dishwashing, laundry, household, and personal care products.

GREENING THE CLEANING

Dienviro.com

A line of award-winning, nontoxic household cleaning products developed in 2005 by the Deirdre Imus Environmental Center for Pediatric Oncology, Greening the Cleaning products are available nationwide, and all after-tax profits support The Imus Cattle Ranch for Kids in Ribera, New Mexico.

METHOD

Methodhome.com

Method's nontoxic, biodegradable cleaning products look as good as they act, and smell good too. The all-purpose and specialty surface cleaners, dishwashing and laundry detergents, air fresheners, and hand and body washes are packaged in stylish bottles designed by Karim Rashid. You won't want to stow them.

MRS. MEYERS

Mrsmeyers.com
Fresh-smelling, hardworking, nontoxic cleaners are what you can expect from Mrs. Meyers. All the company's cleaning supplies are biodegradable and incorporate natural essential oils to provide a pleasant, fragrant cleaning experience.

RESTORE

Restoreproducts.com
Using renewable plant-based ingredients like soy, orange, coconut, and corn, Restore offers a full range of nontoxic cleaning products. Restore Filling Stations enable customers to use the same bottle over and over again by bringing it back to their supermarket and refilling it.

SEVENTH GENERATION

Seventhgeneration.com
Seventh Generation is an industry leader in providing products that make your home healthier. Renowned for its nontoxic cleaning products, Seventh Generation also offers garbage bags made from recycled plastic, as well as paper towels, toilet paper, and tissue paper made from recycled paper. Personal care products include healthy chlorine-free diapers and baby wipes, and feminine care products.

SOY CLEAN

Soyclean.biz
Soy Clean offers a full line of soy-based, nontoxic, biodegradable cleaning supplies. The products can take care of your household cleaning needs and also take on tough tasks like paint stripping.

Cleaning Services

For lazy environmentalists who prefer to have others clean for them, green cleaning services that utilize nontoxic cleaning products are sprouting up around the country. Here's a list to get you started. For additional results, try searching Google.com by entering "green cleaning" in the search box and the name of your town or city.

ANNIE MAIDS

Anniemaids.com
Weston, Florida

AZ HEALTHY HOMES

Azhealthyhomes.com
Tempe, Arizona

ECO CLEAN
Eco-clean.info
Portland and Beaverton, Oregon

ENVIROSHINE
Enviroshine.net
Boulder, Colorado

GREEN & CLEAN
Greencleanhome.com
Atlanta, Georgia

GREEN & CLEAN
Greencleanhome.com
Chicago and Champagne, Illinois

GREEN CLEAN
Greencleanla.com
Los Angeles, California

GREEN CLEAN
Greencleanusa.org
Baltimore, Maryland, and
Washington, DC

GREEN CLEAN
Greencleannc.com
Charlotte, North Carolina

GREEN CLEAN
Greencleannyc.com
New York, New York

GREEN CLEAN PLANET
Greencleanplanet.com
Phoenix, Arizona

GREEN FRIENDLY CLEANING
Greenfriendlycleaning.com
Ann Arbor, Michigan

**GREEN HOME CLEANING
SERVICES**
Greenhomecs.com
Washington, DC

**IMMACULATE CLEANING
SERVICE**
Myimmaculate.com
San Bernardino County, California

MAID NATURALLY
Maidnaturally.com
Spokane, Washington

**NATURAL HOME CLEANING
PROFESSIONALS**
Naturalhomecleaning.com
Oakland, California

ORGANIC CLEANING SERVICES
Organiccleaningservices.com
San Francisco, California

ZEN HOME CLEANING
Zenhomecleaning.com
Brooklyn, New York

14

THE GREENEST
GREEN THUMB

Gardening

Good-bye, gas-powered lawnmowers and synthetic fertilizers and pesticides that encourage things to grow by poisoning others. These days when it's time to go outside to beautify your natural surroundings, you can rely upon eco-advanced products that nature would approve of.

Right now an army of a billion worms are munching on garbage in the heart of downtown Trenton, New Jersey, working to produce some of the most potent plant fertilizer available today. Tom Szaky and Jon Beyer hit upon the idea for Terracycle Plant Food during their freshman year at Princeton University. Garbage is recycled on the front end when their worms eat it, and waste is recycled on the back end when the worms poop it into reclaimed Coca-Cola and Pepsi bottles. The product is so effective that studies consistently show it outperforming its conventional synthetic-based competition. Investors have poured millions of dollars into the company to help hone its eco-friendly fertilizing solutions, and executives have left corporate jobs to join the upstart entrepreneurs who are now in their mid-twenties. Home Depot, Wal-Mart, and CVS carry the entire line. You can spray it on your indoor and outdoor plants and even on your lawn. It's all good because it's all organic, and you don't have to worry about over-applying because it's completely nontoxic. While the contents of Terracycle might not be familiar upon first use, the packaging definitely will be. Terracycle reuses twenty-ounce Coca-Cola and Pepsi bottles that are sent to its headquarters by churches, schools, and nonprofit organizations around the country. Terracycle has created a true win-win situation.

Organic gardeners who detest dirt, tools, and hassle can still nurture a green thumb. These days you don't need tools and soil in order to grow organic herbs, flowers, fruits, and vegetables. All you need is a glass of water and a Garden-in-a-bag made by Potting Shed Creations. Pour some water and the accompanying seeds into the bag and presto! You've got yourself your very own organic garden. The wide selection of choices includes organic oregano, parsley, basil, thyme, mint, tomatoes, strawberries, tulips, and daffodils. Place your Garden-in-a-bag on any countertop or windowsill inside your home. Watch TV with it. You can even take it for walks. Your grow-in-a-bag organic garden is your newfound pal.

Gardens aren't the only outside area gaining eco-attention. Lawn care is changing too. Homeowners who turn to Naturalawn of America are catching bugs, eliminating unwanted insects and weeds, and growing beautiful lawns using products and lawn management programs that reduce pesticides by more than 80 percent. Naturalawn of America's advanced organic-based biological lawn care products have been developed through extensive research and development over the past twenty years. The combination of reduced synthetic pesticides and reliance upon organic-based biological products leads to healthier plants and soil, safer lawns for children and pets, and healthier groundwater supplies for all of us. The company operates in twenty-four states, through more than seventy franchises that provide ongoing lawn care management. A list of franchise locations is available through Naturalawn.com. For individuals in locations that aren't serviced by a franchise, or for do-it-yourselfers, Naturalawn products can be purchased directly through the company's website, and experts are available by phone to answer any questions.

Speaking of grass, imagine delegating the task of cutting it to an automated robot. Dreams do come true. The RoboMower by Friendly Robotics is a small, compact lawnmower that would have definitely befriended R2D2 and C3PO. The RoboMower operates entirely on its own. You simply lay the included wire around the perimeter of your yard to set the boundary and press "go." The RoboMower programs itself to systematically cut your entire lawn by relying upon sensors that identify the established perimeter as well as rocks, trees, and other lawn obstacles, in order to work around them. It's equipped with child and pet safety features and password and disabling mechanisms that discourage theft. The basic model can be stored indoors. The top-of-the-range model comes with an outdoor docking station that allows for total automation. The RoboMower will depart from the docking station day and night based on the time schedule you program and, once finished, return to the docking station to recharge.

Because the RoboMower is powered by rechargeable batteries, it emits zero pollution while operating. Gas-powered lawnmowers, on the other hand, are responsible for 5 percent of all air pollution in the United States. The typical gas-powered lawnmower emits as much pollution in one hour as do forty cars. Switching to an electric-powered lawnmower is the energy-efficient and eco-aware choice. But it's not a total eco-victory. When plugged into an electric socket, any appliance draws energy from the power grid, which is primarily supplied by fossil fuels like coal, oil, and natural gas. However, studies by the California Air Resources Board have found that operating electric mobile vehicles (in this case lawnmowers) can reduce emissions by 60 percent.

Another way to reduce greenhouse gas emissions while stylishly accentuating your lawn is through the use of solar-powered lamps and fountains. Silicon Solar offers waterproof, solar-powered garden lanterns and yard lights that are easy to install in the ground and are equipped with bright, long-lasting LED bulbs. The LED bulbs are powered by internal batteries that receive their energy from a solar panel integrated directly into the top of each lantern. A photo sensor automatically turns the light on at dusk and off at dawn, providing a maintenance-free and emissions-free way to light your garden or footpath. Silicon Solar also offers a range of automated solar-powered flood lamps and motion detection lamps to further light your outside areas at night by relying exclusively upon the power of the sun.

Give your outdoor areas a splash of charm with Silicon Solar's wide selection of solar-powered garden fountains. The HP 300FX solar power pump will shoot a spray of water six feet into the air, making it a lovely companion for backyard small ponds and wading pools. Silicon Solar's line of cascading fountains create a soothing atmosphere as a gentle stream of water flows downward, passing through a series of open vessels on its way to the basin, where a solar-powered pump redirects the water back to the top. Cascading fountains are perfect for gardens, lawns, and decks. They're a relaxing and inviting way to bring a little solar power into your life.

Garden and Lawn Products

GARDEN-IN-A-BAG
Pottingshedcreations.com
Maker of uniquely packaged living gardens, Potting Shed Creations makes growing organic herbs, flowers, fruits, and vegetables a cinch. Pour water and the accompanying seeds into the Garden-in-a-bag pouch to create your very own organic garden.

MODERN BIRDHOUSES
Modernbirdhouses.com
The traditional birdhouse receives a modern update with this stunning collection of FSC-certified sustainably harvested teak birdhouses. They're architect-designed and handcrafted for the finest quality. Birds will be flocking from all over the neighborhood.

NATURALAWN OF AMERICA
Naturalawn.com
The environmentally sound lawn care company Naturalawn of America has been serving clients throughout the United States since 1987. The company's advanced organic-based biological lawn care products have been developed through extensive research and development over the past twenty years.

ROBOMOWER
Friendlyrobotics.com
The RoboMower by Friendly Robotics is a small, compact, and fully automated electric lawnmower. Lay the included wire around the perimeter of your yard to set the boundary and press "go." The RoboMower automatically cuts your lawn all by itself.

TERRACYCLE

Terracycle.net

Tom Szaky and Jon Beyer hit upon the idea for Terracycle Plant Food during their freshman year at Princeton University. Garbage is recycled on the front end when their worms eat it, and waste is recycled on the back end when the worms poop it into reclaimed Coca-Cola and Pepsi bottles. Home Depot, Wal-Mart, and CVS carry the entire line.

Retailers

CLEAN AIR GARDENING

Cleanairgardening.com

This Dallas-based online retailer offers eco-aware lawn and garden products ranging from electric lawnmowers and snowblowers to rainwater barrels and composting bins. You'll also find organic fertilizers and innovative space-saving planters like the Topsy Turvy, which lets you grow vegetables upside down.

GAIAM

Gaiam.com

One of the leading eco-lifestyle retailers in the United States, Gaiam offers a wide selection of outdoor and gardening products. You'll find quality solar accessories like sensor lights and lanterns, as well as outdoor products like hemp garden gloves and hammocks made with fibers spun from recycled soda bottles.

SILICON SOLAR

Siliconsolar.com

Silicon Solar offers a wide selection of solar energy–enhanced outdoor products. Solar-powered garden lanterns and yard lights are easy to install in the ground and are equipped with bright, long-lasting LED bulbs that automatically light at night and shut off during the day. Solar-powered floodlights and security lights are also available, as are solar-powered water fountains.

SMART HOME

Smarthome.com

Smart Home offers a wide selection of electronic home improvement and home automation products. Type "solar" into the search box on the website and you'll find about 150 products that utilize the power of the sun. Look for innovative products like in-ground and above-ground solar-powered pool heaters. And pick up a set of solar-powered stepping stone lights that illuminate the path beneath your feet.

15

Animal Accessories
PETS ARE PEOPLE TOO

Pets, the furriest (hopefully) of our family members, can tap into the latest eco-trends in style, design, and healthy organic living. Being a pet no longer means lounging on a hand-me-down rug, scratching on a cardboard computer box, and nibbling on nutrition-challenged "treats." Twenty-first-century pets are making waves on eco-fashion runways and leading healthy, green lives.

Eco-fashion designer Deborah Lindquist has dressed celebrities like Gwen Stefani, Demi Moore, Jessica Simpson, and Sharon Stone, and now your pooch can share the same stage thanks to Lindquist's delightful recycled cashmere sweaters designed specifically for four-legged fashion mavens. The sweaters are made to order and come in multiple sizes. Color options include gray, black, red, burgundy, purple, pink, lavender, blue, and peach, and feature a choice of appliqués, including a crown, skull, cross, peace symbol, star, and fleur-de-lis. Your furry friend will be praying for cool weather, and there are more than enough combinations to dress to impress throughout the winter.

Eco-stylish pet interiors are in vogue thanks to forward-thinking designers like Jonathan Holden, Elizabeth Paige Smith, and Susan Kralovec. Holden's company, Holden Designs, takes the dining preferences of dogs into consideration with the sculptural beauty of its contemporary raised bowl feeders. The rounded, organic shapes use a single piece of plywood formulated with a super-efficient furniture technique known as bent-ply. Imagine peeling a tree like you would a carrot, layering the peelings atop one another, gluing them together, and then bending them into elegant rounded shapes. That's the bent-ply process, and it enables furniture to be made with one-eighth the amount of wood used in conventional furniture making. Holden Designs offers single and double feeders of varying heights to accommodate small and large pets. Holden has also designed an ergonomic, sleek, space age pet bed—the Jetsons' dog, Astro, would be absolutely drooling. Okay, he's a dog, so he probably drools anyway, but you get the drift.

Elizabeth Paige Smith elevates the life of a cat with her line of corrugated cardboard Kittypod cat beds that do double duty as scratching posts. Since corrugated cardboard is made primarily of recycled cardboard, these eye-catching conversation pieces are also eco-invincible. The Prrrounge is a chaise lounge for cats that love stretching out. The Couchette is a double-sided pedestal that resembles an hourglass and provides a contoured cat perch on top and a hiding space underneath. The Archipod evokes the raw power of modern architecture with its rugged, angular design of multiple platforms for climbing and scratching and a covered shelter for lounging. The Kittypod, the signature piece in the Kittypod line, is an elevated, rounded, egg-shape pod that will delight cats, their owners, and guests, who will definitely try to sit on it. That's okay, because the Kittypod has the structural integrity to withstand the weight of humans too.

Susan Kralovec also serves up design treats for cats and dogs. Her company, Everyday Studios, creates raised drinking feeders made of laser-cut stainless steel—very efficient use of a material that contains recycled content. The Dog Dish is a bi-level, wall-mounted raised feeder that keeps the food off the floor and provides customized dining positions for your dog. The Pet Dish is designed similarly to the Dog Dish but is a minimalist freestanding feeder suitable for both dogs and cats. Everyday Studios' cat scratching posts come in clean, contemporary forms that would satisfy the most discerning Scandinavian design fan and are made of heavy-duty corrugated cardboard. The Cat Tree is an easy-to-install, modern wall-mounted post, and the Claw, Nap, and Pounce are freestanding scratching posts of dazzling geometric shapes.

For pets who prefer to lounge on something a little softer, Big

Shrimpy designs dog and cat beds that combine fleece or faux suede sleeping surfaces with an interior filling made of 100 percent recycled fleece scraps that are also odor- and water-resistant. The fleece scrap filling maintains its shape much longer than conventional pet bed fillings and is softer too. The bed cover and the inner filling can also be replaced separately. Once your pet is rested, give him or her DoubleDoodle, NoodleDoodle, FlopaDoodle, SquaDoodle, or CircaDoodle to play with—Big Shrimpy's line of funky, organically shaped stuffed toys made of faux suede and filled with 100 percent recycled fibers.

Other eco-stylish pet toy options include the SimplyFido organic plush toy collection from Miyim. Choose from Wally the bear, Lolly the lamb, Oscar the monkey, Lucy the rabbit, or Maggie the caterpillar. All of the ten-inch stuffed animal characters are made from organic materials and treated with natural plant- and mineral-based dyes, such as gardenia seed, clove, and chestnut bur. Your pet can chew on these nontoxic toys all day. SimplyFido also enables you to throw your dog a stuffed toy bone from its Bone collection, made with all-organic, nontoxic materials. All SimplyFido plush toys come with removable squeakers, letting you control the noise factor.

Toys are far from the only organic option for your pet. Pet food, like people food, is going organic in a big way. OnlyNaturalPet.com offers a tremendous selection of natural and organic pet foods and treats. For co-founder Marty Grosjean the imperative for feeding our pets healthier organic foods is clear. "With conventional pet food, we're basically feeding our pets the nutritional equivalent of a Big Mac three times a day," says Grosjean. And while Big Macs are undeniably delicious, they're not exactly the health equivalent of Grape-Nuts or, in this case, Newman's Own Organics cat and dog foods. The Newman's Own brand, along with other organic pet foods brands, such as Wellness, Innova, Honest Kitchen, Nature's Variety, Merrick, and Natural Balance, are all available at OnlyNaturalPet.com.

In browsing the Boulder, Colorado–based company's online store, it's clear that a veritable pet food revolution is under way.

In addition to pet food, OnlyNaturalPet.com offers nutritional pet supplements, holistic remedies, natural flea and tick control products, and natural grooming products like herbal shampoos and conditioners. And a holistic veterinarian is on staff to consult by phone to customers around the country. OnlyNaturalPet.com also features a holistic pet health-care library with informative articles covering subjects like "Seasonal Allergies and Itching," "Pancreatitis in Companion Animals," and "Weight Management for Dogs and Cats." Grosjean readily acknowledges that serving pets natural and organic food costs more than conventional pet food choices, but he contends that doing so not only makes pets happier and healthier, but also serves as the best preventative medicine available to avoid more costly veterinarian bills down the road.

When taking your pets on the road, keep them hydrated with Pup Cups, portable purified water cups designed exclusively for pets. Available in two-pack, four-pack, and twenty-four-pack quantities, Pup Cups provide a convenient way to give your pets purified drinking water in a sturdy makeshift bowl. Throw them in your purse or backpack and whip them out whenever your pet needs a quick refresher. For pets with small thirsts, the eight-ounce Pup Cups come with leak-proof resealable lids that enable your pet's water supply to stay fresh throughout the day. Pup Cups are so well designed that they were awarded Best New Product of 2005 by Progressive Grocer. That same year, Pup Cups' parent company, Out of Home (OOH) Pet Products, donated ten thousand Pup Cups to animals affected by Hurricane Katrina.

Pet Products and Retailers

BELLA DOGGA

Belladogga.com

Instill a little design savvy and colorful pattern into your dog's life. Bella Dogga offers a range of pet products, including eco-aware dog beds constructed of organic cotton, with patterns created from low-impact dyes and fluffy interiors filled with kapok.

BIG SHRIMPY

Bigshrimpy.com

Big Shrimpy designs dog and cat beds that combine fleece or faux suede sleeping surfaces with an interior filling made of 100 percent recycled fleece scraps that are also odor- and water-resistant. Big Shrimpy's line of fun-shaped pet toys are made of faux suede and filled with 100 percent recycled fibers.

DEBORAH LINDQUIST

Deborahlindquist.com

Eco-fashion designer Deborah Lindquist has dressed celebrities like Gwen Stefani, Demi Moore, Jessica Simpson, and Sharon Stone, and now your pooch can share the same stage thanks to Lindquist's delightful recycled cashmere sweaters designed specifically for four-legged fashion mavens.

EARTHDOG

Earthdog.com

Earthdog offers a wide range of quality eco-intelligent hemp products for your pet. Select from hemp collars, hemp and recycled fleece blankets, hemp beds, and hemp-stuffed bones.

EVERYDAY STUDIOS

Everydaystudios.com

Founder Susan Kralovec creates modern design treats for cats and dogs, like geometric corrugated-cardboard (recycled content) scratching posts and laser-cut stainless steel (recycled content and material-efficient) dog dishes.

HOLDEN DESIGNS

Holdendesigns.com

Holden Designs takes the dining preferences of dogs into consideration with the sculptural beauty of its contemporary raised bowl feeders. The rounded, organic shapes use a single piece of plywood formulated with a super-efficient furniture technique known as bent-ply.

KITTYPOD

Kittypod.com

Elizabeth Paige Smith elevates the life of a cat with her line of corrugated cardboard Kittypod cat beds that do double duty as scratching posts. Since corrugated cardboard is made primarily of recycled cardboard, these eye-catching conversation pieces are also eco-invincible.

ONLYNATURALPET.COM

OnlyNaturalPet.com offers a tremendous selection of natural and organic pet foods and treats. Look for organic pet foods, nutritional pet supplements, holistic remedies, natural flea and tick control products, and natural grooming products like herbal shampoos and conditioners. A holistic veterinarian is on staff to consult by phone to customers.

PUP CUPS

Pupcups.com

Pup Cups are portable purified water cups designed exclusively for pets. Unseal the lid and let your pet drink directly from the sturdy, makeshift bowl. The eight-ounce Pup Cups come with leak-proof resealable lids so your pet's water supply can stay fresh throughout the day.

SCKOON

Sckoon.com

Sckoon sets the style trends for canines with its kimonos for dogs, made of 100 percent organic cotton. Wrap your dog in bright red or navy blue. The striped organic cotton dog T-shirts give your dog that casual pet-about-town nautical look. Very Ralph Lauren. Organic pet toys and bedding are also available.

SHORE DOG COLLARS

Shoredog.com

Colorful hemp dog collars and leashes are available from Shore Dog Collars. Hemp is a durable, organically grown natural fiber. Now you can walk your dog in eco-aware style.

SIMPLY FIDO

Simplyfido.com

The Simply Fido organic plush toy collection from Miyim features ten-inch stuffed animal characters made from organic materials and treated with natural plant and mineral-based dyes such as gardenia seed, clove, and chestnut bur.

GREAT GREEN PET

Greatgreenpet.com

A shopping blog for quality, eco-aware pet products. The bloggers have a keen eye and showcase everything from gourmet organic pet treats to healthy, nontoxic pet shampoos.

16

Babies and Kids

IT'S NEVER TOO SOON TO START

When it comes to eco-styling, it's never too early to start. Young immune systems are particularly vulnerable to toxins, and recent innovations in eco-design now give parents the opportunity to protect their little ones while maintaining a strong aesthetic. Whether biting on a chair leg, stuffing building blocks in their mouths, or cooing on a crib mattress, today's children can do it all in safe, healthy eco-style.

It starts with a diaper. Rather, 25 billion diapers. That's the number bought in a single year in the United States. Since the majority of these are disposable, quite a lot of synthetic fibers and baby poop are piling up in our landfills. Enter gDiapers, the super-convenient diaper solution that helps prevent diaper rash while dodging landfills. The diapers are a two-part system. A flushable inner refill fits into a pair of colorful "little g" pants. When the inner refill is soiled, simply flush it down the toilet and replace it with a fresh one. Good-bye, mess. So long, stinky garbage bins. Since the gDiapers lining is biodegradable, it breaks down through normal water sewage treatment processing. With fun colors like gumdrop purple, giggle pink, grateful red, and global blue, gDiapers will keep your kid cute and your home clean, and the planet too. Soon you'll be asking yourself how parents ever survived without such supreme diaper convenience.

Now that we've got the mess out of the way, it's time to hook a baby up with some stylish eco-aware duds. For clothing that's naturally antimicrobial, hypoallergenic, and thermal-regulating, check out Bamboosa's line of bamboo wear. This quick-growing wonder grass provides a deliciously soft, plush fiber for babies and children.

Bamboosa's lineup of bamboo baby products includes bodysuits, socks, beanies, hooded towels, washcloths, blankets, and fitted crib sheets. Colors range from pale pink to tahiti blue.

Organic cotton also plays a key role in babies' and kids' clothing. Speesees keeps the chemicals and pesticides sprayed on conventional cotton away from your little one's skin. The toxin-free, organic cotton clothing is outrageously cool. Yoga pants, flap skirts, kimonos, and lamb jackets (with fun, fuzzy ears) complement the bodysuits and lap shoulder T-shirts. Seal pups, sea horses, and giraffes are a few of the animal designs that you can choose from. Or choose pumpkins, pears, or trees.

Positively Organic keeps the organic cotton fashion vibes flowing. Baby hipsters will dig the organic corduroy infant cargo pants available in chocolate brown with contrasting stitching and cuffs in olive, blue, or pink. Pants can be coordinated with long-sleeve infant T-shirts that feature colorful nature-inspired patterns. Varsity T-shirts are totally "rad" and come in sizes for babies, infants, and toddlers. Bodysuits, knotted caps, and baby booties are but a few more of the many stylish items available.

For cooler weather, turn to Llamajama and the thermal-regulating properties of natural wool and alpaca—think a sheep with a really tall neck—to keep your little ones warm, healthy, and superstylish. The company's line of colorful longies, shorties, sweaters, and jumpsuits are über adorable. In an effort to avoid the toxicity of traditional dying, the folks at Llamajama have developed an innovative color process for their clothing. It's called Kool-Aid. When mixed with the right amount of water and vinegar, the sweet drink creates a safe dye that is easily absorbed by wool and alpaca fibers. For do-it-yourselfers Llamajama.com walks you through creating dye potions at home. Llamajama's yarns and finished products come from developing countries in South America, where the company honors its fair trade pledge to pay fair wages to its all-women labor force, as well as engaging in ecologically aware practices and creating healthy and safe working conditions.

Creating a fun, safe, eco-aware room for your kids is a snap thanks to thoughtful furniture companies that are designing modern collections specifically for kids. Argington's Wonders Collection—named for the wonders of the world—is designed to grow with your child. Cribs convert to toddler beds. Seats and tables are height-adjustable. Platform beds can be supplemented with storage space or trundle beds. Furniture pieces like the Delphi changing table with built-in storage units and the Sahara crib share the exact same height and width dimensions, making them a perfect, space-saving match when paired together. High chairs, rocking chairs, toy boxes, and shelves round out the collection. Cofounders, designers, and husband-and-wife team Andrew Thornton and Jenny Argie share a passion not only for quality contemporary design, but also for the health of both children and the planet. Argington gets its wood from FSC-certified sustainable forests. Products are assembled using low-VOC glues and nontoxic finishes. This is furniture that will follow your kids through elementary and middle school—who knows, some of it might even make it to high school graduation.

Give your little ones a safe haven for sleeping with Coyuchi's organic cotton fitted crib sheets and jacquard-woven baby blankets, shams, bumper covers, and crib skirts. The George Baby Collection adds an adorable eco-twist with organic cotton blankets, shams, and bumper covers that depict playful animals and jungle settings. Also available in the George Baby Collection are playful lion jumpsuits, elephant bibs, hooded towels, receiving blankets, and T-shirts.

Lifekind goes all out in the baby nursery. The company offers an entire line of fun, animal-themed organic cotton bedding which extends into organic cotton changing pads and covers, play mats, organizers, diaper stackers, stuffed animals, and prop-up pillows that are filled and covered with organic cotton. Lifekind has also built much of its reputation on providing state-of-the-art organic mattresses, and babies get to benefit from this expertise too. Options include innerspring mattresses or natural rubber soft-core mattresses. Both feature healthy, nontoxic fillings made of organic cotton and pure wool, and each comes with a twenty-year warranty (which is great, though there's a good chance your young ones will have outgrown it by then).

Toys can also be fun and eco-aware. Miyim's plush characters and stuffed animals are cozy, soft, and safe. John Chae, founder of Miyim's parent company, Hosung, had been running a family toy business for thirty years when his wife was diagnosed with cancer. During her recovery, the family began thinking about ways to lead healthier lives. This reevaluation led to the creation of Miyim—a company dedicated to designing toys made of organic materials and toxic-free dyes. Four collections of stuffed characters and animals are currently available—storybook, puppet time, sleepytime, and peaceful dreams—and more are on the way.

Remember back when we were kids and building blocks and Lincoln Logs were the playroom rage? Well, twenty-first-century kids are about to get a dose of 1970s goodness, and I'm not talking about disco. Tree Blocks are hand-cut wood blocks that provide kids with solid wooden toys with which to stack, build, play, and learn. The collection includes building blocks, tree houses, dollhouses, dollhouse furniture, and algebra learning kits. The wood comes from the discarded root systems of apple, cherry, and hazelnut trees, purchased from orchards once the useful production life of the trees is over.

For future eco-engineers, Thames and Kosmos have created a series of alternative energy science kits that entertain kids while they learn about the energies of the future. Kids can learn all about hydrogen as they safely use it to power a fuel cell car with the Fuel Cell Car & Experimentation Kit, or they can harness the energy of the sun to power all sorts of vehicles, including cars, helicopters, boats, gliders, and blimps, with the Solaro Kit. Or build a model house that runs on solar and wind energy with the Power House Kit. Soon your kids will know more about the eco-solutions of the future than you do.

Clothing

BABY BEEHINDS

Babybeehinds.com.au

An Australia-based company that ships its stylish, colorful organic cotton/
hemp and bamboo fleece nappies to customers around the globe. Also
features bear hug carrying slings, skin care products by MooGoo, and
nappie accessories.

BABYSOY

Babysoyusa.com

A line of baby clothes made from soybean fiber, a sustainable textile made
from renewable natural resources that has superior warmth retention and
moisture transmission, keeping babies warm and dry. Aside from clothing,
Babysoy supplies an array of toys, nursery decor items, books, blankets, and
more.

BAMBOOSA

Bamboosa.com

Outfit your baby in bamboo clothing and accessories from Bamboosa. Cute
colors are matched by great comfort plus all the other benefits of bamboo
fiber—it's naturally antimicrobial, hypoallergenic, bacteriostatic, thermal-
regulating, and odor-free.

BLUE CANOE

Bluecanoe.com

Blue Canoe offers select high-quality organic cotton baby clothing items
that are super soft for babies' sensitive skin. The bright colors are the result
of fiber-reactive dye, which is the least toxic of dyes and Earth-friendly.

BOSSY BABY

Bossybaby.com

Started by a Florida mother upon the birth of her daughter, Bossy Baby is
a line of clothing for babies and children made from organic cotton, hemp,
and recyclable fabrics. The collection includes playwear, dressy items, and a
line of newborn clothing.

GDIAPERS

Gdiapers.com

The flushable diaper solution that helps prevent diaper rash while dodging
landfills, gDiapers are a two-part system. A flushable inner refill fits into a
pair of colorful "little g" pants. When the inner refill is soiled, simply flush
it down the toilet and replace it with a fresh one. The gDiapers lining is

biodegradable so it breaks down through normal water sewage-treatment processing.

GREMBO ORGANICS

Grembo.com
Grembo offers a line of stylish, organic cotton clothing for babies and children. Grembo Bags are an innovative, organic sleeping solution for babies. Zip your little one into the Grembo Bag and give her a pure, healthy, restful night's sleep. Various thermal weights are available for different climates and seasons.

HANNA ANDERSON

Hannaanderson.com
Hanna Anderson is a Swedish-inspired company that sells a variety of toys, accessories, and apparel made with cotton certified by the Oko-Tex Standard 100 for its low chemical content. The company offers a wide selection of clothing, from jumpers to dresses, and even Swedish moccasins for babies!

JOMAMACO

Jomamaco.com
JoMama offers fun, funky styles, including little girls' dresses of vintage materials with organic cotton linings. The company also offers cute T-shirts and bottoms. The handmade organic cotton retro tracksuit is rocking.

KATE QUINN

Katequinnorganics.com
Kate Quinn has organic fashions for babies, kids, and women that are hip, stylish, and 100 percent certified organic for a cleaner, kinder earth. Colors are earthy, and designs have a Zen vibe, with kimono-style dresses and onesies. The company also offers luxury bath and bedding items.

KEE-KA

Keekababy.com
This Brooklyn-based company offers unique Earth-friendly gifts and apparel made from 100 percent certified organic cotton and low-impact dyes. Items are fun, adorable, and one of a kind, including signature ready-to-mail brown box packaging.

LLAMAJAMA

Llamajama.com
Llamajama makes baby clothing, such as slippers and diaper covers, using all-natural wool, which is known to have amazing antibacterial properties.

Wool is naturally fire-resistant and absorbs up to 30 percent of its weight in moisture, keeping baby's skin dry.

POSITIVELY ORGANIC

Positively-organic.com
Positively Organic offers a collection of stylish baby and toddler clothes made from organic cotton in sweatshop-free environments. Available items include bodysuits, yoga pants, hats, booties, and gift baskets.

PURE BEGINNINGS

Purebeginnings.com
Pure Beginnings offers clothing, bedding, and personal care products for babies made with pure, 100 percent organically grown cotton and untreated natural wool. Available items include the pesticide-free organic Babēcology skin care product line.

SAGE CREEK NATURALS

Sagecreeknaturals.com
Sage Creek has organic cotton baby clothes, bedding, and body care products, plus baby gift baskets that include a handmade bamboo basket, signature embroidered nightgown, hat, and receiving blanket. Collections feature fun designs and patterns, such as bears, bunnies, and ladybugs, and a kimono-style line.

SCKOON

Sckoon.com
Sckoon gets your baby off to a stylish, eco-savvy start with its line of 100 percent organic cotton products. Plum Tee and Monkey are great paired together. Zen booties are the height of adorable. The Baby Underwear Blue Nightprint is an absolute charmer.

SPEESEES

Speesees.com
Speesees offers a collection of baby products made with organic cotton that is locally grown and handpicked by farmers, then spun, knit, and dyed with low-impact dyes in a sweatshop-free factory in Southern India. The collection features adorable pictures of baby animals from all over the world.

UNDER THE NILE

Underthenile.com

Children's apparel, diapers, and toys made with 100 percent certified organic Egyptian cotton are available here. Garments are pesticide-free and naturally dyed, while buttons and zippers contain organically friendly elements such as wood, shell, and nickel-free metals.

WOOLY LAMB ORGANICS

Woolylamborganics.com

Wooly Lamb Organics has trendy, Earth-friendly clothing for infants newborn to twenty-four months, in a variety of cute collections like Bear, Seashore, Animal Kingdom, and Nature Kids. Apparel is made from certified organic fabrics woven in the United States and is free of harsh chemicals.

Furniture

ARGINGTON

Argington.com

Argington makes modern green furniture for children produced with sustainable, renewable, and nontoxic materials. Trademark designs include the Fuji Toy Box, inspired by Japan's Mount Fuji, and the ultra-cool Fundy Play Table, which offers either a dry-erase or chalkboard top for extra fun play.

CELERY FURNITURE

Celeryfurniture.com

Modern yet timeless designs take form in the Lullaboo children's furniture line from Celery. Crafted from bamboo and formaldehyde-free medium density fiberboard and treated with low-VOC finishes, Celery is the stylish, healthy choice for young ones. Products like cribs, changing tables, and rocking chairs ship flat and are easily assembled without any need for tools or hardware.

DUCDUCNYC

Ducducnyc.com

The DucDuc line of contemporary children's furniture makes parents very envious. Beautiful lines and quality-constructed solid wood furniture—from sustainably managed forests—are what you get from DucDuc. Products are also treated with nontoxic finishes to foster healthy living.

IGLOOPLAY

Iglooplay.com

Iglooplay offers trendy furniture designs for children that, along with being super-fashionable, are also made from sustainable materials. The unique Tea Pods are multi-use and can serve as a stool, a side table, a bench, an ottoman, or a lounger by easily flipping the pieces into different positions.

LILIPAD STUDIO

Lilipadstudio.com

Lilipad Studio offers a line of vibrant children's furniture that is handcrafted using responsibly forested hardwood and hand-painted with nontoxic paints. The line includes tables, chairs, and step stools, which are colorful and interesting as well as completely functional.

OEUF

Oeufnyc.com

Oeuf provides clean, contemporary, European-style nursery furniture using eco-responsible materials and finishes. The signature Oeuf crib is made of a solid birch base and MDF, a wood composite made from recovered wood sources, and treated with a nontoxic, white lacquered finish. There's also a collection of stylish knitted baby apparel made from natural alpaca by a women's cooperative in Bolivia.

Q COLLECTION

Qcollection.com

Founded by Anthony Cochran and Jesse Johnson, Q Collection offers high-end, stylish design furniture and furnishings made with the purest and most environmentally friendly materials available. The Junior collection features baby furniture and bedding to help design a stylish, healthy, and eco-aware bedroom.

Bedding

COTTON MONKEY

Cottonmonkey.com

Cotton Monkey aims to create environmentally sensitive items for children. Offering designer bedding for babies with organic cotton and wool bumpers and organic cotton quilts, throw blankets, crib skirts, and fitted sheets.

COYUCHI

Coyuchiorganic.com

Coyuchi's George Baby collection offers fun, embroidered animal patterns on organic cotton crib blankets, bumper covers, shams, fitted sheets, bibs, T-shirts, and jumpsuits.

LIFEKIND

Lifekind.com

Lifekind offers organic cotton changing pads and covers, crib bumpers, crib sheets, mattress pads, and blankets. The company's organic mattresses, made of cotton, wool, and natural rubber, are also available in baby crib sizes.

NATUREPEDIC

Naturepedic.com

NaturePedic makes organic, hypoallergenic mattresses and bedding for infants featuring a natural, healthy, and nontoxic design. Mattresses are waterproof, fire-safe, and filled with natural or organic cotton.

Toys

CRISPINA FUSCHIA

Crispina.com

Crispina offers blankets, throws, pillow shams, placemats, table runners, and Ragamuffin stuffed animals made from recycled clothing. Used wool sweaters are cleaned, softened, and cut into strips to make Crispina's brightly colored Pot Holder Rugs.

HORIZON FUEL CELL TECHNOLOGIES

Horizonfuelcell.com

Horizon is the creator of a unique miniature fuel-cell car with a hydrogen refueling system, named H-racer. This tiny car, measuring sixteen by seven centimeters, can run in a straight line for more than one hundred meters, using fuel from externally produced hydrogen. The H-racer is about to spread awareness to children and adults everywhere.

KENANA KNITTERS

Kenanausa.com

Kenana offers various products made with homespun wool produced by rural Kenyan women, including toys and clothing. Each item is signed by the artisan, and the proceeds are given as income directly to the knitter.

MIYIM

www.miyim.com
Miyim has toys and infant clothing made from cotton that is organically grown and processed using only all-natural ingredients, clean and pure. Products are long-lasting and kid-safe.

PRANG CRAYONS

Prang.com
Good-bye conventional wax crayons. Hello nontoxic crayons made from soybeans. Prang soy crayons are both stronger and brighter than wax crayons.

SMENCILS

Smencils.com
Smencils are gourmet scented pencils made from recycled newspapers instead of wood. Choose from scents like cherry, cinnamon, grape, bubble gum, and orange. Each comes in a tube to keep the smell fresh.

STUPID CREATURES

Stupidcreatures.com
These stuffed-animal sock creatures are handmade from old socks, fabric remnants, buttons, and neckties, and filled with recycled polyester. Each creature is unique and sure to bring smiles to children's faces.

THAMES & KOSMOS

Thamesandkosmos.com
This specialty toy and educational company offers twenty-eight science kits on a range of topics, including alternative energy, fuel cells, and solar-power technology. The Fuel Cell Car & Experimentation Kit, the Solaro Kit, and the Power House Kit will transform your children into veritable alternate energy geniuses, and entertain them for hours too.

TREE BLOCKS

Treeblocks.com
Tree Blocks are hand-cut wood blocks that provide kids with solid wooden toys with which to stack, build, play, and learn. The collection includes building blocks, tree houses, dollhouses, dollhouse furniture, and algebra learning kits. The wood comes from the discarded root systems of apple, cherry, and hazelnut trees purchased from orchards once the useful production life of the trees is over.

Retailers

BETTER FOR BABIES

Betterforbabies.com

Better for Babies offers a wide selection of organic baby accessories, including Didymos and Ellaroo baby slings, specially woven for holding your baby close, secure, and hands-free. The Little Beetle hemp and organic cotton fitted diapers are innovatively designed for customizable absorbency based on your baby's needs.

BRANCH

Branchhome.com

If the MoMA Store carried only sustainably designed products, it would be Branch. Superbly designed modern and contemporary products demonstrate how fine attention to detail and aesthetics can easily align with environmental awareness. Branch offers furnishings for nearly the entire home, as well as outstanding gifts for men, women, and children.

THE CLEAN BEDROOM

Thecleanbedroom.com

Superior bedding options for children of all ages can be found here. Supplying natural, organic, and chemical-free mattresses for use in cribs and beds, the company also offers organic blankets, linens, and room purifiers.

GREEN NEST

Greennest.com

Green Nest has a wide selection of products for healthier homes, including air purifiers, water filtration items, nontoxic cleaning and home improvement supplies, and educational items. The company also presents a collection of organic baby products, such as clothing, bedding, bottles, and diapers.

GREENLOOP

Thegreenloop.com

Greenloop offers stylish baby products from various brands, including Hug, Lauren Celeste, and the NUI Organics organic merino wool collection. The company carries brands that make use of eco-friendly practices such as utilizing sustainable materials, energy-efficient production, and organic farming.

HANNA'S DREAM

Hannasdream.com

A family-owned and -operated company started in order to provide organic, sustainable clothing that is fashionable and eco-friendly, Hanna's Dream offers a small selection of gently used items, in addition to its extensive collection of new items, including baby apparel and toys.

HIP & ZEN

Hipandzen.com

Hip & Zen presents organic clothing, bibs, and yoga pants for children sizes 0–3 months to 3T, with an eclectic sense of style. The company is a great online retailer for all your organic, recycled, vegan, and generally Earth-friendly whims, with items for babies, women, men, and around the home.

MOMMY AND KAI NATURALS

Mommyandkainaturals.com

Organic products from a number of green designers, including Earth Creations, Kate Quinn Organics, and Under the Nile, are available here. Baby leg warmers, organic bedding, organic stuffed plush toys, and a complete line of apparel are among items that you can find on this site. A line of clothing knitted with alpaca yarn is also available.

THE NATURAL STORE

Thenaturalstore.co.uk

Based in the U.K., the Natural Store carries organic baby products from eco-friendly brands worldwide. Available are hemp, cotton, and bamboo woven nappies, bath items and baby balms, furniture, 100 percent certified organic cotton clothing, sustainable school supplies, and much more. The store ships to the U.S.

PUR BÉBÉ

Purbebe.com

Pur Bébé is an eco-friendly baby boutique with a wide selection of clothes for children ages zero to twenty-four months, as well as a variety of baby products that are Earth-friendly. Products are labeled with green features, including items that are made with 100 percent organic cotton and items containing natural or nontoxic ingredients or made with recycled materials.

SAGE BABY

Sagebabynyc.com

Sage Baby offers numerous organic products, including everything from clothing, bed, and bath items to toys, gift sets, and stationery. Products are superior and stylish in addition to being organic and nontoxic.

YIRO

Yirostores.com

An upscale, eco-aware baby and children's boutique located in the Georgetown neighborhood of Washington, DC, Yiro carries clothing, toys, and gifts made from natural and organic materials.

Skin Care

BABĒCOLOGY

Babecology.com

The Babēcology collection includes shampoo, body wash, baby oil, and balms for infants, made with organic plant and fruit extracts. Free of artificial dyes, fragrances, or harsh synthetics, the Babēcology line is based on twenty-eight years of botanical skin care experience, to bring the safest, most natural products to your baby.

Information/Education

THE COMPLETE ORGANIC PREGNANCY

Written by Alexandra Zissou and Deidre Dolan, this book provides step-by-step instruction on how to identify and avoid dangerous chemicals before, during, and after pregnancy, to protect children. It also contains a collection of writings from well-known authors, as well as recipes from organic chefs.

OEKO-TEX

Oeko-tex.com

Issued by an organization dedicated to establishing ecological standards for textiles, the Oeko-Tex label identifies products that have been evaluated and screened for the presence of harmful substances prior to contact with consumers.

17

TECHNOLOGICAL
ADVANCEMENT

Electronics
That Simplify

If Mother Nature were a chief technology officer—some might argue that she is *the* chief technology officer—she would make sure that every single employee on the planet owned a smartphone. The Treo, the Motorola Q, and the T-Mo Dash are just a few of the electronic devices that bring the digital convergence revolution to your fingertips and reduce your use of items like paper notepads, photo prints, CDs and DVDs, and CD and DVD cases. Smartphones bring the features of an MP3 player, digital camera, digital video recorder, GPS navigation device, and laptop computer together in a single device that fits in the palm of your hand. Of course, you can use them to make phone calls too. The all-in-one design of a smartphone eliminates the need to own multiple electronic devices, which means fewer products have to be produced to deliver the same number of features and benefits. Purchasing fewer products without sacrificing productivity or pleasure is an essential tenet of lazy environmentalism, which holds that you can have your gear and your planet too.

At home you can reap the lifestyle and environmental benefits of digital convergence through the emergence of home media centers—super-smart all-in-one home computers that combine the TV, TiVo, and stereo system with your home computer so you can watch television and videos, record your favorite television shows, listen to music, surf the Internet, chat with friends, and send email while preparing an Excel spreadsheet for tomorrow's presentation. PC manufacturers like HP, Sony, and Dell all offer home media centers. So now you can cut down on clutter, merge your home electronics into a single device with just one remote control, and also give a nod to the planet. Less stuff to buy not only means less stuff to produce, but it also means less stuff to recycle.

While digital convergence enables you to do more with less, you can also look for electronic devices that use a smaller amount of energy. The easiest way to find energy-efficient electronics— from televisions to computers—is to consult the Energy Star website at Energystar.gov. Energy Star is a joint program of the U.S. Environmental Protection Agency and the U.S. Department of Energy that bestows the Energy Star label on products that meet its energy-efficiency performance guidelines. Thousands of products can currently be found through the website. Choosing Energy Star–rated products can reduce your energy bill and greenhouse gas emissions by up to 30 percent. From Sony to Samsung, most major manufacturers make high-performance products that qualify.

In the grand scheme of energy consumption, electronic devices are tiny offenders when compared to the energy consumption of your home heating and cooling systems, as well as lighting and refrigeration. Seeking out the Energy Star label is an easy way to ensure that your electronic devices are part of the broader eco-solution. The exception to this rule, however, is flat-screen TVs. Here, in addition to Energy Star, you'll want to pay particular attention to the model you choose, because flat-screen TVs are major energy guzzlers. Sharp has staked a claim to the most energy-efficient flat-screen LCD TV with its Aquos line, and in flat-screen plasma TVs Panasonic is making energy-efficient strides. Also be on the lookout for next-generation low-power flat-panel TVs coming soon from companies like Samsung, Pioneer, and Hitachi.

Getting the gear is one thing. Getting rid of it is another. Properly disposing of outdated electronics products is a challenging environmental task. While electronic devices enhance your lifestyle, they do come with an environmental price tag. Gadgets are host to a variety of toxic chemicals that are best left inside the machine, where their environmental harm is mitigated. But most discarded electronics end up in landfills, where the toxins inside them can eventually seep into the air, soil, and groundwater. Fortunately, lead is being phased out of most machines. However, mercury, cadmium, and other toxic elements are still in use.

Enter RipMobile, a company that believes recycling your cell phones, PDAs, BlackBerries, and pagers ought to be as simple as a few mouse clicks on the computer. A visit to Ripmobile.com reveals drop-down menus that simplify the process of locating and selecting your product model. RipMobile then calculates the residual value of your item and shows you how much it's willing to pay you in exchange for it. For example, as of this writing a Motorola RAZR V3m from Verizon could be recycled for $75. The Motorola Q smartphone could be recycled for $125. Older models have value too. Once you agree to the terms, RipMobile provides you with a free shipping label to mail your phone to their facility. When it arrives, the RipMobile team inspects the phone to verify that it's still in proper working condition. Upon confirmation, RipMobile either pays you cash via Paypal or issues you an electronic gift certificate for the value of your phone, which can be redeemed through the stores of its vendor partners, which include companies such as Circuit City and Starbucks. Your phone remains in good use—and out of the landfill—because RipMobile is able to identify buyers in developing countries where the telecommunication infrastructure is lacking, and cell phones provide the only effective way to communicate. RipMobile also works with disaster relief organizations that need cell phones for agents in the field.

If the product model you want to recycle no longer works, RipMobile won't pay you for it, but the company will still send you a free shipping label and see to it that it is recycled to the greatest extent possible. According to founder and CEO Seth Heine, "The whole notion is that you should be able to do something that's good for the planet and do it very quickly without having to leave your home. All you need is access to a mailbox." Heine also runs CollectiveGood, a sister company to RipMobile that enables consumers to donate the value of their phones to charity. Phones can be sent back to the company via Collectivegood.com or dropped off at CollectiveGood pickup locations available at more than seventeen hundred participating Staples stores.

Cell phones aren't the only electronics that can have a second life. eBay's Rethink trade-in center enables you to send in electronic devices like old desktop and laptop computers, PC servers, digital cameras, Apple Ipods, and PDAs and quickly receive payment from eBay in return for your product based on its residual value. So if the prospect of auctioning your electronics on eBay is too time consuming or technologically daunting, just visit the website for eBay's trade-in center at Ebay.eztradein.com and follow the easy steps to receive guaranteed payment for your products provided that they are still in reasonable working condition. By compensating you for the electronics you no longer want, eBay's trade-in program shifts the recycling paradigm away from something that we feel morally compelled to do and toward something that is clearly in our enlightened self-interest to do. It's the easy recycling solution that pays.

Electronics manufacturers are beginning to recognize the value of designing products that can be easily recycled. Companies like Dell, Apple, Lenovo, Gateway, Sony, and Hewlett-Packard (HP) have implemented programs to encourage customers to return products to them for recycling at the end of their useful life. Sony and HP will even offer you the trade-in value of your product, which can be redeemed when upgrading to new models.

As a manufacturer of computers, printers, and peripherals, HP also operates several of its own recycling facilities, which financially motivates the company to make recovery and recycling as quick, easy, and inexpensive as possible. HP initiatives include transitioning to modular designs that enable individual product components to be easily removed, upgraded, or replaced as necessary. HP is also moving toward snap-in product components and away from glues and adhesives, to make it easier to remove components when recycling. And to simplify the overall recovery and recycling process, HP is reducing the number and types of materials it uses to make its products.

In 2006, the Institute for Scrap Recycling Industries (ISRI) awarded HP the first ever Design for Recycling Award. According to ISRI president Robin Wiener, "We chose HP because of its documented efforts to reduce the use of hazardous substances, to simplify component design, and to build computers and printing products for easy disassembly and recycling." In 2005, HP recycled 140 million pounds of electronic products and supplies. As we move toward a cleaner future, supporting companies that reduce their use of hazardous chemicals and pursue innovative recycling strategies is a very logical choice.

Electronics Products

DELL MEDIA CENTER
Dell.com
Dell's super-sleek home media center computers do double duty as televisions, personal video recorders, and stereos. Using the wireless keyboard, type emails and documents on one-half of the screen while you watch your favorite movie on the other half. It's one device that does it all.

HP MEDIA CENTER PC
Hp.com
Hewlett-Packard's home media center computers simplify your home electronics needs. Combining the functionality of the television, TiVo, stereo, and DVD player with your home computer, HP's Media Center PCs enable you to enjoy all your entertainment in one simplified home electronics device.

HYBRIO
Hybriousa.com
Power your gadgets with rechargeable batteries that eliminate the need to continually purchase and dispose of standard alkaline batteries. Hybrio's rechargeable Nickel-Metal Hydride (Ni-MH) batteries last up to four times longer than standard alkaline batteries with each charge and can be recharged up to 500 times. Perfect for cameras, MP3 players, and the like.

MOTOROLA Q
Motorola.com
The Motorola Q delivers smartphone productivity on one of the slimmest designs ever made. The keyboard is user-friendly for typing emails, sending text messages, or editing word documents. The phone is also compatible with virtually all formats for audio, images, and video, making it a very handy digital convergence leader.

PANASONIC PLASMA TV

Panasonic.com

Panasonic is the first company in the world to eliminate the use of lead in its plasma display panels for TVs. Panasonic's flat-screen plasma TVs are also industry leaders in reducing energy while delivering a high-quality HDTV viewing experience.

SHARP AQUOS

Sharpausa.com

The Sharp Aquos line of LCD flat-screen televisions delivers great color quality and clarity and top-ranked energy efficiency. The HDTV-compatible televisions are also manufactured in a production plant that draws approximately one-third of its power from solar energy and an onsite co-generation system, and recycles all manufacturing wastewater using a state-of-the-art water purification process.

SONY DIGITAL LIVING SYSTEM

Sonystyle.com

Sony's integrated home media center is a computer that's also a television and even a jukebox with the integrated two-hundred-disc CD changer. The included remote control lets you easily manage all of your entertainment.

SONY READER

Sonystyle.com

Sony's lightweight, handheld digital e-book reader is a great way to take hundreds of books with you on the go. The digital reading experience is very enjoyable thanks to numerous technological advances that enable the e-book to closely mimic the experience of reading print on paper.

T-MOBILE DASH

T-mobile.com

The T-Mobile Dash bundles everything you need to stay productive on the go into a small, beautifully designed package. Phone quality is great and is complemented by the ability to send email, watch videos, snap photos, and listen to music. Almost anything you do on your computer can be accomplished on this handheld device.

THE TREO

Palm.com

The Treo series of smartphones by Palm are designed with integrated features for greater productivity. In addition to making phone calls, you can surf the web at broadbandlike speeds, send emails, listen to MP3s, snap pictures, watch videos, and even create office documents.

Electronics Recycling

CALL2RECYCLE

Call2recycle.org

Call2recycle makes it easy to recycle the rechargeable batteries found in your cordless and cell phones, camcorders, cordless power tools, laptop computers, digital cameras, and two-way radios. Instead of throwing them away, drop them off at more than thirty thousand locations available throughout the United States, at retail stores like Best Buy, Office Depot, RadioShack, Sears, Staples, and Target.

EBAY RETHINK

Ebay.eztradein.com

eBay's Rethink trade-in center enables you to send in electronic devices like old desktop and laptop computers, PC servers, digital cameras, Apple Ipods, and PDAs and quickly receive payment from eBay in return for your product based on its residual value. It's the easy recycling solution that pays.

COLLECTIVEGOOD

Collectivegood.org

CollectiveGood makes it easy to recycle your cell phone, PDA, BlackBerry, or pager and donate the proceeds to the charitable cause of your choosing. Visit Collectivegood.com to be guided through the simple step-by-step process.

RIPMOBILE

Ripmobile.com

RipMobile makes recycling your cell phone, PDA, BlackBerry, or pager easy, convenient, and profitable. Visit Ripmobile.com, select your device model, and print out the free-shipping label. Once RipMobile receives the phone and verifies its working condition, you get paid. Nonworking devices can be recycled free of charge.

Cool and Unique

THE $100 LAPTOP

Laptop.org

Affordable, hand-powered computers are coming to schools throughout the developing world thanks to the techno-visionaries at MIT who formed the One Laptop Per Child nonprofit organization. The $100 (or thereabouts) laptops —dubbed the XO computer—provide a quality computing experience in a system that requires 90 percent less energy than standard computers.

Information/Education

CNET

CNET.com

CNET provides electronics product reviews, technological news, and a lively community that weighs in on the performance of all the latest gadgets. It's a great place to research products that let you take advantage of digital convergence.

ENERGY STAR

Energystar.gov

Energy Star is a program administered jointly by the EPA and the U.S. Department of Energy to promote greater energy efficiency. Visit Energystar.gov to quickly locate the most energy-efficient home electronics like televisions, computers, stereos, fax machines, and printers. You can also scan for energy-efficient home appliances, lighting, heating and cooling systems, and building products.

ENGADGET

Engadget.com

To stay current on the latest electronics and electronics trends throughout the world, turn to Engadget.com. Peter Rojas and crew scour the globe for news and tidbits to keep a readership of more than 5 million people per month updated in real time on the fast-moving trends in digital convergence.

METAEFFICIENT

Metaefficient.com

Eco-gadget and technology lovers will have a field day reading this blog that covers products that maximize efficiency (usually energy efficiency). Whether it's hot water systems, LED lighting, or MP3 players, Metaefficient tracks products that offer elegant solutions for minimizing resource consumption.

WIRED MAGAZINE

Wired.com

New technologies are being created to address eco-challenges, and *Wired* magazine is often a great place to read about them. Look for insightful coverage and analysis of the unprecedented eco-innovation taking place in electronics, transportation, building, and urban planning.

18

Business and Office

You don't have to work in the offices of the Sierra Club or the World Resources Institute to make your workstation a bastion of planet-saving possibilities. Creating an eco-aware office comes down to a few simple principles that are easy to implement. For starters, reduce your energy consumption by opting for energy-efficient office machines like computers, printers, copiers, and fax machines. You don't have to crawl behind your computer to determine how energy-efficient it is. And you don't have to take apart your photocopier and examine its internal operations. You just have to look for the Energy Star label. All energy-efficient products are noted as such through this program administered by the Environmental Protection Agency in conjunction with the Department of Energy. Every major electronics company, from Sony to HP, makes Energy Star–rated products that you probably already use. It's that easy.

Next, start using products that are made with recycled materials. These products include printer and copy paper, envelopes, notepads, Post-it notes, calendars, manila folders, clipboards, storage boxes, and garbage cans. You can even find scissors made with recycled plastic handles. Where are you going to find such a bounty of recycled office supplies? Someplace really familiar: Staples has a private-label line of recycled-content multipurpose paper and also offers recycled-content paper from familiar name brands like Boise Cascade and Hammerhill. A more complete Staples eco-shopping list looks like this:

- ♻ Multiuse and copy paper—between 30 and 100 percent recycled content
- ♻ Yellow lined notepads—100 percent recycled content
- ♻ White lined writing pads—100 percent recycled content
- ♻ Drafting paper—100 percent recycled content
- ♻ Post-it notes—100 percent recycled content
- ♻ Five-subject wirebound notebooks—50 percent recycled content
- ♻ Airmail envelopes—100 percent recycled content
- ♻ White envelopes—100 percent recycled content
- ♻ Desk calendars—100 percent recycled content
- ♻ Wall calendars—100 percent recycled content
- ♻ Monthly planners—100 percent recycled content with print using soy-based inks
- ♻ Manila file folders—100 percent recycled content
- ♻ File jackets—100 percent recycled content
- ♻ Hanging file folders—100 percent recycled content
- ♻ Magazine file storage bins—65 percent recycled content
- ♻ Cardboard storage boxes—100 percent recycled content
- ♻ Shipping peanuts—100 percent recycled content
- ♻ Plastic clipboards—100 percent recycled content
- ♻ Stainless steel scissors—plastic handles of 70 percent recycled content
- ♻ Steel garbage bins—25 percent recycled content

Office Depot offers a similar selection of recycled office products. At both stores you'll also find garbage bags—kitchen and heavy-duty—made of 100 percent recycled content, as well as recycled-paper towels and napkins. Finding paper products made of recycled materials is getting so much easier—a victory for lazy environmentalists. Making paper from recycled materials requires 60 percent less energy than making paper from virgin tree stock, and since the average office worker uses the paper equivalent of an entire tree every year, finding ways to substitute recycled materials for virgin tree stock can save a whole lot of forest. We need trees because they help fight global warming by feeding on climate-changing carbon dioxide gas and storing it in their extensive root systems beneath the ground. It's a good idea to keep as many trees around as possible.

To fill in the gap where larger stores like Staples and Office Depot are lacking, turn to specialized eco-office supply companies. Thegreenoffice.com can fill your recycled paper demands and also help with heavier eco-needs like file and storage cabinets. Opting for steel is a good choice because it is usually made at least in part from other recycled steel. Thegreenoffice.com features Office Impression's line of heavy-duty steel storage cabinets constructed with 50 percent recycled content. The cabinets can be as tall as six feet and are equipped with a single-point locking mechanism for security. Thegreenoffice.com also offers steel file cabinets made by Hon, a company that matches strong attention to design detail with commitment to a cleaner planet. Hon uses at least 25 percent recycled steel in its products and eliminates all VOCs from its cabinet paint.

As for eco-aware desks, you can remove a door from its hinges and place it atop two sawhorses, or you can opt for something more sleek and functional. Legare Furniture makes sturdy, easy-to-assemble FSC-certified sustainable wood desks and shelving units. The jigsaw-like components slide together in minutes and require absolutely no hardware or tools to assemble. ModernLink offers a series of expansive desks, made from fast-growing, rapidly renewable bamboo, that are equipped with integrated pockets and drawers to keep you fully organized. Offi offers its curvaceous Wave Desk made from material-efficient bent-plywood—a process that is nine times more efficient than conventional furniture making. For a top-of-the-line selection, check out the Kidney Shaped Desk handcrafted out of FSC-certified sustainable wood by John Wiggers.

The desk features pencil trays made of sassafras and a small lidded box made of hawthorn—woods that possess natural aromatherapy qualities. The curvilinear shape and dimensions of the Kidney Shaped Desk are proportioned to be consistent with holistic design principles of feng shui and the vastu shastra of the ancient Vedic tradition in India. Wiggers's thoughtful furniture craftsmanship would perhaps be more aptly labeled as a "functional work of art."

It's in eco-aware office chairs that the art of function is most visibly on display. Check out J. Persing's Cricket Chair, an ergonomic wonder that utilizes rolls of rubber—made from recycled automobile tires—beneath the chair seat and behind the chair back to create a sleek, minimalist design that conforms and responds to your body's movements. Herman Miller's Aeron Chair is probably the most eco-advanced office chair known to mankind. Made largely of recycled materials and designed for long life and recyclability, the chair combines state-of-the-art ergonomics with an entirely unique aesthetic that is at once modern and timeless. The Steelcase Think Chair is also an award-winning eco-wonder that intuitively adjusts itself to maximize your support and comfort. It's composed of at least 44 percent recycled content, is up to 99 percent recyclable by weight, and can be disassembled for total recycling in about five minutes with common hand tools. The Think Chair is Greenguard-certified, which guarantees toxin-free material choices that promote superior indoor air quality.

When lighting your eco-conscious office, it may be time to opt for next-generation LED (light-emitting diode) lamps. LED lightbulbs are like compact fluorescent bulbs on steroids. Comparing them with incandescent lightbulbs is like comparing Michael Jordan's game with the moves of the leading scorer on your eighth-grade basketball team. Good luck. LED bulbs last about sixty times longer than standard incandescent lightbulbs and use about thirty times less energy, which makes them ideal for conserving energy. They're best used for directional lighting—which is perfect for desks. C.Crane offers LED lightbulbs with Edison bases—the same as on incandescent bulbs—that can be screwed into any standard lamp. Design companies have begun introducing high-design

LED lamps. The Solo desk lamp by Mindspring is a white gloss or gray, minimalist design that looks great next to your iPod. Gaiam's Gooseneck LED lamp has an adjustable, flexible neck that helps to achieve the ideal light beam angle. The Leaf LED Light designed by Yves Behair for Herman Miller has dazzled design fans since its debut in 2006. And Koncept offers a range of sleek, adjustable LED lamps that are perfect for bedrooms or offices. In 2006, the Z-Bar LED Desk Lamp received the prestigious "best in category" award by *I.D.* magazine. The Koncept line also features one of the first LED floor lamps.

Office Supplies

THE GREEN OFFICE
Thegreenoffice.com
A one-stop shop for eco-office needs, the Green Office offers eco-aware office supplies, electronics, furniture, janitorial products, and products for the break room like biodegradable plates made from sugarcane. Products are prescreened and all eco-credentials are clearly marked.

OFFICE DEPOT
Officedepot.com
You'll find hundreds of office supplies made from recycled materials through Office Depot's website. Type "recycled" into the search box to see the entire inventory of green office products.

STAPLES
Staples.com
Staples has a private-label line of recycled-content multipurpose paper and also offers recycled-content paper from familiar name brands like Boise Cascade and Hammerhill. Many other office products made from recycled content can be found by visiting the website and typing "recycled" into the search box.

Furniture

HERMAN MILLER
Hermanmiller.com

Furniture industry leader Herman Miller is known for its design, quality, and eco-integrity. The Aeron Chair is made largely of recycled materials and designed for long life and recyclability. The chair combines state-of-the-art ergonomics with an entirely unique aesthetic that is at once modern and timeless. The Leaf Light designed by Yves Behair is a forward-thinking design that utilizes LED bulbs for superior energy efficiency.

J. PERSING
Jpersing.com

J. Persing offers eco-modern furniture, with many of the pieces designed by eco-visionary Peter Danko. The Cricket Chair is an ergonomic wonder that utilizes rolls of rubber—made from recycled automobile tires—beneath the chair seat and behind the chair back to create a sleek, minimalist design that conforms and responds to your body's movements.

LEGARE FURNITUE
Legarefurniture.com

Legare Furniture brings FSC-certified wood furniture to the home office with its innovative furniture that requires no screws or glues to assemble. The modular, easily expandable furniture collection includes desks, bookcases, and file carts. Modular media centers are also available and are great for supporting flat-screen LCD or plasma televisions.

MIO CULTURE
Mioculture.com

Mio Culture creates eco-friendly lighting, wallpaper, flooring, seating, and accessories with a whimsical touch. The Grid Organizer is a wall-mountable organizer made from recycled felt. The poster-size design is easy to install.

MODERNLINK
Modernlink.com

Modernlink offers sleek, contemporary bamboo furniture that places equal emphasis on aesthetics and functionality. Their credenzas, bookshelves, dressers, beds, and desks are as enjoyable to gaze upon as they are to use.

OFFI
Offi.com

Offi offers functional, modern designs that easily fit our lifestyles. The Wave Desk is made from material-efficient bent-ply wood—a process nine times more efficient than conventional furniture making—and treated with nontoxic water-based finishes.

STEELCASE
Steelcase.com
Steelcase designs and manufactures office furniture for superior performance. The Think Chair intuitively adjusts itself to maximize your support and comfort. It's composed of at least 44 percent recycled content, is up to 99 percent recyclable by weight, and can be disassembled for total recycling in about five minutes with common hand tools. Like all Steelcase seating, the Think Chair is Greenguard indoor air quality certified.

WIGGERS FURNITURE
Wiggersfurniture.com
John Wiggers is a studio furniture maker who specializes in contemporary and art deco–inspired designs. The Kidney Shaped Desk is handcrafted out of FSC-certified wood and features pencil trays made of sassafras and a small lidded box made of hawthorn—both woods that possess natural aromatherapy qualities.

Lighting

C. CRANE
Ccrane.com
For thirty years C. Crane has been providing consumers with quality electronics and home products. Find here a wide selection of eco-advanced LED lightbulbs that will help create an energy-efficient home.

KONCEPT
Konceptech.com
Koncept offers a range of sleek, adjustable LED lamps that are perfect for bedrooms or offices. In 2006, the Z-Bar LED Desk Lamp received the prestigious "best in category" award by *I.D.* magazine. The Koncept line also features one of the first LED floor lamps.

MINDSPRING
Mindspring-lighting.com
The Solo desk lamp by Mindspring is a minimalist design that packs a lot of technology to create an LED desk lamp that is both heat- and energy-efficient. Taiwan-based Mindspring is a leader in LED technology. The Solo is the first in a series of LED lights that the company is planning.

Cool and Unique

ATLANTIC INKJET
Atlanticinkjet.com
Altantic Inkjet carries recycled printer ink cartridges for all major printer brands. The recycled cartridges work as well as new cartridges, but they cost a lot less.

GEAMI
Geami.com
Geami is the eco-aware office shipping solution that makes shipping peanuts obsolete. Kraft paper is die-cut with tiny slit patterns. When flat, it looks just like regular paper. But pull it so it stretches and the perforations force the paper to expand into a honeycomb, giving it three-dimensional structure. Wrap the expanded paper around your items for protection, and they'll be sure to arrive undamaged. The Kraft paper is recyclable and completely biodegradable.

Information/Education

CRADLE TO CRADLE
Mbdc.com/certified.html
Cradle to Cradle is a certification awarded to eco-intelligent products that use environmentally safe and healthy materials, are designed for a continuous life cycle, incorporate the use of renewable energy in manufacturing as well as energy and water efficiency, and also consider social responsibility. The certification program was created and is managed by MBDC, the design firm of noted sustainable architect William McDonough and chemist Michael Braungart, and is dedicated to revolutionizing product design.

ENERGY STAR
Energystar.gov
Energy Star is a program administered jointly by the EPA and the U.S. Department of Energy to promote greater energy efficiency. Visit Energystar.gov to quickly locate the most energy-efficient home electronics, like televisions, computers, stereos, fax machines, and printers. You can also scan for energy-efficient home appliances, lighting, heating, and cooling systems, and building products.

FOREST STEWARDSHIP COUNCIL (FSC)
FSC.org
The FSC is an international network that promotes responsible management of the world's forests. An easy way to ensure that forestry products (including paper) come from responsibly managed forests is to check for the FSC certification label when purchasing.

GREEN SEAL
Greenseal.org
Green Seal is a nonprofit organization that oversees the Green Seal science-based environmental certification program. Certification is awarded to products and services that meet Green Seal's rigorous testing standards. Purchasing Green Seal–certified products is an easy way to make eco-aware purchasing decisions.

19

IT'S YOUR
MONEY,
USE IT
WISELY

Investing

Many savvy investors believe that the biggest financial returns to be realized in the twenty-first century will come from investing in companies that are building a green future. Even as you read this, the pursuit of profits is merging with the pursuit of a cleaner, healthier planet as institutional investors, venture capitalists, and private individuals around the globe allocate billions of dollars toward next-generation green companies. This includes a diverse range of businesses working on a wide spectrum of eco-challenges, from clean energy, water, and transportation to greater material and energy efficiency. The investment community refers to these companies with terms like cleantech, greentech, renewable energy, alternative energy, and sustainable business. They essentially mean the same thing—companies that are pursuing the same goal of a safer and cleaner planet. As eco-oriented companies list publicly on stock exchanges around the globe, investors can choose to align the pursuit of profits with the pursuit of a clean planet—a lazy environmentalist win-win.

A promising way for investors to get in on the action is through mutual funds that specifically target green sectors. The New Alternatives Fund (ticker: NALFX) is a mutual fund that invests in companies that are creating a positive impact on the environment. The oldest green-focused mutual fund in existence, New Alternatives was established in 1982 and seeks investments in companies focused on renewable energies like wind, solar, hydro, ocean, geothermal, and biomass. The fund also considers investments in fuel-cell and hydrogen technology companies as well as companies developing battery storage capabilities that are compatible with these new alternative energy sources. Other investment areas cover recycling, natural foods, transportation, clean water, clean air, and natural gas. Though the fund provides investors with exposure to the diverse range of companies that comprise the green sector, it openly skews toward green energy companies, where the number of public companies is growing quickly. Just a few years ago there were about thirty publicly traded renewable energy companies in the entire world. Now there are more than four hundred, and the pace shows no sign of slowing.

Which led to the 2006 introduction of the Guinness Atkinson Funds Alternative Energy Fund (ticker: GAAEX), created to capitalize on new global investment opportunities in renewable energy. The Alternative Energy Fund is a pure play that offers investors a way to invest in the global renewable energy industry through companies specifically focused on renewable energy production, energy efficiency, and energy storage and distribution.

Guinness Atkinson Funds has been investing in emerging markets for years and was one of the first companies to create mutual funds focused on China for individual investors who wanted a way to tap the country's rapid economic growth. The firm's experience with high-growth, and correspondingly high-risk, emerging global markets provides it with a seasoned lens through which to evaluate investments in renewable energy companies that are still in their early stages. And the reach is impressive. While the bulk of investments are in firms operating in industrialized countries, fund managers scour the globe for investment opportunities. Says financial manager Ed Guinness, "We look at firms in Malaysia making biodiesel from palm oil. In China we came across a company that uses recycled cooking oil from restaurants to make biodiesel. These are real businessmen with business savvy developing viable and competitive businesses."

For a green fund with a proven track record, check out the Winslow Green Growth Fund (ticker: WGGFX), which invests in small- and medium-size companies. Managed by Winslow Management Company, the diversified fund targets companies in the green energy, healthy living, health care, medical, technology,

Internet and software, financial, and communications sectors. It includes companies that are actively introducing eco-aware solutions to the marketplace as well as companies that are environmentally benign—they don't harm the environment, but they don't necessarily improve it. The Green Growth Fund stacks up well not only against its green competition but also against the entire mutual fund industry. In 2006, *Barron's* ranked Jack Robinson, the Green Growth Fund manager, as the number one aggressive growth fund manager in the U.S. and the number nine equity mutual fund manager overall. Winslow Management has also recently partnered with Europe-based Jupiter Investment Management to launch the Jupiter Green Investment Trust (ticker: JGC), the first cross-continental mutual fund collaboration to invest in a global portfolio of green companies. The fund selects companies that fall into six categories: clean energy, green transport, sustainable living, waste management, water management, and environmental services.

For investors who prefer index funds to actively managed funds, green options are also available. The Cleantech Index (ticker: CTIUS), launched in 2006, provides coverage of a wide range of public companies, including those focused on clean energy, water, and air, as well as transportation, recycling, agriculture, and nutrition.

The Wilderhill family of green benchmark indexes provides several interesting vehicles for investing in the environment. The Clean Energy Index tracks companies that work to further renewable energy and prevent pollution. The Progressive Energy Index tracks companies that develop ways to reduce pollution from fossil fuels. The New Energy Global Innovation Index focuses on clean energy companies based outside the United States. While the three indexes cannot be invested in directly, a company called Powershares offers index-tracking funds for both the Clean Energy Index (ticker: PBW) and the Progressive Energy Index (PUW). Check Wildershares.com for developments on an index-tracking fund for the New Energy Global Innovation Index.

The options presented so far will take you to the cutting edge of green investment and offer you plenty of access to upstart green technology and energy companies. Should you want to allocate funds toward global companies that are true leaders in their commitment to environmental responsibility through their own operations, then consider Portfolio 21, a mutual fund that invests in those companies that are designing superior ecological products, developing efficient production methods, and using renewable energy. Many of the companies in Portfolio 21 are household names like Dell, Hewlett-Packard, Whole Foods, Nokia, and Sony. These companies are linked by a commitment to consistently green their business practices, which puts them at the head of the pack in their respective industries. For companies that need encouragement to do better, Progressive Investment Management, the firm that manages Portfolio 21, will engage its portfolio companies on green initiatives through shareholder activism and advocacy. This follows the understanding that one of the most effective ways of influencing a company's environmental choices is through owning its stock and participating as an owner.

Staying on top of the rapidly evolving green investment landscape is no small task. Tracking new technologies can be a full-time job (of course, for professional analysts it actually is). Sustainablebusiness.com is a terrific resource for investors seeking to learn more about the companies and technologies at the center of the green investing buzz. The website tracks all publicly traded green stocks so investors can easily monitor daily fluctuations across the entire sector from one location. Founder Rona Fried has been tracking green industry developments for nearly twenty years. Fried's monthly newsletter, the *Progressive Investor*, gives you the inside skinny on the eco-investing landscape, covering green trends, companies, and investment opportunities. The *Progressive Investor* relies upon Fried's keen insights and also features interviews with top green analysts at leading investment management firms around the country. It provides performance updates on green stocks and discusses which ones are in buying position. It also addresses tough issues like the eco-merits of investing in companies like General Electric, a key player in the wind industry but also a defense contractor, begging the pertinent question "How green is enough?" The *Progressive Investor* offers insightful guidance to enable you to reach your own informed conclusions.

Green Mutual and Index Funds

ALTERNATIVE ENERGY FUND
Gafunds.com
The Alternative Energy Fund is managed by Guinness Atkinson Funds and offers investors a way to invest in the global renewable energy industry through companies specifically focused on renewable energy production, energy efficiency, and energy storage and distribution.

CLEANTECH INDEX FUND
Cleantechindex.com
This index fund launched in 2006 and provides coverage of a wide range of public companies, including those focused on clean energy, water, and air, as well as transportation, recycling, agriculture, and nutrition.

JUPITER GREEN INVESTMENT TRUST
Jupiteronline.co.uk
Jupiter Investment Management, in partnership with Winslow Management, created this fund to invest in a global portfolio of green companies. The fund selects companies that fall into six categories: clean energy, green transport, sustainable living, waste management, water management, and environmental services.

NEW ALTERNATIVES FUND
Newalternativesfund.com
The oldest green-focused mutual fund in existence, New Alternatives emphasizes investments in renewable energies like wind, solar, hydro, ocean, geothermal, and biomass. The fund also considers investments in fuel-cell and hydrogen technology, and other areas cover recycling, natural foods, transportation, clean water, clean air, and natural gas.

PORTFOLIO 21
Portfolio21.com
This mutual fund invests in companies that are designing superior ecological products, developing efficient production methods, and using renewable energy. Portfolio 21 companies include household names like Dell, Hewlett-Packard, Whole Foods, Nokia, and Sony. These companies are considered leaders of their respective industries in terms of commitment to green business practices.

WILDERSHARES

Wildershares.com

Widershares offers a family of indexes to track the green sector. The Clean Energy Index tracks companies that work to further renewable energy and prevent pollution. The Progressive Energy Index tracks companies that develop ways to reduce pollution from fossil fuels. The New Energy Global Innovation Index focuses on clean energy companies based outside the United States. Mutual fund investments that mirror the composition of the Clean Energy Index and the Progressive Energy Index are available through Powershares.com.

WINSLOW GREEN GROWTH FUND

Winslowgreen.com

This mutual fund invests in small- and medium-size companies in the green energy, healthy living, health care, medical, technology, Internet and software, financial, and communications sectors. In 2006, *Barron's* ranked Jack Robinson, fund manager, as the number one aggressive growth fund manager in the U.S. and the number nine equity mutual fund manager overall.

Information/Education

ALT ENERGY STOCKS

altenergystocks.com

A comprehensive website for investors interested in green energy. The site features daily news updates and analysis about happenings in the world of green energy. Public stock prices for green energy companies are also listed and can be tracked daily.

CLEAN EDGE

Cleanedge.com

A leading green energy research and consulting firm co-founded by green business gurus Joel Makower and Ron Pernick, CleanEdge provides research and published reports on green energy trends for interested investors. The website is updated daily with green energy industry news. A newsletter delivers monthly news, analysis, and insight into trends in green energy, transportation, water, and materials. You can also track the green energy industry through the NASDAQ Clean Edge U.S. Index launched in 2006 and accessible through this website.

PROGRESSIVE INVESTOR NEWSLETTER
Sustainablebusiness.com
Newsletter publisher and Sustainablebusiness.com founder Rona Fried
has been tracking green industry developments for nearly twenty years.
Fried's monthly newsletter gives you the inside skinny on the eco-investing
landscape, covering green trends, companies, and investment opportunities.
The website is an excellent resource for investors seeking to learn more
about the companies and technologies at the center of the green investing
buzz.

RESPONSIBLE SHOPPER
Responsibleshopper.com
Monitor the environmental and social behavior of major corporations
through Responsibleshopper.com. The initiative is overseen by Co-Op
America, an organization dedicated to an environmentally sound and
socially just society. Visit the site and see how well the companies in your
portfolio are really performing.

SEEKING ALPHA
Seekingalpha.com
Seeking Alpha provides market commentary and analysis across all major
sectors. The energy section of the website often features coverage of green
energy stocks and topics.

20

READ ALL ABOUT IT

Media

Getting good green info is getting easier every day.

Across all major mediums—television, radio, print, and Internet—media companies are providing coverage of the eco-issues and trends, as well as the products and services, technologies and high-impact designers, entrepreneurs, and visionaries who are making eco-living understandable, actionable, and hugely relevant to our lives.

Sundance Channel is parading green living directly into our living rooms with the launch of Sundance Channel Green, the first regularly scheduled weekly primetime block of eco-programming. No misplaced yawns please. Each week's three-hour block features original television shows that uncover action-driven eco-innovators who are on the front lines of the eco-revolution, along with full-length feature documentaries that entertain as much as they inform. Noted eco-activist, renowned actor/director, and Sundance Channel pioneer Robert Redford is spearheading the initiative. So count on quality, informative television that will make you want to laugh, cry, and slug an oil executive in the teeth.

A newcomer to eco-infotainment television and a company making a big splash across radio and Internet channels as well is LIME. Billing itself as "healthy living with a twist," LIME makes healthy, balanced eco-aware living fully accessible, exciting, and empowering. Danny Seo, author, activist, and eco-fashion consultant to the stars, is often referred to as the Martha Stewart of green living. His LIME television show, *Simply Green with Danny Seo*, anchors an expanding eco-themed television lineup. On *Simply Green*, Danny highlights simple things we can all do to add fun, flair, and a touch of whimsy to our lives in ways that tread a little lighter on the planet. You don't have to go far to watch it. All of LIME's video programming is available directly via its website—Lime.com —on its state-of-the-art broadband video player.

LIME's radio channel is available through Sirius Satellite Radio and directly through Lime.com where you can catch broadcasts of my daily radio show, *The Lazy Environmentalist,* which showcases cutting-edge, eco-aware products and services and features in-depth interviews with high-impact designers, entrepreneurs, and visionaries who are building a green future. Topics span the subjects covered in this book, so the show is a way to stay current on all the innovation that's making green living easy, stylish, and extremely relevant to our lifestyles.

Elsewhere on the radio spectrum is Betsy Rosenberg's program *EcoTalk,* airing nationally on the Air America Network. *EcoTalk* covers a broad range of issues, from the connection between energy efficiency and national security to the positive and potentially lucrative impact of socially responsible investing. It's the daily eco news discussed in a format that breaks down complex issues and helps us recognize how closely intertwined eco-matters are with our own lives.

Over on newsstands, *Plenty* magazine will help you explore how green issues intertwine with twenty-first-century developments, and how green inventors, businesses, and culture creators are serving up far-reaching solutions. *Plenty* avoids doom and gloom while illuminating the pressing eco-topics of the day. The green gear section is also great for finding gifts and cool gadgets.

Also on the green magazine shelf is *Verdant,* an eco-lifestyle magazine that tracks eco-trends across design, art, fashion, and travel. *Natural Home* magazine provides great information and pictorials on greening our homes without sacrificing style, and includes in-depth articles about topics ranging from choosing the right eco-insulation to finding the best organic bedding. *Ecological Home Ideas* delivers precisely what its name implies—information and tips on bringing our homes into balance with nature.

Outside magazine features quality coverage on eco-travel adventures and green gear, and frequently taps ace eco-reporter Amanda Griscom Little for feature articles on topics ranging from the greening of Wal-Mart to the making of influential green activist Laurie David—co-founder of Stopglobalwarmingnow.org, producer of the movie *An Inconvenient Truth*, and better half to *Seinfeld* creator Larry David. *Body & Soul* magazine now sprinkles green tips and content throughout its pages. *Dwell* magazine, one of the premier modern design and shelter magazines, does too. *House & Garden* magazine features eco-aware furnishings inside each issue. *House & Garden* green editor Zem Joaquin is something of a style arbiter and also spotlights green home furnishing finds through her online blog, Ecofabulous.com. *Nylon* regularly features green designers and materials in its fashion pages, which can also be accessed through the magazine's website.

Which leads us to the Internet, where the pace is fast and the eco-getting is good. The eight-hundred-pound gorilla of the online eco-blog world is Treehugger.com. No, you don't have to swear allegiance to trees to peruse its web pages. You just have to want the inside skinny on modern eco-trends. With more than a dozen writers contributing daily content from their posts around the world, Treehugger.com keeps industry insiders, design fans, techies, hipsters, policy wonks, and window shoppers current on the latest eco-happenings and product introductions. The website draws more than six hundred thousand visitors per month, many of whom make it their primary web destination as they start their day. With more than ten thousand categorized posts created since its launch in 2004, Treehugger.com is an extraordinary resource and tool for eco-minded consumers and researchers. Surfing the website is a fast way to see what all the eco-hubbub has been about these last few years, and discover products, services, or organizations that match your interests. There really is something for everyone, and that is part of the point. Treehugger.com founder Graham Hill says, "We are focused on the green future and bringing sustainability mainstream." And Treehugger.com is also focused on using multiple media platforms to do it. In addition to its daily blog content, Treehugger.com is moving into online television.

Simran Sethi, whose on-air credentials include MTV and PBS, leads an award-winning television team that is making Treehugger.com a dynamic entertainment destination.

The Sustainable Style Foundation offers a wealth of continuously updated information on the merging of style and substance. Collin Dunn and crew keep the daily blog and product spotlights fresh and always interesting. SSF also publishes a quarterly online magazine called SASS and hosts the annual Outstanding Style Achievement Awards. Past winners include Armani for creating hemp apparel and Gibson Guitars for utilizing FSC-certified wood.

Inhabitat.com offers in-depth coverage of green design and architecture. Founded by Jill Fehrenbacher while she was an architectural graduate student at Columbia University, Inhabitat.com has become a key resource with a strong following among those who are exploring how our homes and buildings can integrate new technologies, materials, and aesthetics that enhance our lifestyles while bringing them into greater balance with nature. Many of the contributing writers hail from the design and architectural fields, so coverage is consistently informative and insightful.

Jill Danyelle of Fiftyrx3.com is on the front lines of eco-fashion and dishes out tasty finds that she uncovers while combing trendy boutiques throughout New York City and beyond. Readers also get juicy updates about her triumphs and challenges in pursuit of greening her own daily wardrobe in super style.

Bradley Berman at Hybridcars.com enables you to fuel up on cutting-edge eco-transportation developments. From hybrid to hydrogen, Hybridcars.com gives you the scoop on the automobiles and the eco-advanced technologies behind them that are driving green transportation forward.

The godfather of gritty, gripping eco-journalism and commentary, Grist.org delivers news, opinion, and in-depth features and profiles of the key green issues and trends, and the people who are at the forefront of the environmental movement. Grist is where the critical points of the eco-debate are hashed out and where pragmatic and idealistic environmentalists converge. Grist's journalists delve into gritty issues like the cost of climate change, and also report on the happenings at swanky parties where the denizens of green living gather to sip organic martinis.

For the most comprehensive view of the broader themes of sustainability and how they all interconnect, turn to daily commentary at Worldchanging.com. Executive editor Alex Steffen and crew work with a veritable "who's who" of contributing writers who go in depth on green living, transportation, urban development, politics, community building, and so much more. The website is superbly organized to allow for quick access to the information available. And while you're there pick up a copy of the companion book, *WorldChanging: A User's Guide for the 21st Century*.

If logging on to a website is too far to travel to get your share of eco-living insight, then sign up for IdealBite's daily eco-living email tips and let co-founders Jen Boulden and Heather Stephenson deliver their fun and irreverent eco-tips directly to your inbox. IdealBite offers lots of small ways to align your lifestyle with greener values. To hear Boulden describe their low-key eco-approach: "It's ideal like in an ideal world and bite like a small bite of an apple. You don't have to eat the whole thing to be healthy. You can start with small bites."

Television and Radio

BUILDING GREEN
PBS.org
This thirteen-part television series guides viewers through the ins and outs of residential green building, remodeling, and smaller do-it-yourself projects. It's all about the greenest things you can do to remodel the place you live, and it's hosted by actor and green builder Kevin Contreras.

ECOTALK
Airamerica.com / ecotalk
Betsy Rosenberg's program *EcoTalk* airs nationally on the Air America Network and through XM Radio, covering a broad range of issues ranging from the connection between energy efficiency and national security to the positive and potentially lucrative impact of socially responsible investing.

E-TOPIA

Leonardodicaprio.org

Leonardo DiCaprio is the co-creator and executive producer of this reality green TV series that chronicles the reconstruction of a typical American town into a "green utopia of tomorrow." Check the website of DiCaprio's foundation for airing details, environmental videos narrated by DiCaprio, and resources for greening your lifestyle.

GET FIT WITH SARA SNOW

Health.Discovery.com

Discovery Health Channel's resident natural living expert Sara Snow leads viewers on a journey toward stylish, practical, and accessible green living. In *Get Fit with Sara Snow,* Snow introduces viewers to companies and people who are creating green living solutions and also offers simple tips for improving wellness and health.

THE LAZY ENVIRONMENTALIST

Lazyenvironmentalist.com

Catch my daily radio show on the LIME Channel of Sirius Satellite Radio and Lime.com. *The Lazy Environmentalist* showcases cutting-edge, eco-aware products and services and features in-depth interviews with high-impact designers, entrepreneurs, and visionaries who are building a green future. Topics span the subjects covered in this book, so it's a way to stay current on all the innovation that's making green living easy, stylish, and extremely relevant to our lifestyles.

LIME

Lime.com

LIME makes healthy, balanced eco-aware living fully accessible, exciting, and empowering. LIME Television features eco-aware shows like *Simply Green with Danny Seo.* LIME Radio features green programming like my radio show, *The Lazy Environmentalist.*

SIMPLY GREEN WITH DANNY SEO

Dannyseo.com

Author, activist, and eco-fashion consultant to the stars, Danny Seo is often referred to as the Martha Stewart of green living. His LIME television show, *Simply Green with Danny Seo,* anchors an expanding eco-themed television lineup. On *Simply Green,* Seo highlights simple things we all can do to add fun, flair, and a touch of whimsy to our lives in ways that tread a little lighter on the planet. LIME is currently available nationwide through DirectTV and the Dish Network and in many cities via cable television providers. Visit Lime.com to see how you can get LIME TV in your area.

SUNDANCE CHANNEL GREEN

Sundancechannel.com

Sundance Channel offers a regularly scheduled weekly primetime block of eco-programming. Each week's programming features original television shows that uncover action-driven eco-innovators who are on the front lines of the eco-revolution, along with full-length feature documentaries that entertain as much as they inform.

Magazines

BODY & SOUL MAGAZINE

Bodyandsoulmag.com

Personal health and eco-awareness are so intertwined that it's no wonder *Body & Soul* sprinkles green tips and commentary throughout its pages. The magazine is published by Martha Stewart Living Omnimedia and focuses on the healthy, natural, "whole living" lifestyle.

DWELL MAGAZINE

Dwellmag.com

Since its launch in 2000, *Dwell* has been a champion of thoughtful, intelligent contemporary design and architecture. The magazine informs about design's ability to positively influence our lives and society, and it's within this context that green content—design and architecture—is almost always prominently featured in every issue.

ECOLOGICAL HOME IDEAS

Ecologicalhomeideas.com

Ecological Home Ideas delivers precisely what its name implies—information and tips on bringing our homes into balance with nature. It features green remodeling ideas and tons of green products to align your home with a cleaner planet.

GOOD MAGAZINE

Goodmagazine.com

Good magazine covers the people, places, and trends that merge idealism with capitalism to create solutions that work and fit the way we want to live. In a conversation like this, green issues naturally figure prominently.

HOUSE & GARDEN MAGAZINE

Houseandgardenmag.com

This magazine features eco-aware furnishings inside each issue. *House & Garden* green editor Zem Joaquin is something of a style arbiter and also spotlights green home furnishing finds through her online blog, Ecofabulous.com.

LUCIRE MAGAZINE

Lucire.com

Lucire is a global fashion magazine that features regular eco-fashion content and commentary, including the "Behind the Label" column written by eco-fashion guru Summer Rayne Oakes.

METROPOLIS

Metropolismag.com

Metropolis magazine offers a sophisticated viewpoint on how design influences our lives and is capable of creating cost-effective and efficient products, buildings, cities, and societies that are ecologically sound and socially just. The pictures are pretty too.

MOTTO MAGAZINE

Whatsyourmotto.com

Motto magazine covers the new paradigm of work where values meet profits. Read about companies, entrepreneurs, and business people who are finding ways to create positive social, environmental, and financial returns.

NATURAL HOME

Naturalhomemag.com

Natural Home magazine provides great information and pictorials on greening our homes without sacrificing style, and includes in-depth articles on topics ranging from choosing the right eco-insulation to finding the best organic bedding.

NYLON MAGAZINE

Nylonmag.com

This über-hip fashion magazine regularly features green designers and eco-materials in its pages. You can also access the green content through the magazine's website.

ODE MAGAZINE

Odemagazine.com

Ode is news filtered through a realistic yet optimistic lens to focus on people and ideas that are changing the world. The subject matter is wide and often hits upon topics that help readers to consider ways to make the world a greener, healthier place.

OUTSIDE MAGAZINE

Outside.away.com

This active lifestyle and adventure travel magazine often features eco-travel adventures and green gear, and frequently taps ace eco-reporter Amanda Griscom Little for feature green articles covering the people, companies, and trends catapulting green into the mainstream.

PLENTY MAGAZINE

Plentymag.com

Plenty helps you explore how green issues intertwine with twenty-first-century developments and how green inventors, businesses, and culture creators are serving up far-reaching solutions. The magazine avoids doom and gloom, while illuminating the pressing eco-topics of the day.

VERDANT MAGAZINE

Verdantmag.com

Verdant covers eco-lifestyle trends across design, art, fashion, and travel. It's the upscale green lifestyle magazine that provides great ideas for better living.

Internet

ECOGEEK.COM

It's *Wired* magazine for environmental techies and is updated daily, tracking the latest trends in environmental technologies.

FABULOUSLY GREEN

fabulouslygreen.blogspot.com

Fabulously Green tracks the latest trends, styles, and products in eco-fashion and accessories and green interior design. Find products ranging from the newest clothing fashions to hip handbags to plant-able greeting cards that will sprout organic herbs like basil or chives—it's the gift that keeps on giving.

FIFTYRX3.COM

Jill Danyelle's eco-fashion blog is an essential destination for tracking the fast-moving product introductions and trends at the crossroads of fashion and the environment.

G LIVING NETWORK

Gliving.tv

G Living is a contemporary green lifestyle broadcast network delivered via its website. Each week millions of viewers watch *GLivingLive*, an hour-long show covering topics in green design, fashion, architecture, business, food, sports, and more. Gliving.tv also provides updated daily articles and coverage of the modern green living movement.

GREAT GREEN GOODS

Greatgreengoods.com

A dedicated green shopping blog, Great Green Goods scours the Internet for stylish and funky green finds. Products highlighted are typically made from recycled or sustainable materials.

GREENLIGHT MAGAZINE

Greenlightmag.com

Greenlight is the online magazine for better, healthier, eco-aware choices and a stylish, guilt-free lifestyle. The quarterly magazine is delivered to you via email, and the website features plenty of additional articles.

GRIST.ORG

The godfather of gritty, gripping eco-journalism and commentary, Grist delivers news, opinion, in-depth features, and profiles of the key green issues and trends, as well as the people who are at the forefront of the environmental movement. Grist is where the critical points of the eco-debate are hashed out and where pragmatic and idealistic environmentalists converge.

HYBRIDCARS.COM

From hybrid to hydrogen, Hybridcars.com gives you the scoop on the automobiles and the eco-advanced technologies behind them that are driving green transportation forward.

IDEALBITE.COM

Get your daily share of eco-living insight by signing up for IdealBite's fun, irreverent, bite-size eco-tips emailed directly to your inbox.

INHABITAT.COM

Jill Fehrenbacher, who founded Inhabitat.com while she was a Columbia University architectural graduate student, and her team of writers have created a key resource that offers in-depth coverage of green design and architecture. Explore how our homes and buildings can integrate new technologies, materials, and aesthetics that enhance our lifestyles while bringing them into greater balance with the planet.

METAEFFICIENT

Metaefficient.com

Eco-gadget and technology lovers will have a field day reading this blog, which covers products that maximize efficiency (usually energy efficiency). Whether it's hot water systems, LED lighting, or MP3 players, Metaefficient tracks products that offer elegant solutions for minimizing resource consumption.

PORTOVERT

Portovert.com

An online magazine for eco-savvy brides and grooms, *Portovert* delivers all the tips you need to green your bridal shower, bachelor party, wedding reception, and all the details in between.

SUSTAINABLE STYLE FOUNDATION

Sustainablestyle.org

If it's stylish and green, you'll probably find it here. The daily showcase features green products. The daily spotlight covers sustainable style information and resources. The online sourcebook provides yet another resource for great products and services to plug into your eco-lifestyle. SSF also publishes a quarterly online magazine called *SASS* and hosts the annual Outstanding Style Achievement Awards.

TREEHUGGER.COM

The top green destination on the web, this fast-paced blog is dedicated to everything that's green with a modern aesthetic. Get the latest updates on green trends and search more than ten thousand categorized posts. Check out TreehuggerTV for quality green video programming.

WORLDCHANGING.COM

For the most comprehensive view of the broader themes of sustainability and how they all interconnect, turn to daily commentary at WorldChanging. com. And while you're there pick up a copy of the companion book, *WorldChanging: A User's Guide for the 21st Century.*

21

ECO LIVING 101

Programs,
Classes,
and Degrees

It's one thing to bring greater eco-awareness to the way you live, but it's another to infuse an eco-sensibility into the way you work. I'm not talking about how much recycled paper you feed into your printer—see Chapter 18 for that—but about choosing a career based on improving our relationship with the environment. Eco-driven employment no longer requires that you chain-link yourself to a nuclear reactor or gulp saltwater while on a Greenpeace ship. Today you can go to engineering school and learn how to design streamlined, super-efficient ships that require less fuel, or you can study how to build green buildings and join the ranks of the more than six thousand U.S. Green Building Council LEED (Leadership in Energy and Environmental Design)–accredited professionals who are developing the eco-intelligent buildings of the future. You can pursue studies in green business at business schools around the country and use that expertise to help global corporations green their business operations, or even start your own green-minded company. Across all industries, the rising interest in solving environmental challenges presents exciting, well-paid career opportunities. As with most emerging trends, breaking in isn't always easy, but it's always possible. And an education is a great place to start.

Business schools throughout the United States are increasing their focus on green business. At the George Washington University School of Business in Washington, DC, green business education is a focal point for emerging professionals seeking opportunities with global corporations or international organizations, or preparing to launch their own eco-ventures. The eco-emphasis is spearheaded by Dr. Mark Starik, professor of strategic management and public policy, who has been educating undergraduate and MBA students about green business, sustainability entrepreneurship, and international environmental policy for nearly fifteen years. Courses include strategic environmental management and environment, energy, technology, and society. Counted among recent alumni to come through the program are Jennifer Boulden, co-founder of IdealBite, a rapidly growing media company providing bite-size daily green living tips, and Marty Silber, co-founder of Stella Capital, a company that provides financing to large-scale renewable energy projects throughout the United States.

The Beyond Grey Pinstripes survey annually ranks the top full-time MBA programs committed to teaching social and environmental sustainability in their business programs. George Washington University consistently ranks high on the list, as do schools such as Stanford, Notre Dame, the University of Michigan, and the University of North Carolina. The full rankings are available at Beyondgreypinstripes.org.

Specialized green MBA programs are also popping up across the country. For those who want a fully integrated green emphasis, check out New College of California's green MBA program, the Presidio School of Management MBA in sustainable management, the Bainbridge Graduate Institute MBA in sustainable business, and the Green Mountain College MBA with emphasis on sustainable business. Each program gives students the opportunity to study with faculty and peers who are on the cutting edge of green business.

If business school doesn't provide enough green information for your tuition dollars, there are other options. Net Impact is an organization that is committed to developing leaders who will change the world through business. Net Impact chapters can be found on most college campuses, and professional chapters—found in many major metropolitan areas—provide alumni with ongoing social and environmental business education and networking opportunities.

On the sustainable design front, architectural and design programs are beginning to integrate eco-principles into their curriculums. At the School of Architecture at the University of Minnesota, graduate students can pursue a master's of science (MS) in architecture in sustainable design. The program educates students about core green building concepts like energy, indoor environmental quality, green materials, optimal building orientation, and water management. Elective courses cover topics like building energy systems and architecture and ecology. Students can also enroll in eco-themed courses offered by the anthropology, history, and political science departments, among others. For those who wish to become licensed architects, the program can be combined with a master's in architecture (MArch). Other innovative graduate green architectural and design programs around the country include the San Francisco Institute of Architecture master's in ecological design and architecture and Yale University's new master's in environmental management and architecture, offered in a collaboration between the schools of forestry and environmental studies and architecture.

Students who attend colleges that don't offer courses in sustainable/green design can gain exposure to the field through summer workshops and semester-long programs offered at ECOSA Institute in Prescott, Arizona. The institute emphasizes sustainable and ecological design and attracts students from a broad range of design disciplines, such as architecture, landscape architecture, product design, interior design, and planning. Participants learn about the impact that design has on both the natural environment and the built environment (aka buildings) and are introduced to innovative design strategies that reduce our environmental impact and help build sustainable communities. Instructors come from both academia and the design world, and many are at the forefront of their respective fields. Lecturers include Andrew Millison, a permaculture activist who is building the world's first Ecohood in Prescott to retrofit a low- to mid-income neighborhood into a highly sustainable community.

When applying to college, eco-minded high school students can select schools that offer majors in environmental education, engineering, management, policy, science, or more generally in sustainability. The Institute for Sustainability maintains an updated list of universities and colleges offering eco-curriculums. One of the most unique environmental undergraduate curriculums is located amid the tall cornfields in Fairfield, Iowa. The Maharishi University of Management offers a BS in sustainable living/environmental science, teaching students to design and maintain communities "that meet the needs of people and the environment so abundantly they function indefinitely." Students learn about sustainable practices in technology, agriculture, architecture, and landscape design and gain knowledge about the ecology of living systems. It's a whole-systems approach that extends beyond the classroom and the library. Maharishi University of Management was founded by Maharishi Mahesh Yogi, the man who brought Transcendental Meditation (TM) to the United States nearly fifty years ago. So in addition to learning sustainable business practices, students who attend the university also engage in meditation as part of a journey of personal growth and evolution. And as you cultivate your healthy mind, you can cultivate a healthy body too, because all of the food on campus is organic.

Professionals already out in the working world can tap into numerous continuing education opportunities that can help channel careers in a green direction. In building-related fields, the U.S. Green Building Council offers workshops that introduce and explain green building concepts as well as the LEED (Leadership in Energy and Environmental Design) Green Building System, the most widely recognized green building guidelines governing this fast-growing segment of the industry. Those who wish to develop full green expertise can continue onward toward LEED certification.

Design:Green offers continuing education workshops for designers, strategic planners, marketers, engineers, and other professionals who want to learn how to integrate environmental awareness into new product development. Jacquelyn Ottman of J. Ottman Consulting, one of the leading green marketing experts in the United States, masterminds the sessions along with selected industry experts. The goal is to equip professionals with the tools and mind-set to create products that are sustainable, innovative, profitable, and globally competitive.

Those who want to develop skill sets in green construction can head up to Waitsfield, Vermont, where the Yestermorrow Design/Build School offers a certificate in sustainable design and construction. The five-week intensive course introduces participants to sustainable design principles and provides hands-on experience in the design/build process. The course can also be tailored to individual interests, with possibilities to delve into top subjects like super-insulated homes, solar design, green remodeling, landscape design, and natural paints and finishes. Yestermorrow has been drawing nationally renowned experts to its beautiful Vermont campus for more than twenty-five years to teach design/build principles. As its name reflects, the school aims to merge the tradition of craft with modern technologies to create environments that connect people to their natural environment and to one another.

On the West Coast, the Real Goods Solar Living Institute draws thousands of people each year to its twelve-acre Solar Living Center campus in Hopland, California, about ninety-five miles north of San Francisco. Here, students participate in hands-on workshops covering subjects like renewable energy, green building, ecological design, and alternative construction techniques, working with materials like straw bale, cob, and bamboo. If you want to learn how to run your car on veggie oil or master the art of off-grid solar systems, this is the place for you.

Business Education

BAINBRIDGE GRADUATE INSTITUTE
Bgiedu.org
This institute's MBA in sustainable business is a part-time program designed for working professionals. The distance-learning program requires students to meet once a month for a four-day intensive classroom session at its campus on Bainbridge Island near Seattle, Washington. Graduate certificate programs are available for mid-career professionals who wish to learn about sustainable business or green entrepreneurship.

GEORGE WASHINGTON UNIVERSITY SCHOOL OF BUSINESS
Sbpm.gwu.edu
Green business education is a focal point for emerging professionals seeking opportunities with global corporations or international organizations, or preparing to launch their own eco-ventures. The eco-emphasis at GWU is spearheaded by Dr. Mark Starik, professor of strategic management and public policy.

GREEN MOUNTAIN COLLEGE
Greenmtn.edu
Based in Poultney, Vermont, Green Mountain College offers a distance-learning MBA program with an emphasis on sustainable business. The program provides students with traditional business education in the core disciplines and trains them also to consider social and ecological outcomes when making management decisions.

MAHARISHI UNIVERSITY OF MANAGEMENT
Mum.edu
Founded by Maharishi Mahesh Yogi, the man who brought Transcendental Meditation (TM) to the United States, the university offers one of the most unique environmental undergraduate curriculums available. The BS in sustainable living/environmental science teaches students to design and maintain communities "that meet the needs of people and the environment so abundantly they function indefinitely."

NEW COLLEGE OF CALIFORNIA
Newcollege.edu/greenmba
The green MBA program at the New College of California in San Francisco is a two-year full-time on-site program that equips graduates with a traditional business education as well as the skills to create real-world solutions that support a more environmentally and socially just society. The project-oriented learning approach is designed to help students develop critical thinking, leadership, and entrepreneurial skills.

PRESIDIO SCHOOL OF MANAGEMENT
Presidiomba.org
From its idyllic perch overlooking the Golden Gate Bridge in San Francisco, the Presidio School of Management offers an MBA in sustainable management for students who want to combine practical business know-how with tools to transform companies, communities, and countries. Notable recent alumni include key members of the Treehugger.com team, including Nick Aster, who spearheads information technology, and Simran Sethi, who spearheads TreehuggerTV.

Design Education

BOSTON ARCHITECTURAL COLLEGE
The-bac.edu
Offers both on-campus and distance learning courses in sustainable design.
The courses are great for those who are interested in green building or in
developing a general understanding of the sustainable design movement.
Boston Architectural College also offers a Sustainable Design Certificate for
those seeking more in-depth knowledge.

ECOSA INSTITUTE
Ecosainstitute.org
Located in Prescott, Arizona, this institute emphasizes sustainable and
ecological design and attracts students from a broad range of design
disciplines, such as architecture, landscape architecture, product design,
interior design, and planning. Summer workshops and semester-long
programs are available to undergraduate and graduate students.

PARSONS SCHOOL OF DESIGN
Parsons.edu
At Parsons, undergraduate design students are introduced to green design
principles through David Bergman's semester-long sustainable design
course, which delves into the design of green products and also addresses
more fundamental questions about the responsibility of designers to create
products that minimize our environmental impact. Bergman and designer
Erica Doering jointly teach a smart product design course, which instills an
understanding of sustainable design principles and the choices designers
face when creating eco-intelligent products.

SAN FRANCISCO INSTITUTE OF ARCHITECTURE
Sfia.net/ecodes.asp
The San Francisco Institute of Architecture offers a master's of ecological
design. The innovative institute, which focuses on green architecture
and construction, is committed to teaching green design principles to all
comers. Opportunities are also available to enroll in distance-learning
programs.

UNIVERSITY OF MINNESOTA
Arch.cdes.umn.edu/academic_programs/MS/MS_SD/index.html
At the School of Architecture at the University of Minnesota, graduate
students can pursue a master's of science (MS) in architecture in
sustainable design. The program educates students about core green

building concepts like energy, indoor environmental quality, green materials, optimal building orientation, and water management.

YALE UNIVERSITY
Environment.yale.edu
Yale's master's in environmental management and architecture is offered in a collaboration between the schools of forestry and environmental studies and architecture. The program equips students pursuing careers in sustainable or restorative design with the skill sets and technologies to make buildings healthier, smarter, and more eco-aware.

Continuing Education

DESIGN:GREEN
Designgreen.org
Led by green marketing expert Jacquelyn Ottman, Design:Green offers continuing education workshops for designers, strategic planners, marketers, engineers, and other professionals who want to learn how to integrate environmental awareness into new product development.

REAL GOODS SOLAR LIVING INSTITUTE
Solarliving.org
Thousands of people each year visit the twelve-acre Solar Living Center campus, where students participate in hands-on workshops covering subjects like renewable energy, green building, ecological design, and alternative construction techniques, working with materials like straw bale, cob, and bamboo.

U.S. GREEN BUILDING COUNCIL
Usgbc.org
The U.S. Green Building Council offers workshops that introduce and explain green building concepts, as well as the LEED (Leadership in Energy and Environmental Design) Green Building System, the most widely recognized green building guidelines governing this fast-growing segment of the industry. Those who wish to develop full green expertise can continue onward toward LEED certification.

YESTERMORROW DESIGN/BUILD SCHOOL

Yestermorrow.org

Yestermorrow Design/Build School offers a certificate in sustainable design and construction. The five-week intensive course introduces participants to sustainable design principles and provides hands-on experience in the design/build process.

Information/Education

BEYOND GREY PINSTRIPES

Beyondgreypinstripes.org

The annual survey ranks the top full-time MBA programs committed to teaching social and environmental sustainability in their business programs.

GREEN DRINKS

Greendrinks.org

Every month in cities around the world professionals working in (or looking to enter) environmental fields gather through Green Drinks for drinks and casual networking. It's a great way to connect with others who can lead your career in a green direction.

THE INSTITUTE FOR SUSTAINABILITY

Aiche.org

College-bound high school students can search this institute's listings of colleges and universities that offer eco-focused majors in education, engineering, management, policy, science, or more generally in sustainability. Click on the heading "Youth Activities" to view the list.

NET IMPACT

Netimpact.org

Net Impact is an organization that is committed to developing leaders who will change the world through business. Net Impact chapters can be found on most college campuses, and professional chapters—found in many major metropolitan areas—provide alumni with ongoing social and environmental business education and networking opportunities.

O2 NETWORK

O2.org

O2 is an in international network for sustainable design. Loosely headquartered in the Netherlands, O2 consists of local chapters throughout the world that enable designers and those interested in design to share ideas and information about green design.

U.S. ENVIRONMENTAL PROTECTION AGENCY

Epa.gov/enviroed

The environmental education program of the EPA offers age-appropriate eco-learning curriculums for children. Check out the Environmental Kids Club, with fun learning activities for preschoolers through fourth-graders. The Student Center provides middle school students with more sophisticated understanding of eco-issues. The High School Environmental Center offers resources to help students get involved in eco-solutions, whether through volunteering or internships. A career guide is also available, with links to numerous websites where students can explore environmental career opportunities.

22

IT'S NEVER TOO
LATE TO START Death
and Dying

When considering death, you can elect to become part of the circle of life. It's now possible to choose a burial that takes you back to nature and that restores and replenishes the land. The final choice we make upon this Earth can be the ultimate act of recycling—the reusing of ourselves. And choosing this path is not only kinder to the environment, but also kinder to our checking accounts.

Opting for an eco-burial involves a few steps. First, skip the embalming. Every year more than eight hundred thousand gallons of formaldehyde-based embalming fluid are buried inside humans, which are buried inside caskets and deposited six feet deep in U.S. soil. Leakage poisons the soil and degrades groundwater supplies. Contrary to popular belief, embalming is not required by law anywhere in the United States. Human bodies, like all organic matter, naturally decompose and return to the soil except when filled with poisonous embalming chemicals. Refrigeration or dry ice are safe alternatives for open casket funerals.

Second, opt for a nontoxic, biodegradable casket. While most coffins are made of veneered chipboard—wood shavings glued together with formaldehyde-based toxic glues—Ecopod, a U.K.-based company, has developed a sleek, nontoxic, and fully biodegradable coffin made of 100 percent recycled paper. Closely resembling a seed pod, the Ecopod also gives an aesthetic nod to the designs of Ancient Egyptian tombs. Elegant and austere-looking, and deceptively lightweight, these coffins come in a range of colors and styles that suit a wide variety of tastes. Ecopod creator Hazel Selena says, "A funeral could be a colorful celebration of the person's life. I want people to be left feeling 'Wow, that was amazing.'"

The Cocoon coffin by Uono of Germany takes eco-coffin design in new and exciting directions. The modern, cocoonlike organic shape is made of natural jute, a vegetable-based fiber, and finished with a high-gloss water-based varnish that is available in fourteen colors. Steel handles are discreetly integrated into the lightweight frame. Rope handles can also be substituted for a fully biodegradable casket that will decompose in ten to fifteen years, and interior linings are available in cotton or silk. The Cocoon is so stunningly attractive that it begs the question—why wait till you're dead to have something so plush to rest in? Perhaps the Cocoon gives us all something to look forward to.

For those seeking a more traditional aesthetic, Belmont Caskets offers a high-quality eco-aware casket crafted of FSC-certified sustainable solid oak wood and finished with natural, nontoxic shellac. The unbleached organic cotton interior lining is fitted over a plush cotton futon composed of at least 85 percent recycled content. Attention to eco-impact is matched by Belmont Caskets' fine craftsmanship, which makes these caskets aesthetically indistinguishable from other higher-end models.

If greater simplicity is desired, Kent Casket of Brooklyn, New York, offers an FSC-certified sustainable pinewood coffin. The Woodland casket is sanded to a fine, smooth finish that brings out the beauty of the wood, and is treated without toxic glues, varnishes, or finishes. Best of all, the coffin biodegrades over time, giving both its materials and its inhabitant back to the land.

Should you prefer cremation, eco-aware coffins are far more suitable than conventional choices, as they limit the pollutants emitted into the atmosphere during incineration. But even when incinerating healthier materials, cremations still use an energy-intensive heating process that results in carbon dioxide greenhouse gas emissions. Promessa, a Swedish company, has developed an alternative to cremation aptly named Promession. It provides a dignified way to capture the nutrient-value of the human body and return it to the soil. The process involves freezing a corpse at very low temperatures through the use of liquid nitrogen. The procedure makes the body brittle enough to disintegrate into an organic powder when gently shaken. The powder is then filtered through a metal separator to remove any surgical spare parts or mercury. Finally, the hygienic and odorless powder is placed in a biodegradable urn and buried just beneath the soil, which enables the nutrient-rich essence of the human body to return to the land. Promession funerals are already under way in Sweden; the U.K. is debating whether to permit them, and they may soon be coming to America.

Choosing to skip the embalming fluid and opting for a bio-degradable coffin are decisions that are honored by law in all cemeteries in the United States. These measures will garner you immeasurable eco–eternal gratitude, but the final step of the eco-burial journey leads to eco-cemeteries. Here funerals are conducted without embalming fluids, and only biodegradable caskets or burial shrouds—cloths used to wrap a body for burial—are permitted. For the latest in shroud fashion, check out Kinkaraco's Kinkara eco-shroud made of natural silks, cottons, linens, wools, and canvas. The stylish burial garb was featured in an episode of HBO's *Six Feet Under*.

Eco-cemeteries give us an enduring connection to nature. At Fernwood Cemetery in California, just north of San Francisco, flat stones, natural rocks, wildflowers, shrubs, and trees are often used as gravesite markers, in place of upright gravestones. Fernwood provides visitors with handheld GPS devices to locate the gravesites of their loved ones amid the naturally restored surroundings. At GreenSprings Cemetery near Cayuga Lake in the Finger Lakes region of New York, fifteen-by-fifteen-foot burial sites are allotted along a ninety-three-acre rolling hilltop meadow that looks more like a nature preserve than a standard cemetery with traditional rows of headstones. Trails meander through the fields, enabling the families of those buried there to enjoy the beauty of the surroundings. This verdant environment is a gift from the deceased individuals who have chosen to give their nutrient-rich bodies back to the earth. It is the quintessential eco-choice and the wise economic choice too—eco-burials often cost less than half the price of the standard funeral. So always remember that in death there is life, and hopefully a little more cash for your grandkids.

Caskets and Urns

ARKA ECOPOD
Ecopod.co.uk
A revolutionary design in coffins, the strong yet lightweight Ecopod is made of 100 percent recycled paper and is perfect for green burials or cremation. Also available is the Acorn Urn, which is made along the same principles as the Ecopod, overlaid in moss green, handmade paper.

BELMONT CASKETS
Environmentalcaskets.com
Belmont offers the Eco Casket, a high-quality solid-oak casket made from all-natural materials without compromising aesthetics. The wood is FSC-certified, and the interior is comprised of organic unbleached cotton.

BIOS URNS
Urnabios.com
A unique concept, the Urnabios are funeral urns made of coconut, peat, and cellulose, with a seed placed within. This ingenious idea allows you or your loved one to, upon death, "give life," in the form of a newly planted tree.

CARDBOARD CASKET
Cardboardcasket.com
Cardboard Casket presents three designs (and two prop designs) of quite literally cardboard caskets. These affordable, biodegradable boxes provide an eco-aware alternative to the traditional casket.

IN THE LIGHT URNS
Inthelighturns.com
In the Light sells quality biodegradable urns that are suitable for burial at sea or on land. Urns are available in varying sizes, styles, and colors, made of such things as hemp, clay, and various Earth-friendly recycled materials.

KENT CASKET
Kentcasket.com
Kent Casket provides simple, biodegradable pine caskets for natural green burials and cremations, made from FSC-certified wood, using nontoxic glues. It's a no-frills, but eco-enlightened, way to say good-bye.

KINKARACO

Kinkaraco.com

As seen on the hit HBO show *Six Feet Under*, the Kinkara Shroud is one of Kinkaraco's eco-shrouds, 100 percent natural biodegradable fabrics that can be placed in the coffin or directly into the ground (where legal). Shrouds are reinforced for stability and come with biodegradable lowering devices.

PROMESSA

Promessa.se

This Sweden-based company has developed an alternative to cremation, aptly named Promession, that involves freezing a corpse at very low temperatures, making it brittle enough to disintegrate into an organic powder when gently shaken. Promession funerals are available in Sweden and may soon be coming to the U.S.

UONO

Uono.de

A coffin for design mavens, the Cocoon is a futuristic, eco-aware casket made from high-quality, natural materials that biodegrade within ten to fifteen years.

Cemeteries

FERNWOOD

Foreverfernwood.com

Located in Mill Valley, California, adjacent to the Golden Gate National Recreation Area, Fernwood provides a memorial landscape of nature, with rocks, wildflowers, shrubs, and trees. Natural burials at Fernwood use no toxic embalming fluids, only a biodegradable casket or burial shroud, and every grave is locatable via global positioning system (GPS) coordinates.

GLENDALE NATURE PRESERVE

Glendalenaturepreserve.org

The Glendale Memorial Nature Preserve is located in Florida's panhandle area, and provides a natural setting of fields, creeks, ponds, and woods. All burials are mapped using Geographic Information System technology and can be located via a global positioning system (GPS).

GREEN SPRINGS

Naturalburial.org

Located on a hundred acres of rolling hilltop meadows in the Finger Lakes region of New York, Green Springs offers a beautiful and sustainable place where native trees and shrubs may be planted on gravesites to help restore the land to its natural state.

RAMSEY CREEK PRESERVE

Ramseycreekpreserve.com

Located in South Carolina, Ramsey Creek Preserve was the first green cemetery opened in the United States. Owner and operator Memorial Ecosystems is committed to developing memorial nature preserves that are environmentally and socially responsible, as well as inherently spiritual in nature. Ramsey Creek Preserve also offers pet burials for your dearly departed furry family member.

Information/Education

FOREST OF MEMORIES

Forestofmemories.org

Forest of Memories is an organization of volunteers who share its goal of furthering the development of green burial grounds in Canada and in the U.S. Their website is informative, full of resources for locating green cemeteries near you, researching services and consultants, and participating in discussion forums.

GREEN BURIAL COUNCIL

Decentburial.org

Green Burial is a nonprofit founded to encourage sustainable practices in death care by developing a certification program to distinguish eco-aware providers, working to develop green burial grounds, and connecting consumers to green burial professionals. The council maintains a list of approved providers.

ACKNOWLEDGMENTS

I wish to thank my parents, Bill and
Jancy Dorfman, for artfully donning so many hats, ranging from
loving parents to passionate fans to dispassionate investors. To my
brother and sister in-law, Jed and Carolyn Dorfman, thank you for
taco salad Sunday dinners and your insights and feedback throughout the writing stages. To Herb "The Godfather" Sydney, thank
you for all of your gracious wisdom and guidance and for your
exceptionally patient tutelage in my endeavors. To my agent, Mel
Parker, thank you for believing in this project and steering me so
admirably through the exciting adventure of a first-time author. To
Marisa Belger, thank you for your invaluable insights and thorough
edits, chapter by chapter and revision by revision, that gave structure to my voice. To Bob Halper, thank you for opening doors that
made this book possible. To my friends who have put up with me
while I've endeavored to make the world a greener place; Stan and
Rachel Horowitz, Adam Rothenhaus, Jason Venner, Andrew Adler,
Wayde Jester, Jonathan Fernands, Carl and Elizabeth Brown, Taylor
and Melissa Hurt, Brooke Smith, Carrie Norton, Lisa Hunter, Neil
Chambers, Chuck Heckman, and Summer Rayne Oakes. To the
Brofmans—Lynne, Bruce, Peter and Scott—who are my second
family and a constant source of love, laughter, and support. To Lucy
Umberger, who more than anyone else helped me recognize my
true nature as a lazy environmentalist. To Elka Boren, thank you for
aligning my chakras so I could think straight. To Christine Goulden,
thank you for helping me shape chapters when I was stuck. To my
editor, Dervla Kelly, thank you for your constant enthusiasm, guidance, and stewardship throughout this project. To Laura Smith,

Andrew McKenna, and Jonathan Pontecorvo at LIME Radio, thank you for giving me the professional platform to articulate and hone the ideas that inform these pages. To Jodi Fontana, thank you for innumerable kindnesses, constantly keeping the faith, and running my company while I wrote. Lastly, to the environmental entrepreneurs, designers, and visionaries, this book is your story. It is a privilege to be able to share it.